Selected Works of Landscape Architect John L. Wong

From Private To Public Ground
From Small To Tall

Selected Works of Landscape Architect John L. Wong

From Private To Public Ground
From Small To Tall

FOREWORD by Peter E. Walker, FASLA, Partner, PWP Landscape Architecture
INTRODUCTIONS by John L. Wong; David J Neuman, FAIA, LEED BD C – Founding Principal at Neu Campus Planning, Inc.; Adrian Smith, FAIA, Gordon Gill, FAIA, Founding Partners at Adrian Smith + Gordon Gill Architecture; James K.M. Cheng, Founding Principal at James KM Cheng Architects Inc.
INTERVIEW with John L. Wong by James McCown
PRINCIPAL PHOTOGRAPHY by Tom Fox, David Lloyd, Bill Tatham
PRINCIPAL PLANS & DIAGRAMS by John L. Wong and SWA Collaborators
EDITED by Oscar Riera Ojeda

OSCAR RIERA OJEDA
PUBLISHERS

CONTENTS

012	**FOREWORD** By Peter E. Walker, FASLA – Partner, PWP Landscape Architecture
016	**1. LEARNING FROM THE BEST AND OTHERS** Introduction by John L. Wong
040	**2. EARLY WORKS** Introduction by John L. Wong
106	**3. STANFORD UNIVERSITY AND INSTITUTIONAL PROJECT CHALLENGES** Introduction by David J Neuman, FAIA, LEED BD C – Founding Principal at Neu Campus Planning, Inc.
220	**4. LANDSCAPE/GROUNDSCAPE FOR THE WORLD'S TALL AND TALLEST STRUCTURES** Introduction by Adrian Smith, FAIA, Gordon Gill, FAIA, Founding Partners at Adrian Smith + Gordon Gill Architecture
388	**5. DESIGN RESPONSES TO IMPROVE RESILIENCE** Introduction by James K. M. Cheng, Founding Principal at James KM Cheng Architects Inc.
474	**6. RECENT WORKS AND ONGOING CHALLENGES/OPPORTUNITIES** Introduction by John L. Wong
514	**7. RESIDENTIAL GARDENS** Introduction by John L. Wong
558	**INTERVIEW** With James Moore McCown
566	**ACKNOWLEDGMENTS** By John L. Wong
570	**APPENDIX** Project Photography Credits Project Credits John L. Wong Contributors
588	**BOOK CREDITS**

FOREWORD
By Peter E. Walker, FASLA – Partner, PWP Landscape Architecture

John has worked with the SWA Group in all of their developmental stages for more than 50 years. I first met John in 1972 when he joined the Sasaki Walker summer program in their offices in Sausalito, California. Even then John amazed all of us with the quality of his freehand drawings. He had what landscape designers in those days called a "good hand". This he exhibited in all his design work to such a degree that everyone was impressed.

John graduated with a Bachelor of Science from the University of California at Berkeley in landscape architecture in 1974. After graduation he joined Sasaki Walker. In 1976 he was accepted by the Harvard Graduate School of Design, and in 1978 he received a Masters Degree in Landscape Architecture in Urban Design. While at the GSD he worked part-time for the SWA Group East, a small firm set up by SWA to support my "Landscape as Art" teaching at Harvard, and after his graduation John worked full-time for SWA Group East. At that time, the small eastern office was doing mostly experimental work, competitions, and part-time jobs for the various SWA regional offices, such as the design of Burnett Park in Fort Worth, Texas, a rooftop garden for our house in Boston with Martha Schwartz, and a first-time new community project in Saudi Arabia and development projects for the Gerald Hines Company.

In 1980, SWA East was merged back into the West Coast office, which was led by Kalvin Platt, then its president. John became a Principal of SWA in 1980, a Managing Principal in 1987, and in 1999 joined the SWA Board of Directors. He served as Board Chairman from 2012 through 2023, and he is currently a member of the SWA Group Board. During his years at SWA, John served as a visiting critic at Harvard GSD and at the University of California at Berkeley. In addition, he has lectured broadly in the United States and abroad. Over these many years we have remained friendly competitive colleagues.

In 2010 SWA Group opened an office in Shanghai, China. Since then John has designed a distinguished series of projects and plans in China, Korea, Japan, and the Middle East. Over the years the SWA Group has become very large, with offices in Sausalito, San Francisco, Laguna Beach and Los Angeles, California; Houston and Dallas, Texas; New York City (SWA Balsley); Shanghai, China; and the United Arab Emirates. Most importantly it has grown to be the largest completely independent design firm practicing landscape architecture, planning, and urban design in the world today. They have been, since their beginning, entirely employee owned.

An important aspect of John's tenure has been expanding projects in China, Southeast Asia, and the Middle East. The size, scope, and quality of these designs have made a unique contribution to landscape design.

There are far too many projects of John's to discuss in this introduction, but a few of the most important ones over the years will indicate their range and quality, gardens and urban spaces that reach such a high level of design sophistication they elevate a flowering of modern urban design worldwide.

- The 1991 Ronald Reagan Presidential Library, Semi Valley, California, sits on a 180-acre site with a long view to the Pacific Ocean. Eighty mature oaks were transplanted from the adjacent Reagan Ranch to transform the library site, providing a sense of instant permanence.

- XIQU Center in Hong Kong, China (2018) near the ferry station lifts its theater so that the plaza continues level out to the city beyond.

- The Al Wasl Expo Plaza in Dubai, finished in 2020, is a series of projects that include a central plaza, a metro arrival plaza, an inner-loop pedestrian way, and several parks thus providing a largely shaded public campus for the Expo. Included is the flamboyant structure that projects bird shadows down onto the elegant stone plaza below.

- Stanford University, Stanford, California, has transformed large parts of the historic Olmsted-designed campus over the last 30 years with projects such as the Cantor Art Center (1996), the Lasuen Mall (2000), and the Panama Mall (2019), to name but a few. John's designs include completion of malls and outdoor corridors as well as Olmsted sub-campus centers joined to make a grand overall plan, both formal and informal parts, into the human-scale campus we see today.

• The 2018 University of California at Davis West Village in Davis, California, creates the largest planned zero-net energy community in the United States.

• Guthrie Green in Tulsa, Oklahoma (2016), utilizes a geothermal heat pump system beneath the park that provides both heat and cooling for the park and the surrounding non-profit arts tenants.

• The 2008 gardens for Burj Khalifa in downtown Dubai, UAE, are among the tallest buildings in the world. The garden at the tower's base combines entryway and plaza into a series of gardens – curvilinear, formal, parterre, strolling – which provide a setting for the tower to be seen both from above and from the at-grade automobile arrival. Here John has found ways to humanize and connect this incredible structure to the ground and the city by humanizing the base areas to include expanded pedestrian entry areas (viewed from inside down but especially when viewed from outside). While so many large tower projects are often crowded into the modern surrounds without significant treatment at the base, this setting complements the monumental sculptural presence of the building.

In addition to these projects, John has supervised the design of a series of large distinguished residential gardens in California and Asia, including a 1988 residential sculpture garden in the Bel Air, Los Angeles, neighborhood for the Cantor family.

Looking back, it has been a privilege to have been a small part of John's story and to have been able to watch, with pride, the many contributions he and the SWA Group have made to the art of landscape design.

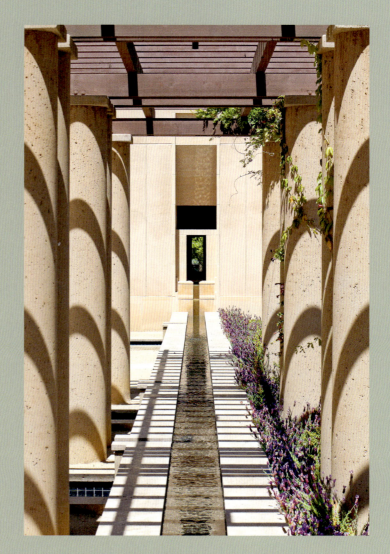

Above Stanford University SIEPR
Below Zifeng Tower, Nanjing Greenland International Commercial Center

1

LEARNING FROM THE BEST AND OTHERS

018 INTRODUCTION by John L. Wong

SELECTED DRAWINGS

- **019** Villa D'Este – Water Organ/Fish Pool, Tivoli
- **020** Villa Medici – Castello
- **021** Il Duomo, Spoleto
  - Il Duomo – Paving Study, Spoleto
  - Streetscape, Spoleto
  - Villa D'Este, Como
  - Villa D'Este, Tivoli
  - Villa D'Este, Tivoli
  - Villa D'Este – The Hundred fountains, Tivoli
  - Villa D'Este – Fountain of the Dragons, Tivoli
  - Villa Adriana – Villa dell Isola, Tivoli
  - Villa Gamberaia, Settignano
  - Villa Gamberaia, Settignano
  - Villa Lante, Bagnaia
  - Corso Vannucci, Fontana Maggiore, Cattedrale, Perugia
  - Isola Bella, Stresa, Lago Maggiore
  - Villa Farnese, Caprarola
  - Villa Farnese, Caprarola
- **022** Villa Gamberaia, Settignano
  - Santa Maria delle Pace, Roma
  - Santa Maria delle Carceri, Prato
  - Villa Medici – Castello
  - Cappella degli Scrovegni, Padova
  - Biblioteca Laurenzian S Lorenzo, Firenze
  - Cappella d Pazzi, Firenze
  - S Lorenzo – Sagrestia Vecchia Cappelle Medicee, Firenze
  - S Lorenzo – Cappelle Medicee Sagrestia Nouva, Firenze
- **023** Piazza del Campo, Siena
- **024** Villa La Rotonda, Vicenza
- **025** Villa La Rotonda, Vicenza
  - Villa La Rotonda, Vicenza
  - Villa Farnese, Caprarola
  - Villa Lante, Bagnaia
  - Basilica Palladio, Vicenza
  - Teatro Olympico, Venezia
- **026** Canal Grande at Ponte Rialto, Venezia
  - Ponte Rialto, Venezia
  - Ca' d'Oro, Venezia
  - Piazza S Marco, Venezia
  - Piazza S Marco, Venezia

	Basilica S Marco, Torre dell'orologi, Piazza S Marco, Venezia		Villa Farnese, Caprarola
	Torre dell'orologi, Piazza S Marco, Venezia		Villa Farnese, Caprarola
	S Giorgio Maggiore, Venezia		Villa Farnese, Caprarola
	Palazzi a Piazza S Marco, Venezia		Villa Barbarigo Dona Delle Rose, Valsanzibio
	Scuola di S Marco – Campo SS Giovanni e Paolo, Venezia		Villa Gamberaia, Settignano
	Scuola di S Marco – Campo SS Giovanni e Paolo, Venezia		Piazza del Comune, Assisi
	Paving & Drainage Study – Piazza S Marco	034	Vaux-Le-Vicomte, Melun

027 Ca' d'Oro Facade, Venezia
028 Basilica S Pietro, Vaticano, Roma
029 La Scala, Piazza di Spagna, Roma
　　Piazza di Spagna – Chiesa Trinita dei Monti, Roma
　　Piazza di Spagna, Roma
　　La Scala della Trinita, Piazza di Spagna, Roma
　　Piazza del Campidoglio, Roma
　　Campidoglio, Roma
　　Villa Adriana – Villa dell Isola, Tivoli
　　Villa Adriana – Grandi Terme, Tivoli
　　Campidoglio, Roma
　　Piazza S Pietro, Vaticano, Roma
　　Piazza S Pietro, Vaticano, Roma
　　Piazza S Pietro, Vaticano, Roma
　　Scala – Cortile d Bellevdere Bramante, Vaticano, Roma
　　Plan of 1748, Roma
　　Pantheon, Roma
　　Colosseum, Roma
030 Piazza Pio II, Pienza
　　Paseo, Todi
　　Via Appia, Perugia
　　Piazza del Popolo, Piazza Garibaldi, Todi
　　Scala della Trinita Studies, Francesco de Sanctis, Roma
　　Scala della Trinita, Francesco de Sanctis, Roma
　　Biblioteca Laurenzian S Lorenzo, Firenze
　　Cappella d Pazzi, Firenze
　　Palazzo Ducale, Urbino
031 Villa Farnese, Caprarola
　　Oval Fountain, Villa D'Este, Tivoli
032 S Antonio – Cappella di S Antonio, Padova
　　Palazzo del Te, Mantova
033 Villa Farnese, Caprarola

　　Parc du Sceaux – Grand Cascade, Sceaux
　　Parc du Sceaux – Grand Canal, Sceaux
　　Chateau de Chantilly, Chantilly
　　Chateau de Fontainebleau – Grand Parterre, Fontainebleau
　　Chateau de Villandry, Loire
　　Versailles – The Grand East West Axes / Fountain of Apollo/Royal Avenue, Versailles
　　Vaux-Le-Vicomte, Melun
035 Pagoda de Chanteloupe, Amboise
　　Palais/Jardin du Luxembourg, Paris
　　Chateau de Courances, Courances
　　Francois I Staircase, Chateau de Blois, Loire
　　Chateau de Courances, Courances
　　Vaux-Le-Vicomte, Melun
036 Step Pyramid of Zoser – Great South Court, North Sakkara
　　Deir el Bahri, Temple of Queen Hatshepsut, Thebes
　　Section Study - Deir el Bahri, Temple of Queen Hatshepsut, Thebes
　　Temple of Kom Ombo, Kom Ombo, Aswan
　　Abu Simbel – South Temple of Ramses II, Abu Simbel
037 Abu Simbel – South and North Temple of Ramses II, Abu Simbel
　　Philae – Temple of Isis, Aswan
　　Temple of Khnum, Esna
　　Medinet Habu Necropolis, Thebes
　　Medinet Habu Necropolis, Thebes
　　Abu Simbel – South Temple, Abu Simbel
038 Temple of Amon, Karnak
039 Grand Gallery - Pyramid Cheops, Giza
　　Necropolis Ramesseum, Thebes
　　Paving Study - Ibn Tulun Mosque, Cairo
　　Temple of Amon, Karnak
　　Plan – Temple of Amon, Karnak
　　Abu Simbel – South and North Temple of Ramses II, Abu Simbel

INTRODUCTION
By John L. Wong

Through early school and college courses in the landscape architecture field, I learned a wide range of subjects: the history of the profession, the technical knowledge of construction, the science of related topics that deal with air, water, plants, soil, and many other phenomena, analytical skills and the process of abstracting information onto the land and environment, and the expressive language of giving form and meaning to solve a problem on a given site. However, beyond courses in a landscape architecture degree program, how does one learn how to design? In my first few years of learning to become a landscape architect, I received mentorship and teachings from some extremely talented and experienced individuals. Do as you're told and ask all the questions on the what, why, and how was certainly a way to learn the design craft.

It was during my third year in college that I applied for the Sasaki Walker Summer Program and was accepted. During that summer, I was exposed to one of the most influential landscape architecture practices at the time. The design projects I worked on were exciting and varied greatly in types, scales, and locales. I learned a great deal just by looking, watching, listening, and having the opportunity to contribute. The most interesting opportunities were the weekend field trips that brought summer students along with office staff to see the leading contemporary projects in the Bay Area from local designers and firms – Frederick Law Olmsted, Tommy Church, Lawrence Halprin, Garrett Eckbo, Dan Kiley, Robert Royston, Sasaki Walkers, EDAW, and many others. These projects ranged from small private gardens to large parks and campuses and from work places to new communities. I learned about the importance of going there to see, observe, and learn about what works and what doesn't. I saw specific designs in their real spatial contexts and came to understand the functional relationships and aesthetic beauty of each place we visited.

Many students asked a lot of questions and took many photo slide pictures – digital photography was not invented yet. After seeing numerous projects every weekend, I started to bring a black notebook to sketch and record the elements that interested me, which included the spatial form, materials, color, and unique design elements. I also began looking at proportion, lines, symmetry, ground plane, and texture. I recorded these elements by drawing the plan of the site, the perspective of the space, and sometimes the details of an execution, and I attached notes to further describe the important aspects of the graphics.

I continued to visit projects of interest after the summer program in order to learn from the best designers. This peaked in 1982 when I spent an eye-opening year at the American Academy in Rome traveling to the many fascinating cities, towns, piazzas, and gardens of Italy. Additionally, I travelled to Greece, Israel, Egypt, Malta, Germany, Switzerland, and France. Chapter 1 illustrates many beautiful places that I had the opportunity to see and record and they helped form the foundation for my selected works in this monograph.

Italy

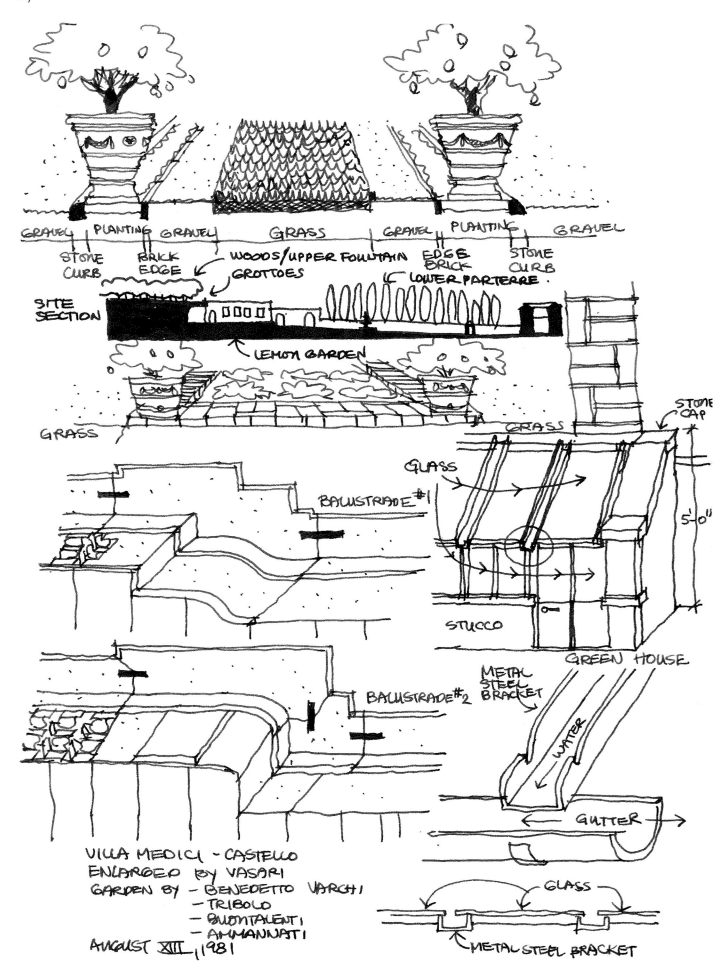

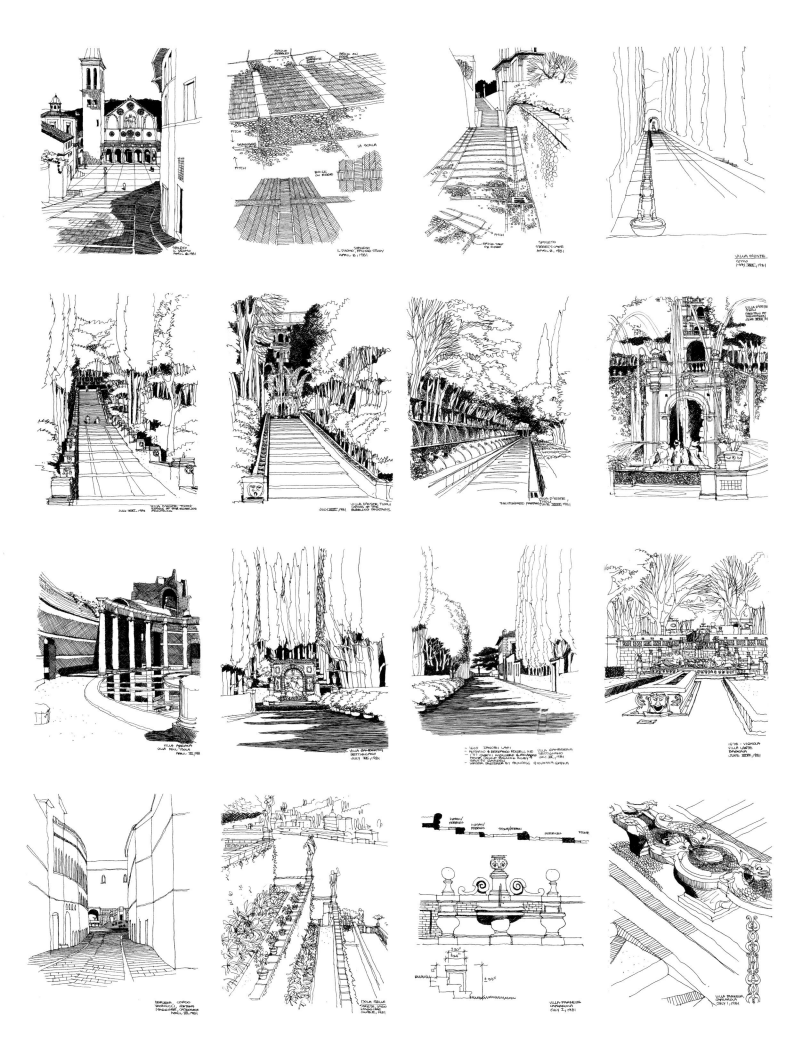

Italy

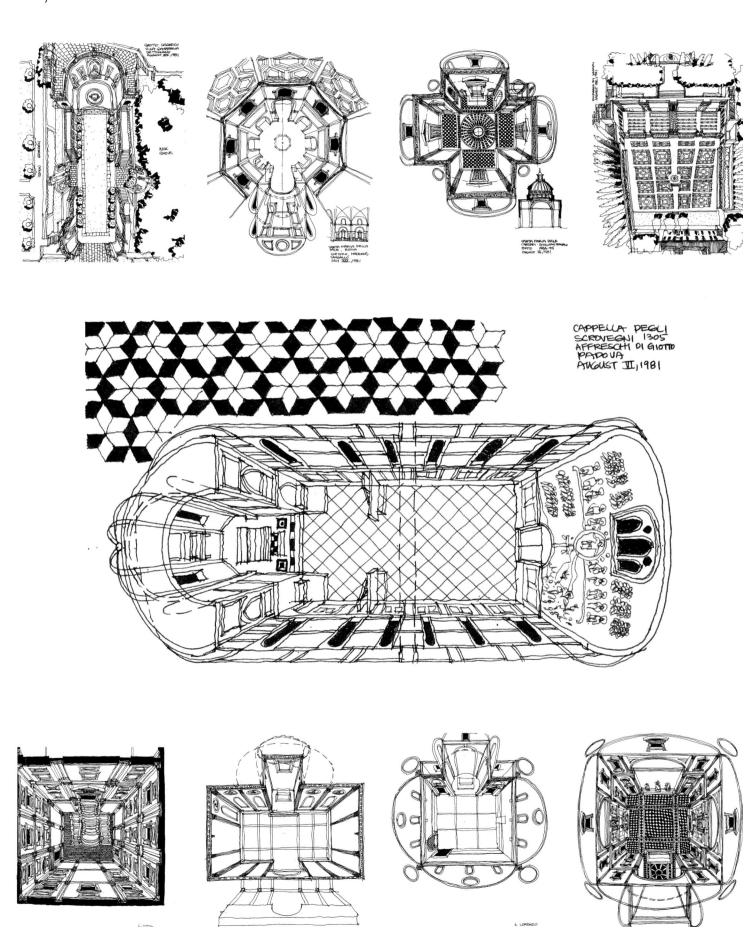

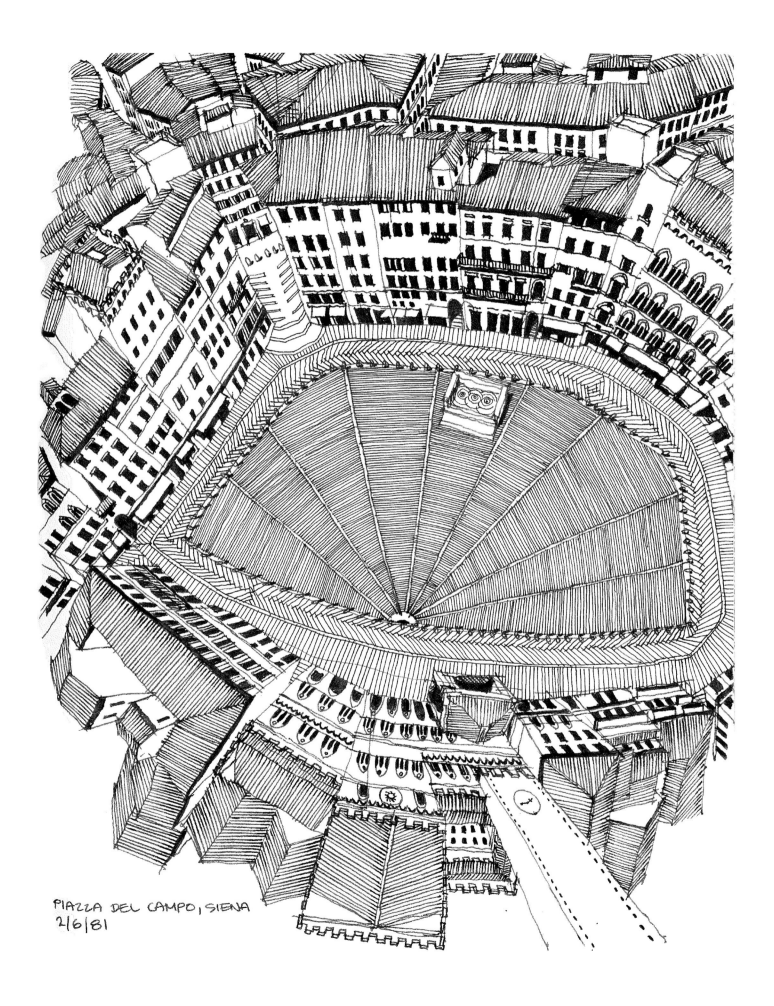

PIAZZA DEL CAMPO, SIENA
2/6/81

Italy

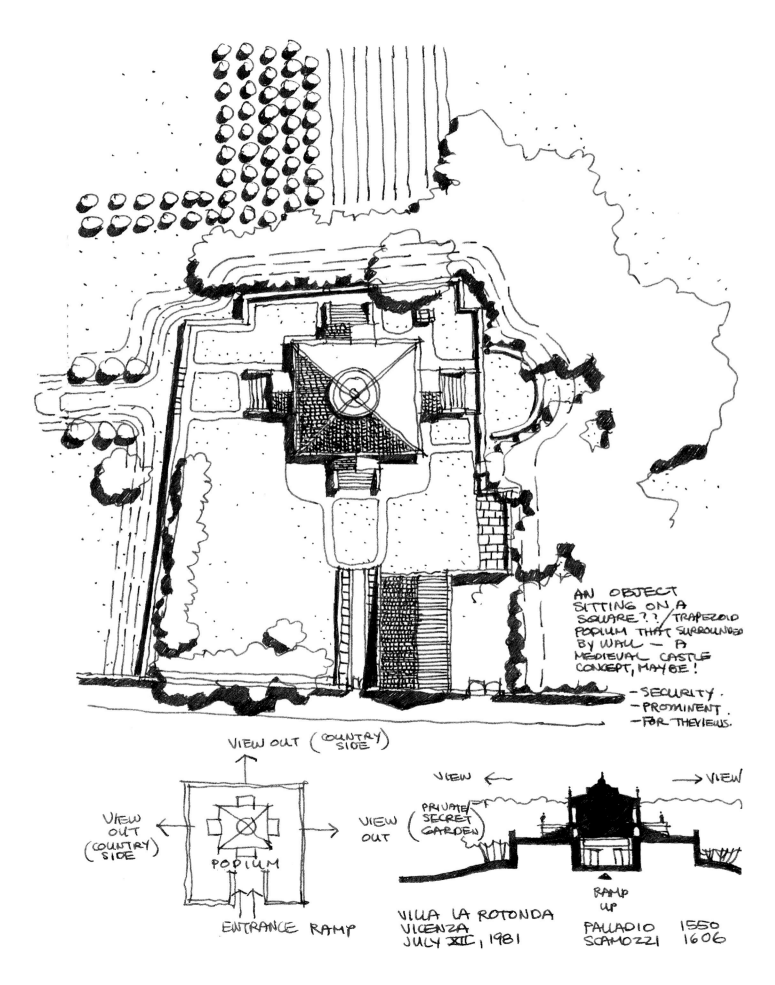

VILLA LA ROTONDA
VICENZA
PALLADIO 1550
SCAMOZZI 1606
JULY VII, 1981

LA ROTONDA,
VICENZA

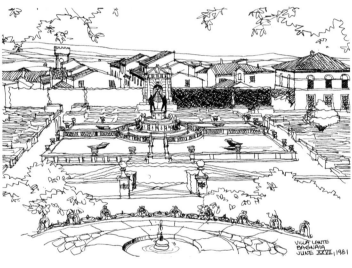

VILLA FARNESE
CAPRAROLA
JULY I, 1981

VILLA LANTE
BAGNAIA
JUNE XXVII, 1981

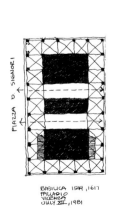

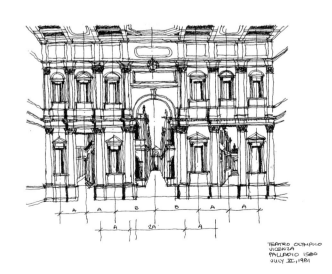

LOGGIA

BASILICA 1549, 1617
PALLADIO
VICENZA
JULY XII, 1981

TEATRO OLYMPICO
VICENZA
PALLADIO 1580
JULY X, 1981

Italy – Venice

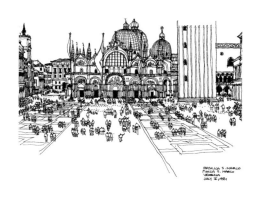
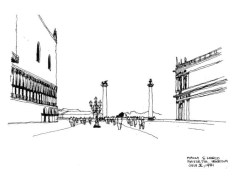

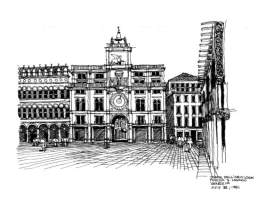

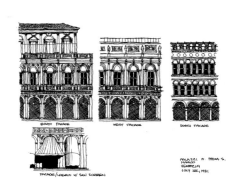

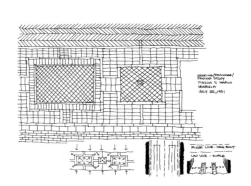

026   1. LEARNING FROM THE BEST AND OTHERS

CA' D'ORO – FACADE
VENEZIA
JULY IX, 1981

Italy – Rome

BASILICA S. PIETRO
VATICANO, ROMA
AUGUST II, 1981

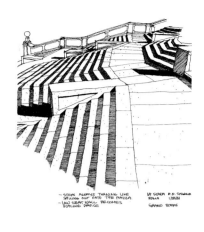

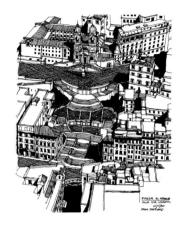
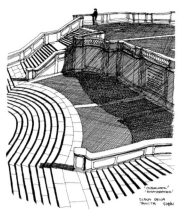
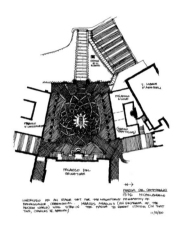
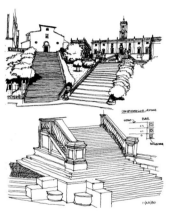

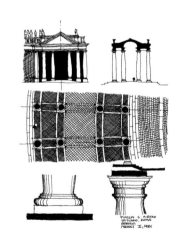
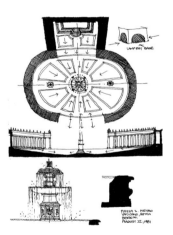
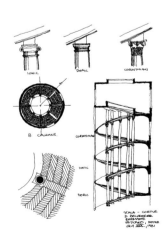
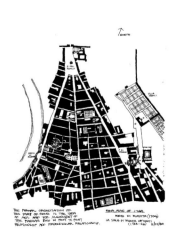
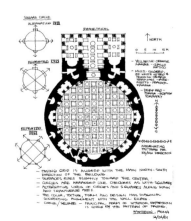
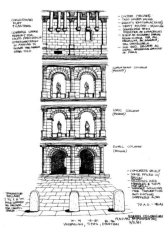

Italy

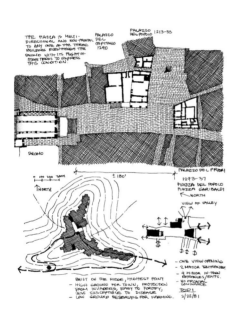
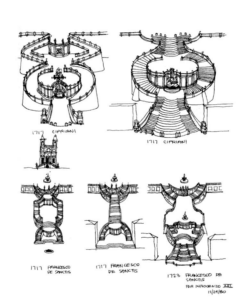
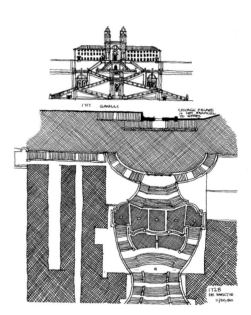

SANGALLO THE
YOUNGER, VIGNOLA
1547-59

ENTRY TERRACE/PLAZA
VILLA FARNESE,
CAPRAROLA
APRIL XXII, 1981

VILLA D'ESTE
TIVOLI
OVAL FOUNTAIN
TIBURTINE SIBYL/
ERCULANEO
JUNE XXIIII, 1981

Italy

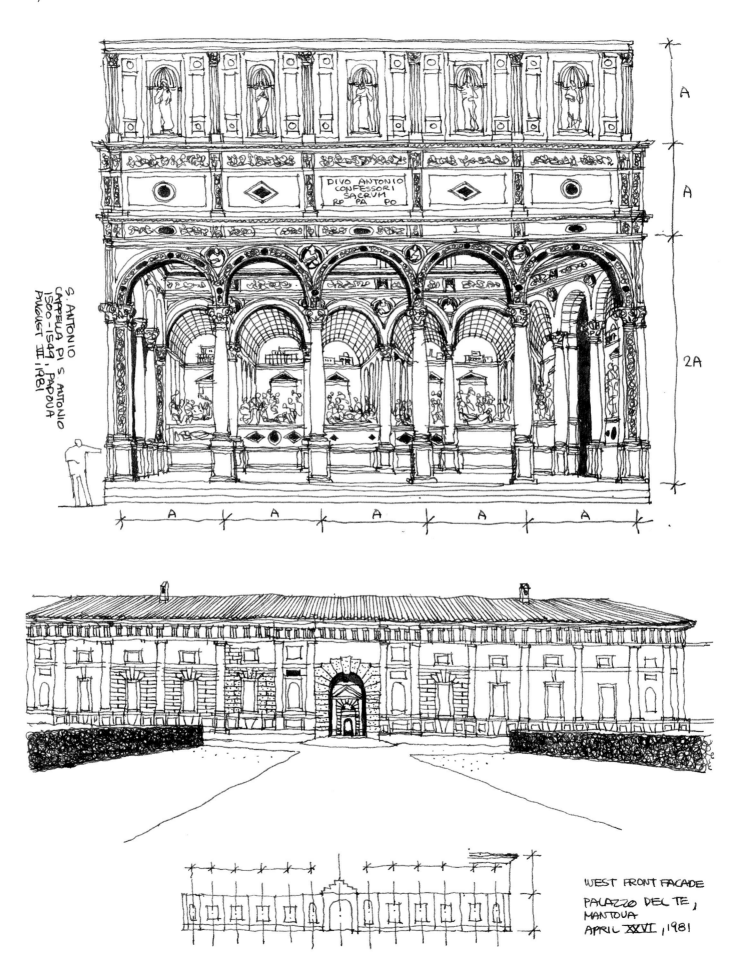

France

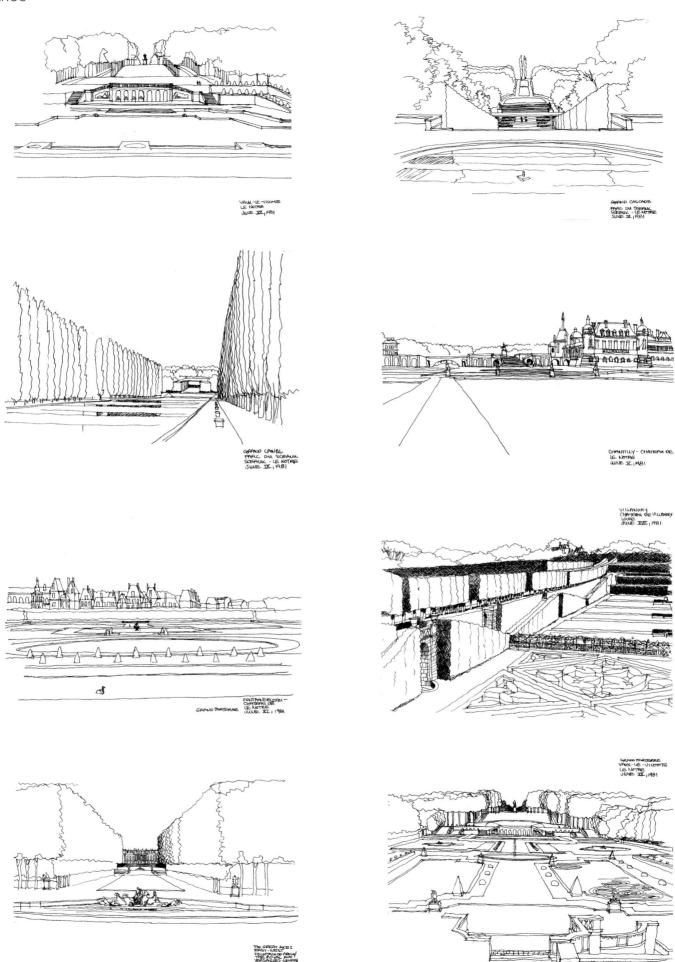

PAGODE DE CHANTELOUP
AMBOISE - LOIRE
JUNE XVI, 1981

PALAIS/
JARDIN DU LUXEMBOURG
PARIS JUNE VII, 1981

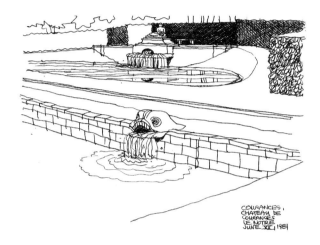

COURANCES,
CHATEAU DE
COURANCES
LE NOTRE
JUNE XX, 1981

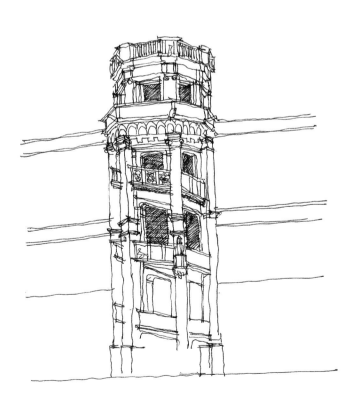

FRANCOIS I STAIRCASE
CHATEAU DE BLOIS - LOIRE
JUNE XV, 1981

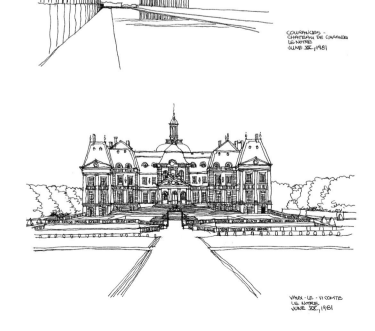

COURANCES -
CHATEAU DE COURANCES
LE NOTRE
JUNE XX, 1981

VAUX - LE - VICOMTE
LE NOTRE
JUNE XX, 1981

Egypt

NORTH SAKKARA, EGYPT
STEP PYRAMID OF ZOSER/
GREAT SOUTH COURT 3/7/81

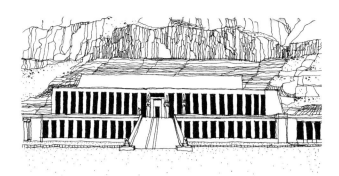

THEBES, EGYPT
DEIR EL BAHRI - TEMPLE
OF QUEEN HATSHEPSUT 3/12/81
MIDDLE TERRACE @ ENTRANCE/ TOP
OF RAMP

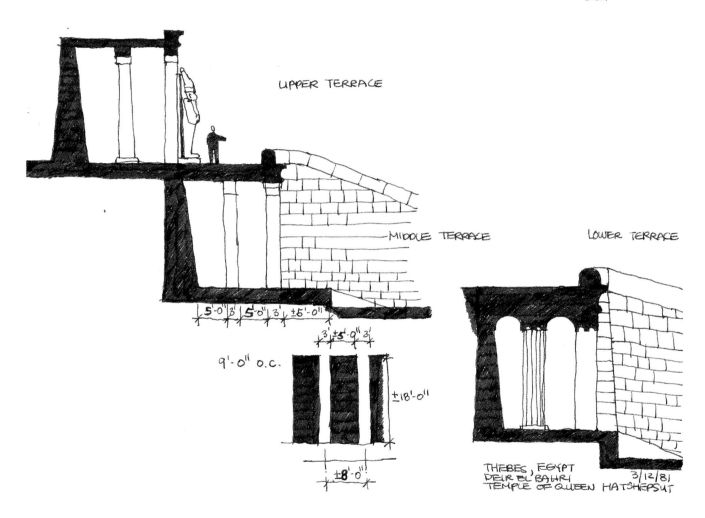

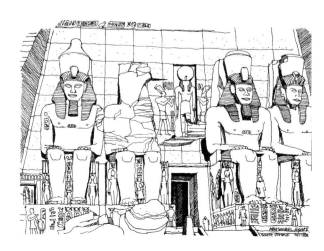

036   1. LEARNING FROM THE BEST AND OTHERS

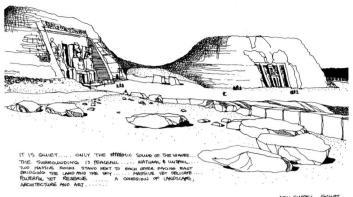

IT IS QUIET..... ONLY THE RHYTHMIC SOUND OF THE WAVES....
THE SURROUNDING IS PEACEFUL...... NATURAL & UNSPOILT.
TWO MASSIVE ROCKS STAND NEXT TO EACH OTHER FACING EAST
BRIDGING THE LAND AND THE SKY...... MASSIVE YET DELICATE...
POWERFUL YET RESERVED...... A COHESION OF LANDSCAPE,
ARCHITECTURE AND ART.......

ABU SIMBEL, EGYPT
THE SOUTH & NORTH TEMPLE
OF RAMESSES II
3/17/81

ASWAN, EGYPT
PHILAE, TEMPLE OF ISIS /
PYLON / COLONNADES
3/15/81

24 COLUMNS
WITH 16 DIFFERENT
TYPES

ESNA, EGYPT
TEMPLE OF KHNUM

DETAILS OF 16 DIFFERENT
TYPES FOR THE 24
COLUMNS IN THE HYPOSTYLE
HALL   3/14/81

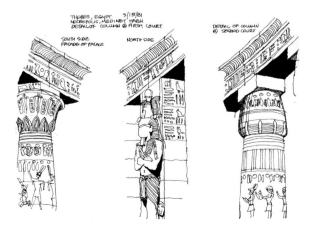

THEBES, EGYPT   3/18/81
NECROPOLIS, MEDINET HABU
DETAIL OF COLUMN @ FIRST COURT

SOUTH SIDE   NORTH SIDE   DETAIL OF COLUMN
FAÇADE OF PALACE   @ SECOND COURT

THEBES, EGYPT
NECROPOLIS, MEDINET HABU
FIRST COURT - ENTRY TO
FIRST HYPOSTYLE HALL   3/18/81

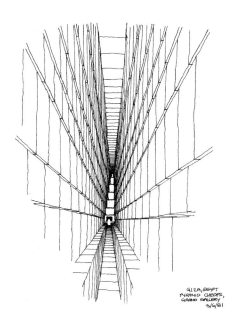

GIZA, EGYPT
PYRAMID CHEOPS,
GRAND GALLERY
3/6/81

THEBES, EGYPT
NECROPOLIS, RAMESSEUM
DETAILS OF COLUMN @
GREAT HYPOSTYLE HALL
3/9/81

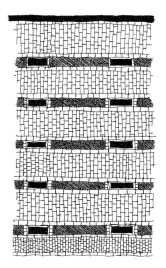

COURT/SAHN

CAIRO, EGYPT
IBN TULUN MOSQUE
DETAIL OF PAVING
PATTERN @ SANCTUARY
3/6/81

KARNAK, EGYPT
TEMPLE OF AMON, PRECINCT,
TEMPLE OF KHONSU / FIRST
COURT WITH HYPOSTYLE HALL,
RECTANGULAR CHAMBER AND
SANCTUARY BEYOND 3/9/81

KARNAK, EGYPT
TEMPLE OF AMON PRECINCT,
PLAN OF TEMPLE OF KHONSU
3/9/81

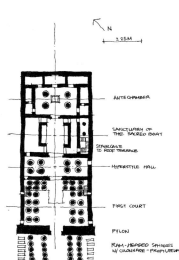

ANTECHAMBER
SANCTUARY OF
THE SACRED BOAT
STAIRCASE
TO ROOF TERRACE
HYPOSTYLE HALL
FIRST COURT
PYLON
RAM-HEADED SPHINXES
W/ COLONNADE - PROPYLAEUM

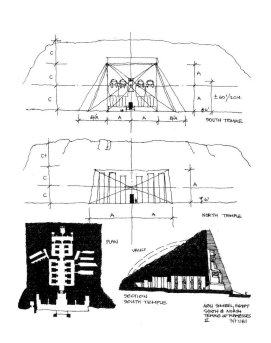

SOUTH TEMPLE
NORTH TEMPLE
PLAN
VAULT
SECTION
SOUTH TEMPLE

ABU SIMBEL, EGYPT
SOUTH & NORTH
TEMPLE OF RAMESES
II 3/17/81

2

EARLY WORKS

042	**INTRODUCTION by John L. Wong**
	SELECTED PROJECTS
044	Burnett Park
044	Boston Pier 1, 2, 3
044	400 S. Hope Street
044	Boca Raton Hotel & Beach Club
044	Citicorp Plaza
045	Disney World Properties
045	Charles Square
045	Bunker Hill
045	LG Beijing
045	Los Angeles Air & Space Museum
045	NeXT Seaport Center
046	Copley Square Competition
047	Pershing Square Competition
048	Federal Triangle Design Competition – 10th Street to 12th Street
049	Todos Santos Plaza
050	190 Marlborough St
051	Lawrence Livermore National Laboratory DPRF/NTTC, NDERF Buildings
054	Fantasy Pointe at Nasu Highland Park
060	Burnaby Civic Square and Library
066	Ronald Reagan Presidential Library
074	Zhongshan International Exhibition Center
078	Suzhou Convention and Exhibition Center
088	Shimao Sheshan Garden E1 & E2
092	SIP Administrative Center
100	Korea World Trade Center – COEX

INTRODUCTION
By John L. Wong

When starting a career, one of the most important ways to develop one's skill is to work on a variety of projects, which creates the valuable opportunity to learn how to solve a design problem and develop a design point of view that responds to the most pressing issues of the time. Another important element is to develop strong relationships with other contemporary colleagues and allied professionals within the field and to continue doing so throughout one's lifetime.

The SWA Group East was my first employer after I completed my two years at the Harvard Graduate School of Design. The work in the beginning was exciting, fast paced, and tremendously demanding. There were many experimental ideas thrown out to push the envelope and test new ground, including a roof garden at 190 Marlborough St., Boston. This was a collaboration between Peter Walker and Martha Schwartz to recapture the untapped potential of our urban rooftops. Other efforts involved entering design competitions to test out new ideas and gain recognition for both lead designers and the firm. These featured projects included the Federal Triangle National Competition, NEA Copley Square National Design Competition, Columbus Carscape Competition, NEA Pershing Square National Design Competition, Todos Santos Plaza Competition, Nagano Master Plan Competition, and the Suzhou Convention and Exhibition Center to name a few.

Then I experienced more traditional project opportunities by working on projects with some of the most prominent architects and designers at the time. During my two years at Harvard and later at the American Academy in Rome, I met with many talented individuals who became not only lifelong collaborators but also friends. It was during these early opportunities that I was able to develop long-term professional relationships with the various younger members of project teams who later became the project leaders for the next generation. They were up-and-coming designers at the top of their field and I was privileged to collaborate with them. Many of these projects were the most noteworthy commissions of the time, namely the Lawrence Livermore National Laboratory Buildings, Ronald Reagan Presidential Library, LG Beijing, SIP Administrative Center, Korea World Trade Center, Burnaby Civic Square & Library, and others.

Aside from generative experimentation and actively searching for new design expression, this period of early works formed the basis and direction for me to develop the tools and knowledge needed for my next body of work, which continually presented new design challenges.

Opposite page Fantasy Pointe at Nasu Highland Park

Burnett Park
Fort Worth, Texas

Boston Pier 1, 2, 3
Boston, Massachusetts

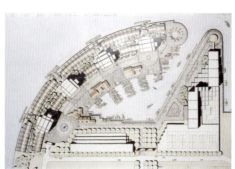

400 S. Hope Street
Los Angeles, California

Boca Raton Hotel & Beach Club
Boca Raton, Florida

Citicorp Plaza
Los Angeles, California

Disney World Properties
Orlando, Florida

Charles Square
Cambridge, Massachusetts

Bunker Hill
Los Angeles, California

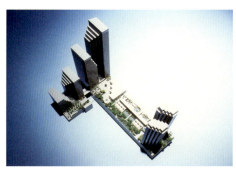

LG Beijing
Beijing, China

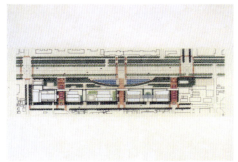

Los Angeles Air & Space Museum
Los Angeles, California

NeXT Seaport Center
Redwood City, California

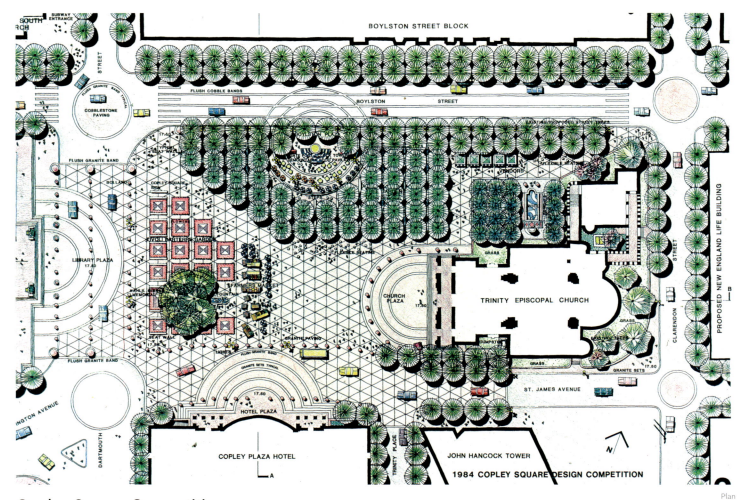

Plan

Copley Square Competition
Boston, Massachusetts

This design submission was a finalist for an NEA-sponsored National Design Competition of an important public square in the heart of the Boston Back Bay neighborhood, which is bounded by Boylston Street, Clarendon Street, St. James Avenue, and Dartmouth Street. Trinity Church, John Hancock Tower, and the Boston Public Library anchor the main space for this 2.4 acre site, which is also the location of the Boston Marathon finish line. The concept for this urban oasis centers on a plaza and an urban park that can flexibly serve community activities and citywide events across all seasons. The design features a plaza for the church, a bosque of pleached Sycamore trees to create a grand public room, and a parterre garden for seasonal display of local native plants. Additionally, in order to maintain the historical significance of the place, it includes a garden to celebrate John Singleton Copley, the painter for whom the square is named.

Study model

Pershing Square Competition
Los Angeles, California

This design, a finalist in a competition for the redesign of a public square in downtown Los Angeles, transforms the site into an outdoor setting for shoppers, office workers, and tourists. The square features strongly defined pedestrian access points and major paths forging strong linkages with downtown streets. Other features of the project include fountains, a water theater, and a botanical garden.

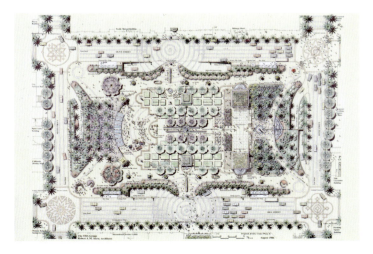

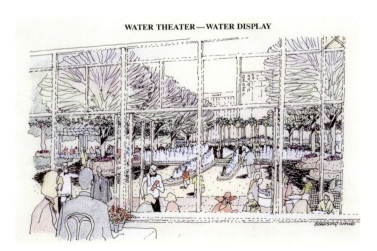

WATER THEATER — WATER DISPLAY

Study model

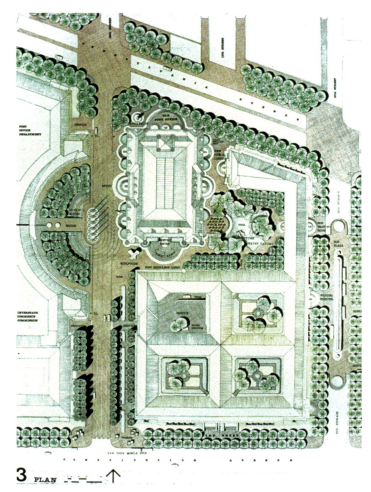

Plan

Federal Triangle Design Competition – 10th Street to 12th Street
Washington D.C.

The Government Services Administration sponsored a design competition to transform and renovate the old Post Office Building and area bounded by Constitution Avenue and Pennsylvania Avenue between 10th Street to 12th Street. This area is where the Interstate Commerce Commission and the IRS are located. The design plan acknowledges and reinforces the special character of the Mall, Pennsylvania Avenue, and the downtown shopping district, as well as the connection between these districts and the existing and proposed uses. The landscape concept improves the visual and formal relationships between individual buildings and throughout the Federal Triangle. The project completes the unresolved ends on 12th Street and Pennsylvania Avenue, improves the landscape and paving design, and provides visual cues for entrances to enhance the office working environment and tourist enjoyment.

Plan

Todos Santos Plaza
Concord, California

An open international design competition to redesign the 122 year-old Todos Santos Plaza, the City of Concord, California, attempted to unite artists and designers in the creation of "place as art". "In the Spirit of Collaboration" was not only part of a search for a new downtown image, but also a way of promoting a greater integration of the arts and design. The renovation of Todos Santos Plaza, the city's oldest park and central core, was planned as the centerpiece of a decade-long civic redevelopment plan. Inspired by the important history and culture of the place, the design team used a miniaturized replica of Todos Santos' original 20-block plan as a central grid, with stone blocks suggesting the early buildings. Stone paving outlining the original town form carries over into the pedestrian walkway and to the promenade framed the historical park. Double allées of California Sycamore strengthened the park edge and linking to the four entry corners and to a curved walkway emphasize the connectivity of different parts of the park. Lawn has been expanded for informal recreation use and community event activities. A linear water feature is placed at the promenade along the main street to welcome visitors and daily park users.

190 Marlborough St
Boston, Massachusetts

The design goal is to recapture the vast areas of our urban rooftops and to focus on them as forgotten resources in the same way that the 1970's focused on abused natural resources. It is not only physically cumbersome but also economically unfeasible to simply recreate a natural landscape in such a synthetic environment as the roof. The preconceived notions of romantic rooftop gardens have kept rooftops from being developed due to the exorbitant cost of construction. The lack of structural support for the added weight to the roof also prevent major intervention to bring in traditional materials to build up a garden on the roof's surface. Through the exploration of new spatial ideas and the use of materials that are not commonly found in traditional gardens, the design team hopes to solve the obstacles that keep this vast open space resource in our cities from being utilized to their full potential.

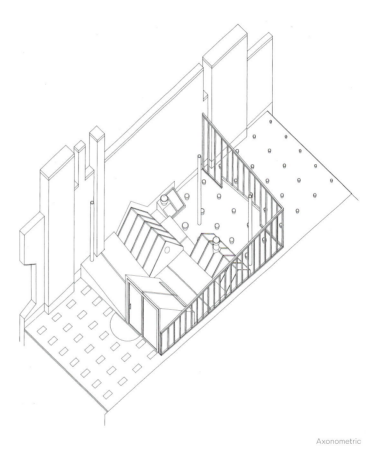

Axonometric

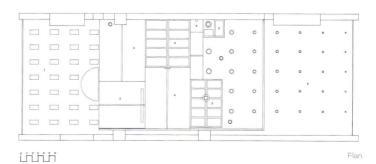

Plan

1. Mirror garden
2. Entry shed
3. Sun deck
4. Dining deck
5. Existing glass sheds
6. Shower
7. Pot garden

Lawrence Livermore National Laboratory DPRF/NTTC, NDERF Buildings

Livermore, California

The design team provided site planning and full landscape architectural services for these two major research and office buildings for over 500 laboratory scientists and technicians and the 2nd Street Mall area at the Lawrence Livermore National Laboratory site, as well as exterior design for five courtyards, an entry plaza, and an open service yard. The design features a series of courtyards with a major central garden for informal use by the building employees. The landscape mitigates the hot interior valley climate with the use of water-conserving and drought-tolerant plant materials.

Plan

Fantasy Pointe at Nasu Highland Park
Nasu, Japan

The landscape design for a 142-acre year-round amusement park and entertainment center featuring eleven themed attractions, as well as diverse retail and commercial spaces, modern sports facilities, and a 200-room luxury resort hotel. A lower plaza serves as an indoor game zone, drawing visitors in from the area's harsh outdoor climate. The original site was on a steep slope in the midst of a forest; the design integrated these existing natural elements into a play area for young children that includes an elaborate "enchanted forest" that incorporates and preserves existing strands of red pines, oaks, and maple trees, supplemented with an extensive understory of flowering woodland plants.

057　FANTASY POINTE AT NASU HIGHLAND PARK

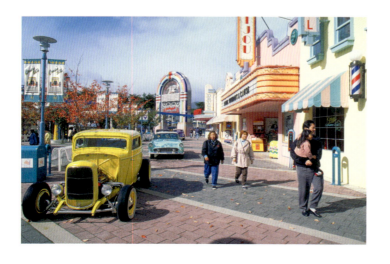

FANTASY POINTE AT NASU HIGHLAND PARK

Burnaby Civic Square and Library
Burnaby, British Columbia, Canada

The design team provided an urban design and development plan for a three-building complex that included a first phase library and civic space for the Metrotown area of the growing city of Burnaby. A strong central lawn, reinforcing pedestrian allées of honey locust, parterre gardens, and the siting and character of the library building, as well as of the civic "bandshell" and flanking colonnades, all combine to instill a strong sense of place. The major portion of the central garden space and the library are over a two-level parking structure that was built as part of the first phase. At the library's ends, an outdoor children's garden for reading and a flower strolling garden allow direct access into the civic square.

Plan

062　2. EARLY WORKS

BURNABY CIVIC SQUARE AND LIBRARY

Ronald Reagan Presidential Library
Simi Valley, California

The rural hilltop location for this 130,000-square-foot building complex includes the library, archives, theater, administration, exhibit hall, and a public affairs center for research and study. The design team arrived at a solution derived from the former president's personal style, as well as the climate and history of his home state, that would have a minimal impact on the surrounding open hillsides of scrub and grasslands. Entrance to the library site winds up through the open hillsides and is landscaped with native shrubs, trees and olive trees typical of private drives of early California ranches. The landscape emphasizes a palette of California native plants and mature California Live Oaks. A generous entry court is enclosed by the wings of the building itself, with a Mediterranean-style low fountain. The view is maximized and highlighted with two major terraces that open out from the interior and provide alternate gathering spaces for visitors. Sensitive grading and site furnishings appropriate to the Mission Style complement the architectural style.

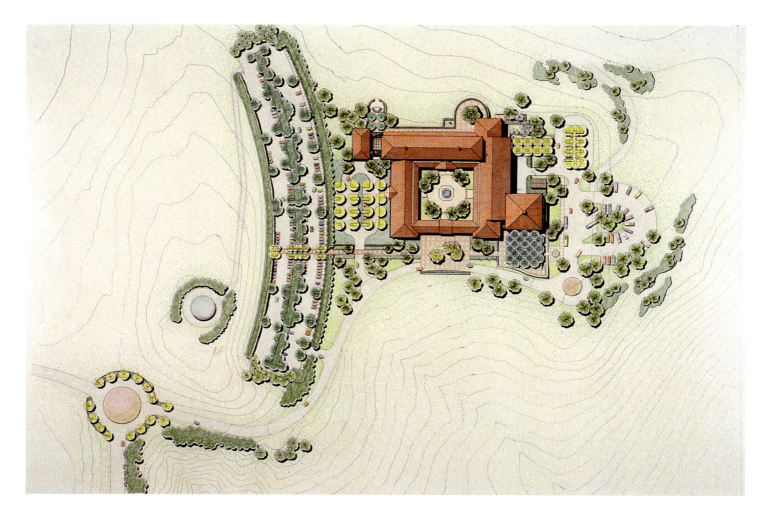

Zhongshan International Exhibition Center
Zhongshan City, Quangdong Province, China

The landscape design for the Zhongshan International Exhibition Center frames the Trade Mart, Exhibition Hall, and Conference Center buildings in a park-like setting that celebrates arrivals, provides a variety of gathering spaces, and complements the functions and design of the buildings. The Public Plaza and amphitheater provide a large, flexible venue for performances and outdoor exhibitions and shows. Encircling the building complex is a water system of shallow, dry creeks to provide an aesthetic feature while collecting stormwater runoff that also functions as a bioswale before returning water to the Chang-Ming river system. The south edge of the river is informally landscaped to create a riverfront park, while the north edge against the buildings serves as a more formal promenade.

Plan

Site plan

Suzhou Convention and Exhibition Center
Suzhou, China

After winning a design competition for a new convention and exhibition center in Suzhou, the design team conceived a design based on a traditional Chinese fan, with a cluster of pavilions that form a central arrival plaza, park, and an outdoor exhibition space. The site is located within the SIP (Suzhou Industrial Park) District, a new industrial city located next to Jinji Lake. The landscape follows the radius pattern of the convention center halls to establish a grand public meeting garden at the heart of the complex. A series of reflecting pools connect the entry lobby with views out toward the lake.

Plan

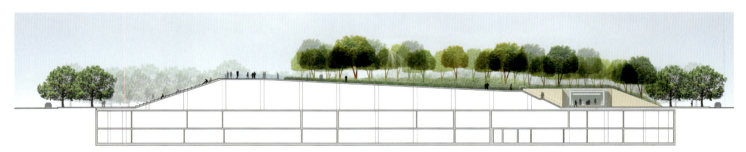

Section - NS Plaza

Section - NS Retail

083　SUZHOU CONVENTION AND EXHIBITION CENTER

086   2. EARLY WORKS

Shimao Sheshan Garden E1 & E2
Shanghai, China

The design team was invited by the architect and client to collaborate on the Shimao Sheshan residential project in Shanghai. The project has a total of 75 units on a flat site with three forested hills and a lake-formed setting. Five prototypes of differing styles were designed based on traditional high-end custom estate homes. The design approach creates estates in a forested setting, with water channels meandering throughout the site and buildings sited to maximize southern exposure. Because the design is intended to create a new standard for high-end residential projects in China, the marketing approach focuses on buyers wanting property elevated by the blending of architecture, interior, and landscape to create a unique setting.

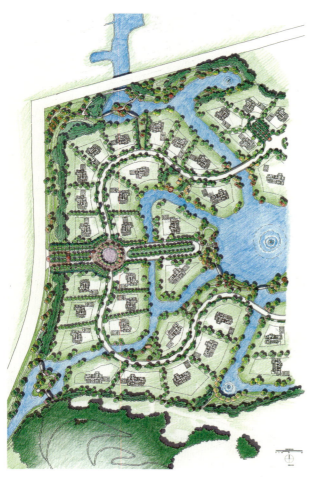

Plan - E1 west

Plan - E2

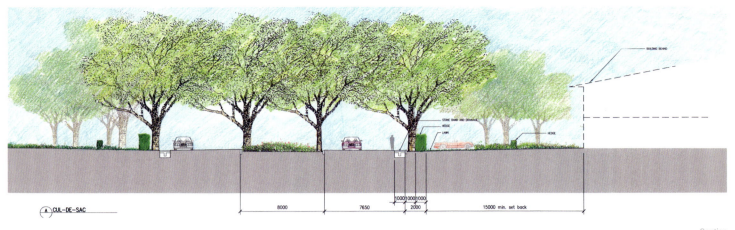

A CUL-DE-SAC

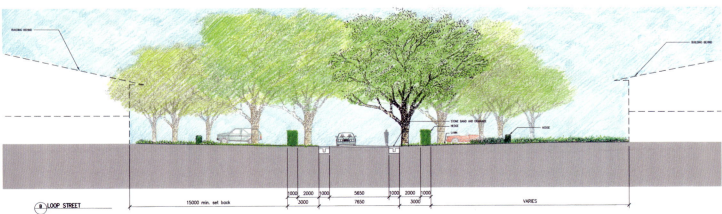

B LOOP STREET

SHIMAO SHESHAN GARDEN E1 & E2

SIP Administrative Center
Suzhou, China

Located on the east bank of Jingji Lake and on the east-west axis of Suzhou City, the Suzhou Industrial Park Administrative Center is the work area for government management departments. There are eight buildings within the site's total eight city blocks, including the Administrative Main Building, Courthouse, Police Headquarters, and Commerce Building, from which government officials serve Suzhou residents. The design team provided the landscape master plan and design for the area with a total of 70 acres, including the civic plaza, parks, central green, canal waterfront, and streetscape. The plan creates identity for the area, integrating its past and future with the central focus on water in this "City of Canals" and linking the site with its natural and historical setting.

Plan

095　SIP ADMINISTRATIVE CENTER

097　SIP ADMINISTRATIVE CENTER

099　SIP ADMINISTRATIVE CENTER

Korea World Trade Center - COEX
Seoul, Korea

This project, an expansion of the existing facilities on the site, includes the convention/exhibition center, hotel, department store and retail arcade. New facilities total 7,496,000 square feet of design and construction. The preliminary phase of study evaluated the development potential and market-driven feasibility of the project. The master plan maximizes the revenue-generating potential of the site while accommodating the expansion of the center required to remain competitive with other international centers. The design features the idea of a forest in an urban setting. The layering of landscape through the use of tree cover and lawn parterre creates a variety of spaces from closed to open and from hard to soft. Major water features are located at north and east entries, with a sunken garden open to subway connections and a lower retail level.

Plan

102   2. EARLY WORKS

3

STANFORD UNIVERSITY AND INSTITUTIONAL PROJECT CHALLENGES

108	INTRODUCTION BY David J. Neuman

SELECTED PROJECTS

110	Stanford Campus Planning and Projects
111	Stanford Liliore Rains Graduate Housing
114	Stanford University DAPER Master Plan
118	Stanford University Arrillaga Plaza and Recreation Center
120	Stanford University Cantor Center for the Visual Arts Expansion
126	Stanford University Ford Plaza
130	Stanford University Campus Center
136	Stanford University Alumni Center
142	Stanford Sand Hill Road and Stanford Shopping Center Expansion
144	Vi Living
152	Stanford West Apartments
158	Stanford University Escondido Village Master Plan
162	Stanford University Lathrop Library
168	Stanford University West Gate
169	Stanford University Lasuen Mall
174	Stanford University Meyer-Buck Estate
178	Stanford University SIEPR (Stanford Institute for Economic Policy Research)
186	Stanford University Terman Park
192	Stanford Hoover Institution, David & Joan Traitel Building
193	Stanford University Graduate School of Education
194	Stanford University Panama Mall
198	Bentley School
200	Tokyo University of Foreign Studies Campus
210	Tarrant County College

INTRODUCTION

By David J. Neuman, FAIA, LEED BD C – Founding Principal at Neu Campus Planning, Inc.

It has been a pleasure working with John L. Wong for many years, especially during my fifteen-year tenure as the University Architect for Stanford. We reacquainted shortly after my being recruited for the position in 1988. The interview panel consisted of two prominent Board of Trustee (BoT) members, who made it clear to me that the BoT was very concerned about the loss of the real character of the Stanford campus, as each new building project asserted itself without respecting the comprehensiveness of the original campus plan and its character-defining features, including the overall environmental setting and its landscape. In addition, the unchecked infiltration of roads, cars and parking into the central fabric of the core campus had diminished the quality of life for faculty, students and staff. It was apparent that the site context and landscape had been generally ignored and the original physical planning intentions had lost direction over time. The campus community now needed to work together to reestablish the *Planning Principles* that the Stanfords, both Leland and Jane, had negotiated and envisioned with Frederick Law Olmsted in the planning and design of the original Stanford campus in the late 1880's.

In 1991, the BoT approved the following *Fundamental Planning Guidelines*, as part of the *Central Campus Design Guidelines* developed by the University Architect's Office:

- Enduring Planning Framework (original Stanfords/Olmsted Plan)
- Compelling Landscape Treatment (native/naturalistic)
- Strong Contextual Architecture (both site-sensitive/current thinking)
- Controlled Perimeter Treatment (buffered boundaries with neighborhood sensitivity)
- Carefully-Designed Interactions (both on-and off-campus).

Given this directive, it was imperative that our small office team sought "consultant partners," who not only could provide project-by-project support, but also could assist us in responding quickly to requests for planning assistance: e.g. an Athletics Area Master Plan in response to a major donor's timeline. Having worked successfully and collaboratively on planning and design issues with the SWA firm's Laguna Beach office during my twelve-year tenure as the Campus Architect at UC Irvine, I had met John, and was impressed with his understanding of both the environmental and the political context of a major university campus. Thus I invited John, as part of a select group of prominent landscape architects, to join us as "partners" as he and I both understood that the situation at Stanford was very complex. It was essential that we addressed, in a significant and consistent fashion, the "public realm" of the Stanford campus, including plant and hardscape materials, as well as a universally accessible and intelligible sense of order of circulation, along with the provision of outdoor spaces for respite and small gatherings. While responding to the basic site, cost and time issues of specific projects, we had to deal sensitively in the direct engagement of a variety of stakeholders, including respective donor partners, as a key part of the project development equation at Stanford. John and I worked together on both the design and the project implementation of many Stanford landscape projects, as well as discussing future opportunities to advance the basic campus *Planning Principles* on various portions of the overall campus, including areas of third-party leasehold development; e.g. Stanford West. He complemented our Office's approach with his unique understanding of both advanced landscape concepts and sustainability principles.

His work continues to flourish at Stanford and other significant college and university campuses due to his vast experience and, more importantly, his thorough understanding of the background and rationale for a university campus that strongly supports a community of learners and scholars in the present and in the future.

Opposite page Stanford Alumni Center

Stanford Campus Planning and Projects
Stanford, California

Over the past 40 years, the design team has been working with Stanford University to reclaim the 100-year-old master plan vision of Leland Stanford and Frederick Law Olmsted for the campus. Through over 300 campus improvement projects, this design intervention has restored the historic axis, open spaces, and landscape patterns in order to juxtapose formal and naturalistic spaces within the central campus. Working with Stanford Land, Buildings, and Real Estate and the Facilities and Capital Planning group, the design team provided planning, approval processing, and landscape design services on a variety of landscape typologies, including private gardens, museum grounds, building courtyards, recreational fields and facilities, corridors, and public realms to enhance the campus ground with special emphasis on alternative transportation (pedestrian ways, bike, and campus transit) options for the student body, faculty, and visitors.

Master plan

Stanford Liliore Rains Graduate Housing
Stanford, California

The design team collaborated on the site plan and landscape architectural design for 780 new housing units, common area facilities, parking for single graduate students on the Stanford University campus, and open greens in an axial relationship, recalling the original Stanford Campus design concepts. The outdoor spaces are used for formal gathering, seating areas, games, and passive recreation. The personality of the project was further developed through the preservation and renovation of the Buttery Building, the oldest structure on the Stanford Campus. This structure is incorporated as the focus of the project, and houses offices, meeting rooms, and special events. Water conserving plant materials were employed throughout the project. Lawn was used primarily in the interior courtyard to visually link the space together and provide areas for outdoor games. Secondary and outer areas were planted primarily with drought-tolerant native plants and wood chip mulch.

Site plan

Stanford University DAPER Master Plan
Stanford, California

The design team prepared an overall master plan for the Department of Athletics, Physical Education and Recreation (DAPER) at the eastern sector of the Stanford University Campus. The plan organizes and unifies all the athletic uses; establishes pedestrian and landscape connections; and locates parking and future athletic facilities. The plan's initial phase included a new Women's NCAA Softball Facility; renovation of the track and field facility; an expansion of DeGuerre Pool; a new parking and arrival plaza; a new competition soccer field; a new artificial turf field; a new rugby field; intramural sports and practice fields; and a pedestrian promenade around the Baseball Sunken Diamond.

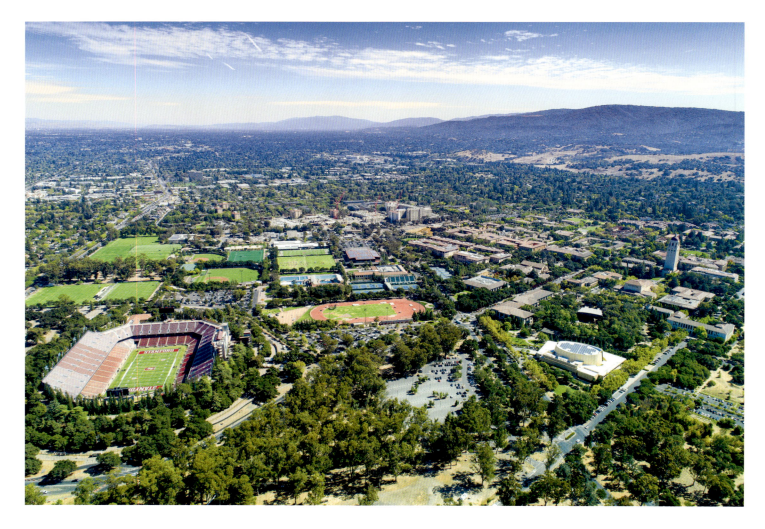

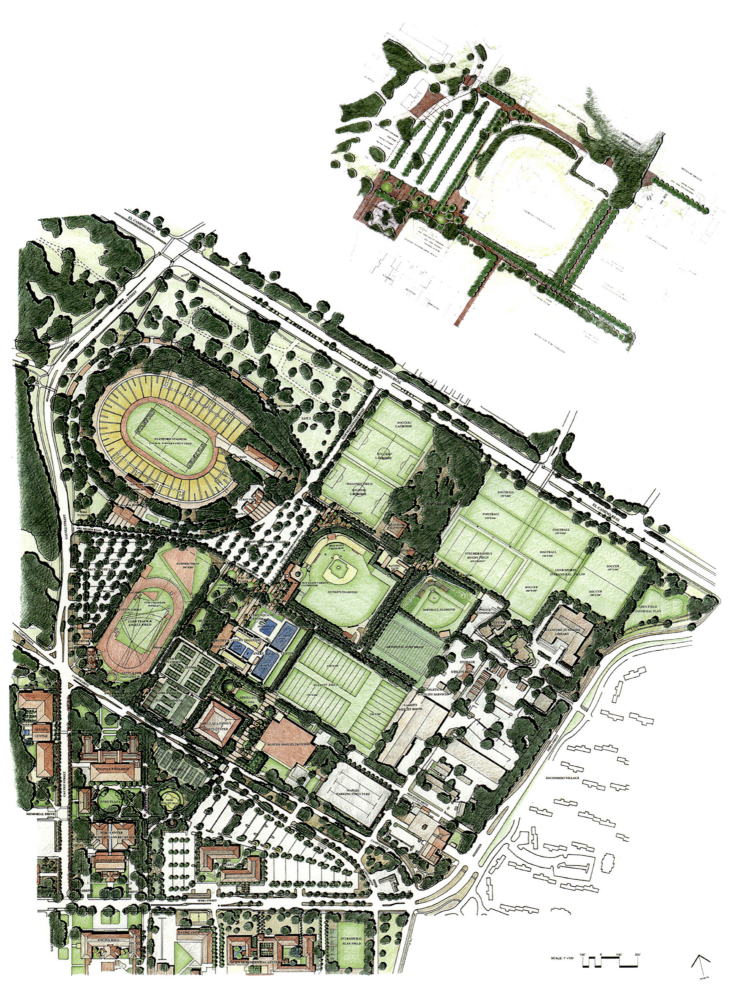

Master plan - Eastern sector

3. STANFORD UNIVERSITY AND INSTITUTIONAL PROJECT CHALLENGES

STANFORD UNIVERSITY DAPER MASTER PLAN

Stanford University Arrillaga Plaza and Recreation Center
Stanford, California

The team was retained to design Stanford University's Athletics Connective Elements Project, an area bordered by the new Arrillaga Family Sports Center, DeGuerre Pool Complex, Maples Pavilions, and Campus Drive. The concept of creating a grove for a new athletics quad was introduced to provide two multi-purpose gathering spaces for special events, informal gatherings, and recreational play. Between the new Sports Center and DeGuerre Pool, a sunken amphitheater was introduced to host major ceremonial events while between the Sports Center and Maples Pavilion, a pedestrian mall was provided for multipurpose gathering. The mall also forms a focal point for athletics toward the east. The two areas are connected with special paving, new lighting, and drifts of California Live Oaks to reinforce the "grove" idea.

The design team provided landscape design for a new intramural sports and recreation center for basketball, fencing, weightlifting, volleyball, rock climbing, racquetball, and sports medicine. The new building is sited within an existing, historic oak grove. The design includes connections to adjacent pedestrian pathways and pedestrian bridges with landscaped banks on the east and west sides to add natural light to the lower level.

Plan

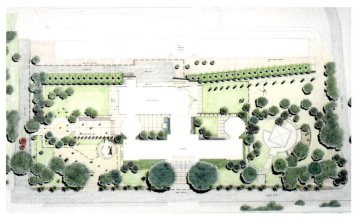

Landscape site plan

Stanford University Cantor Center for the Visual Arts Expansion
Stanford, California

The original Stanford campus museum was damaged in an earthquake in 1989. With help from Mr. and Mrs. Gerald B. Cantor, major donors to the Museum, site improvements, expansion and seismic renovation improvements were accomplished. The design team provided master plan updates and full landscape services for the site including pedestrian pathways; two major terraces for displaying of artwork; a landscaped courtyard; the siting of additional Rodin and other sculptures; and the renovation and integration of the existing Rodin Sculpture Garden with the new center gardens.

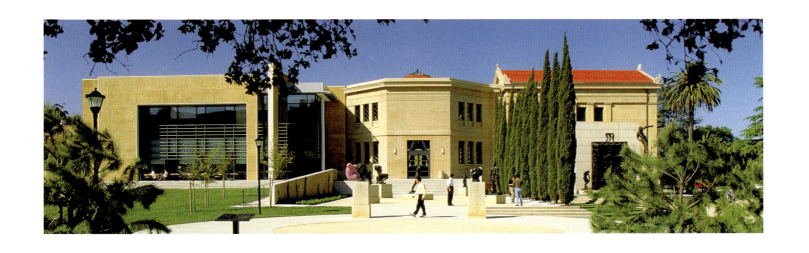

124   3. STANFORD UNIVERSITY AND INSTITUTIONAL PROJECT CHALLENGES

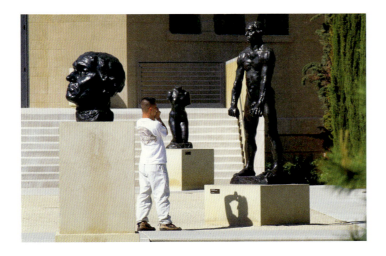

STANFORD UNIVERSITY CANTOR CENTER FOR THE VISUAL ARTS EXPANSION

Stanford University Ford Plaza
Stanford, California

This design reimagined the major outdoor usable space among buildings at the heart of the Stanford Campus, and reintroduced historic axial relationships between buildings as expressed by plantings and pedestrian circulation. The space is a key linkage between the university's academic core and athletic facilities.

Plan

Stanford University Campus Center
Stanford, California

The addition of the Campus Center required historic renovation, seismic retrofit, and a new addition to mark this important center and intersection of the campus. The design worked to preserve important tree specimens: elm, cedar, oak, sycamore and Japanese black pine, which marked the new entries to the Union and Old Bookstore complex. The design team aimed to create public gathering areas connecting to the surrounding buildings and clock tower, to facilitate pedestrian and bicycle flow, and to re-engage the complex to the historic axis of the immediate surroundings. In addition, new courtyard areas were added to the northwest and southeast sides.

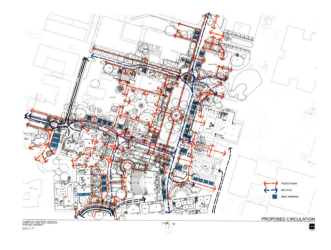

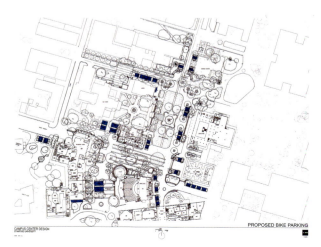

130   3. STANFORD UNIVERSITY AND INSTITUTIONAL PROJECT CHALLENGES

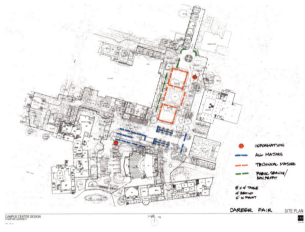
CAREER FAIR SITE PLAN
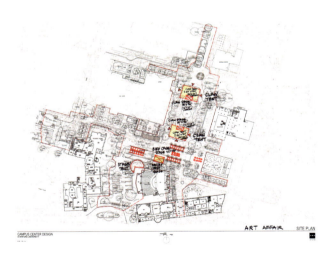
ART AFFAIR SITE PLAN
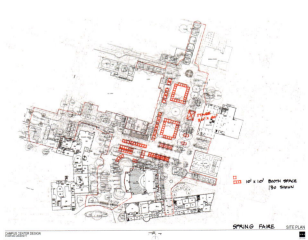
SPRING FAIRE SITE PLAN

PROPOSED ACTIVITY NODES

DEMOLITION PLAN

SITE PLAN

SITE PLAN

Site section

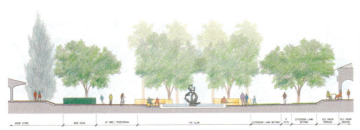 

Site section

Stanford University Alumni Center
Stanford, California

After working on the master plan for this Alumni Center, the design team won a competition for the site design. The project is adjacent to the heavily wooded Frost Amphitheater, and the berm that surrounds the space serves as the backdrop for the project's more private "back yard." This "back yard" is divided into three main spaces: a large lawn adjacent to the Great Hall for flexible outdoor use; a stroll garden near the offices featuring native perennial plantings, a café, and conference rooms; and a large paved area and fountain outside the central "living room." The fountain initially suggests a spring seeping through a stone retaining wall, with the water then traveling through the mortar joints of a stone-paved terrace 2.5 feet above the main paved area, then finally spilling into a large reflecting pool. The design also includes an entry plaza with eight date palms.

Plan

140   3. STANFORD UNIVERSITY AND INSTITUTIONAL PROJECT CHALLENGES

Stanford Sand Hill Road and Stanford Shopping Center Expansion
Stanford, California

The proposed project sites are located along Sand Hill Road from El Camino Real to Pasteur Drive with San Francisquito Creek bordering it to the West and Stanford Medical Center to the East. Beyond creating a new extension of Sand Hill Road, which previously ended in the shopping center's parking lot, the design layout aims to improve the overall circulation of this important corridor by expanding choices for bicyclists, pedestrians, and motorists. The individual projects – Stanford West Apartments, Stanford West Senior Housing (now Vi Living), Stanford Shopping Center Expansion, and related improvements - intend to establish a mix of uses that will complement existing urban patterns and reinforce linkages between jobs, housing, shopping, and recreational activities.

The landscape design integrates the new and expanded facilities into the natural setting established by the San Francisquito Creek, the oak savanna, and the western edge of Stanford campus. The overall design aims to preserve natural features on the parcel, including archaeologically sensitive areas and existing mature trees. Internal street grids, architecture, and landscape elements are designed to recall the traditions of existing older neighborhoods in Palo Alto and Menlo Park. The shopping center design focused on improving parking layout and pedestrian circulation while expanding the natural character of the landscape into the shopping center and road corridor extension. The proposed material palettes consist of native oaks, California natives, and natural field grasses that extend the existing rural character of the roadway south of the projects to the new projects at the north and provide cultural and aesthetic continuity along this important corridor.

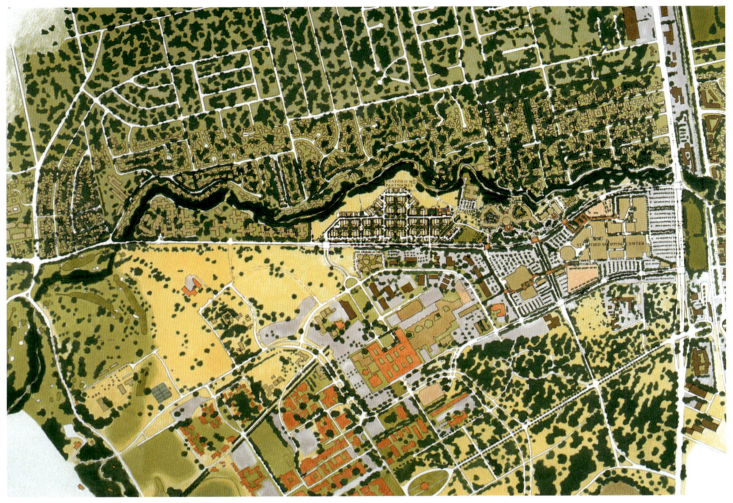
Expansion plan

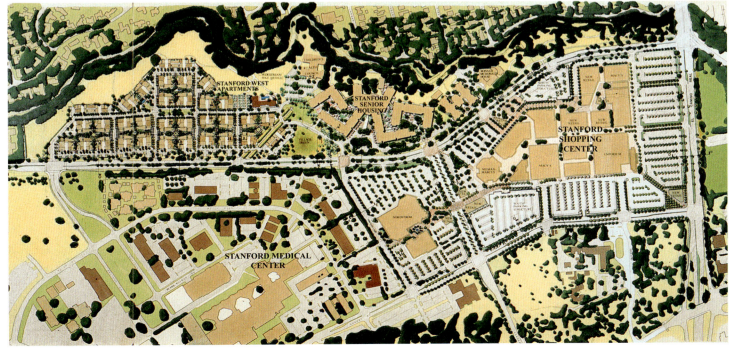
Plan

Vi Living
Palo Alto, California

Vi Living is a continuing-care community that offers senior residents access to many cultural, medical, and community resources. Outdoor trails and garden spaces were designed to create a strong social community and environment for residents to enjoy. The project, built on an existing brownfield site, was designed to preserve hundreds of oaks and redwoods and the environmentally sensitive rare native plants and wildlife habitat, including some endangered species. Drought-tolerant native plants were propagated from local seedlings and planted for native reservation. Rain gardens were designed to recharge 90 percent of the groundwater, filtering runoff before it enters the environmentally sensitive San Francisquito Creek. Recycled local materials, including gravel and boulders from the site's former roads and buildings, were also utilized.

Plan

150   3. STANFORD UNIVERSITY AND INSTITUTIONAL PROJECT CHALLENGES

Stanford West Apartments
Palo Alto, California

The design team provided planning, approvals processing and full landscape architectural services for this project located in the Sand Hill Road corridor of the Stanford University Campus. Stanford West Apartments consists of 630 multifamily units and is oriented to employees at nearby employment centers such as the campus, medical center, and research park.

The new neighborhood preserves natural features on the parcel, including archaeologically sensitive areas and existing mature trees. Internal street grids, architecture and landscape elements were designed to recall the traditions of existing older neighborhoods in Palo Alto and Menlo Park.

Plan

152   3. STANFORD UNIVERSITY AND INSTITUTIONAL PROJECT CHALLENGES

Stanford University Escondido Village Master Plan
Stanford, California

As part of the design team's charge to provide cost-effective, phased strategies for redevelopment and increased capacity in one of Stanford's graduate housing areas, we designed and implemented the first phase of a pedestrian / bike connection and greenway. The spine is located centrally to provide connections to the central open space and recreation areas. New pavement, lighting and landscaping for pedestrian and bike were provided to mark this new entry.

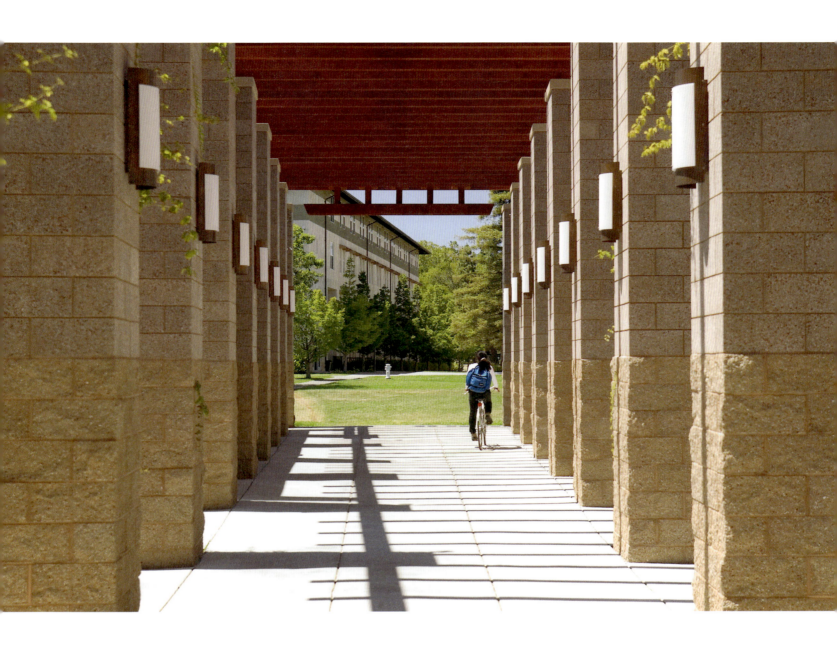

Stanford University Lathrop Library
Stanford, California

This project included a master plan update and full landscape architectural services for the west side of the Graduate School of Business, the Littlefield Center courtyard, the north parking area, and the continuation of Lasuen Mall. Major features of the landscape design realigned the historic north and south axis of Lasuen Mall and sited California Live Oak trees and bike parking courts along the main entry with new seating and pedestrian pathways to connect the various points of entry.

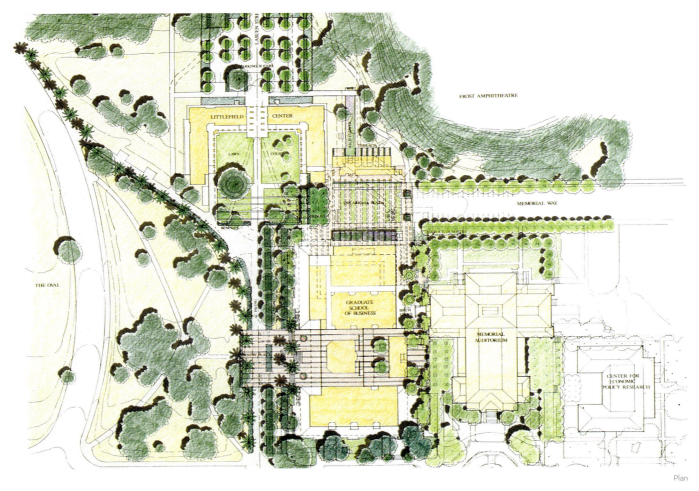

Plan

Plan – First floor

165　STANFORD UNIVERSITY LATHROP LIBRARY

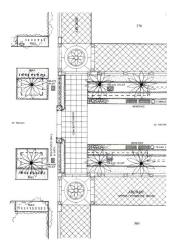
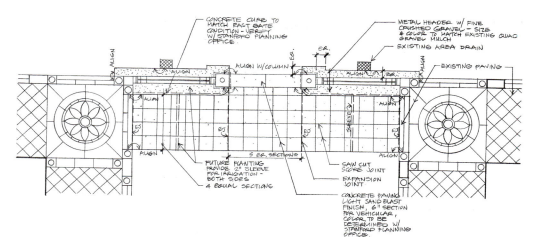

Stanford University West Gate
Stanford, California

The project is located on the Main Quad at the center line of the east-west axis, one of the main cross-axes to the north-south axis framed by Lasuen Mall and Lomita Mall. The design's goal is to set up a symmetrical entry gateway and forecourt aligning to the historic portal of the Main Quad. Five pairs of vertical Mexican Fan Palms framed by paired benches reinforce the architectural arcade while decomposed granite paving and native plants line this important axis, restoring the original design vision for these key entries, which lead to both the extension of the Science Quads to the west and to the historical main entrance to Green Library.

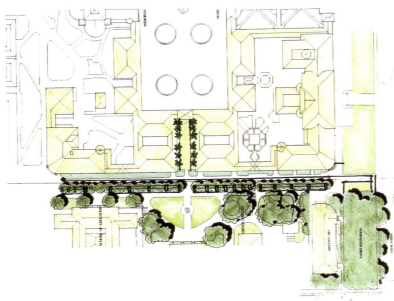

Stanford University Lasuen Mall
Stanford, California

This project is a realignment of the Olmsted historic north-south axis which links up to the former Business School to the north and the Student Union to the south. During the seventies, projects added along the mall ignored this important axial opening. The scheme called for a new pedestrian/bike alignment base walk with granite curb for the historic Main Quad and with new planting and seating. Lighting is added and realigned to reflect the formal layout along with a new bike parking enclosure screened by clipped hedges.

173　STANFORD UNIVERSITY LASUEN MALL

Stanford University Meyer-Buck Estate
Stanford, California

A mansion with a seven-acre site belonging to J. Henry Meyer, a leading San Francisco Financier and a major influence in California's development, was bequeathed as a gift to Stanford University in 1970. A future development plan was drawn up by the design team on a three-acre portion of the site for the future residence of the provost. The project included the restoration of the two-story early 20th-century building and the creation of new gardens based on historical precedents.

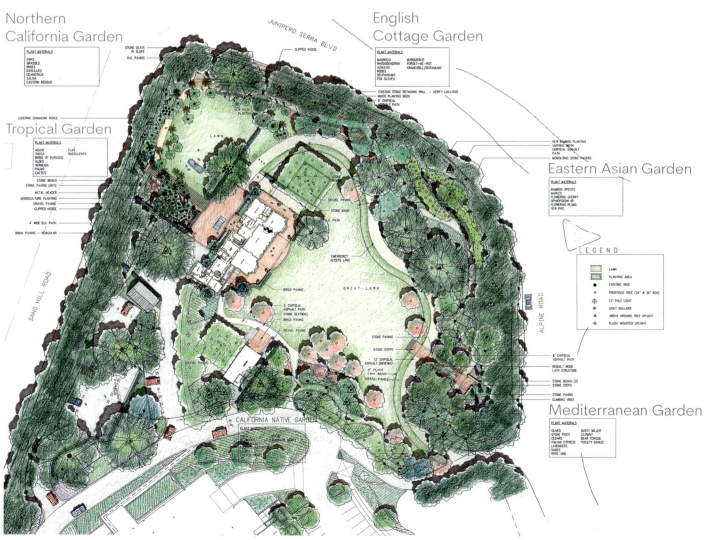

Plan - First floor

Stanford University SIEPR (Stanford Institute for Economic Policy Research)
Stanford, California

The Stanford Institute for Economic Policy Research is an organization designed to unite economists from a variety of entities within the University to analyze, discuss, and debate current economic topics and issues. The institute resides in a 3-story, L-shaped building on a former parking lot, concentrating the building massing along the edge of the site while creating a courtyard and lawn space unifying the landscape space in front of the Landau Economics Building. Beginning in a basin at the building entry and running the entire campus block, a linear water feature and pergola defines interior courtyard and campus streetscape. The curtain wall connector between the building wings frames another view of the courtyard with an allée of mature fan palms, an orange tree grove, and large fountain basin, recognizing the project donor whose keen interest in landscape translated to extensive participation and involvement with the overall design expression and material selection.

185   STANFORD UNIVERSITY SIEPR (STANFORD INSTITUTE FOR ECONOMIC POLICY RESEARCH)

Stanford University Terman Park
Stanford, California

The need to remove an outdated 1970s-era engineering building at Stanford offered unique design opportunities for an interim park space. The project emphasized reuse and utilized salvaged materials, as well as the existing grading and fountain, as key features of the park. As a multifunction performance and recreational space, the project sought to preserve the land for future uses. The design also encompassed the final phase of the Panama Mall Master Plan, enhancing pedestrian and bike circulation along historic Panama Mall. Overall, the new park is a model of efficient site development incorporating many possibilities for recreation and study, making the most of an interim land use.

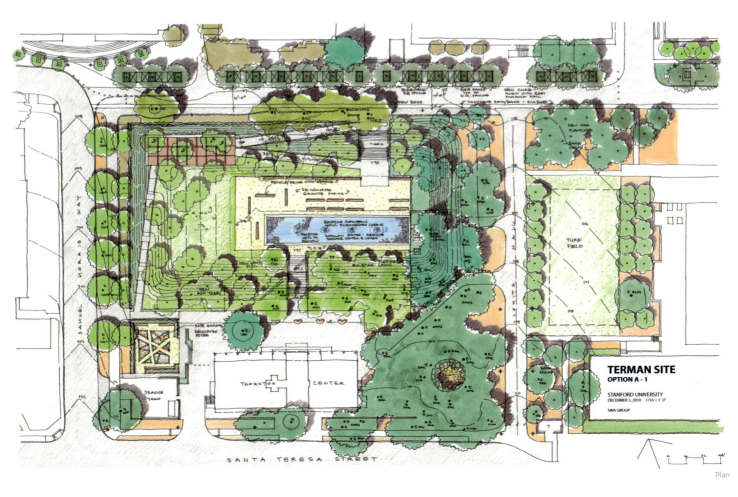

Plan

190   3. STANFORD UNIVERSITY AND INSTITUTIONAL PROJECT CHALLENGES

Site plan

Stanford Hoover Institution, David & Joan Traitel Building
Stanford, California

The Hoover Institution at Stanford University is a public policy research organization promoting the principles of individual, economic, and political freedom. The design team collaborated to create a building and site that helped promote research through open connections and workspaces. The site design serves as an extension of the building itself, bringing conversational thinking and teamwork outside the office environment and facilitating a range of special events. The design team also paid particular attention to work within the established design criteria and traditions of the Stanford campus, while at the same time showcasing the Hoover Institution site as a "campus within a campus." By establishing a hierarchy of courtyards, walkways, and gathering spaces, the landscape design supports the proposed program while reinforcing the identity of the Hoover Institution, expanding its presence, and respecting the campus framework of landscape, landmarks, connections, and destinations. In addition to preserving trees, the design also respects and reinforces existing circulation and use patterns of this important campus district. A proposed new pavilion creates two courtyards that are carefully scaled and designed to support the pavilion's exhibition and reception functions as well as the main building's assembly and dining activities. The main courtyard was designed with pervious paving and tree wells to treat stormwater entirely below the courtyard. The landscape also incorporates low-water-use plants and efficient irrigation systems that tie into the overall campus landscape program.

Section - North-south

Stanford University Graduate School of Education
Stanford, California

Stanford's Graduate School of Education has a new quad that encompasses major renovation to an existing building, a new south building (Barnum), and the consolidation of uses from six separate locations on campus. The central courtyard space created by the two buildings forms the east-west axis and hosts outdoor classrooms while serving as a large event space for people to gather.

Relocated specimen native oak trees form a significant gateway entrance on the Lasuen Mall side, while informal native plantings on the Meyer Green side blend into the existing landscape. The ground plane's paving pattern is inspired by shelves of library books, representing the fundamental concepts of education, knowledge, and information.

Section - East-west

Stanford University Panama Mall
Stanford, California

Located at the southwest side of the Main Quad, Panama Mall was designed to be the major connection between the East Quad and the West Quad. The project converts a utilitarian service route to a main east-west corridor to accommodate pedestrian, bike, emergency and service access; the Mall needed to maintain existing service and emergency access while providing a separate, new pedestrian and bike path. The east end connects to Lausen, a major north-south connector and to the recently completed Campus Center. The west end terminates at the new Terman sunken park and in the future will extend to the west campus. In addition, the linear corridor includes informal seating, picnic units, group study area, and new bike parking. An allee of existing spruce and new trees in the same alignment provides structure to this important campus connection.

Schematic design – Master plan

Bentley School
Stanford, California

The design team provided master planning and landscape architectural services for the expansion and renovation of this private school. The design uses boldly painted seatwalls as art pieces that allow flexible use of courtyard space for outdoor classrooms and gatherings, while preserving the site's native stands of oaks and conifers. The project restores an abandoned school site to a safe and highly functional condition; upgrades existing buildings for energy conservation; and furthers the school's philosophy that the physical environment is integral to its educational mission.

Master plan

A. Existing Classroom Buildings
B. Gymnasium
C. Pool
D. Administration
E. Library
F. Theater/Arts Complex

Tokyo University of Foreign Studies Campus
Fuchu, Japan

The design team provided master planning and landscape architecture for the 10.7-hectare Foreign Studies Campus of Tokyo University, on the site of a former military base on the outskirts of Tokyo. This campus serves Japanese and foreign students pursuing a wide range of degrees in international studies and all aspects of world culture. The design features a clear, hierarchical landscape, with a strong diagonal spine that connects the adjacent town's retail center and transit station through the campus: passing through an entry plaza, a circular central plaza; past interconnected courtyards and gardens; and then to the student housing and playfields. The design sited buildings to preserve as many existing trees as possible. This flexible, functional landscape offers formal and informal outdoor gathering spaces. The design includes a series of outdoor elements to encourage social activity as well as outdoor teaching, reading, and study. The Main Entry Plaza offers seating and bicycle parking; the Central Garden accommodates major gatherings; and a series of smaller garden spaces relate to classroom buildings, serving to draw people outside.

Plan

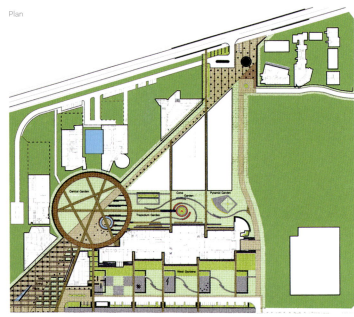

204   3. STANFORD UNIVERSITY AND INSTITUTIONAL PROJECT CHALLENGES

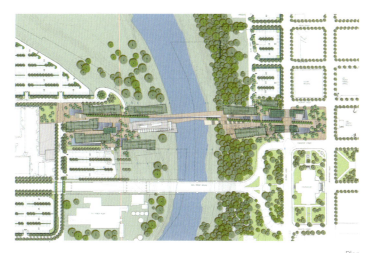

Plan

Tarrant County College
Fort Worth, Texas

The Tarrant County College District (TCCD) created a fifth college campus in downtown Fort Worth to meet the growing needs of the region; the college is expected to serve 10,000 students by 2023. The design team provided the campus master plan and landscape design. The campus site is bisected by the Trinity River and the design features a connecting bridge. Water features throughout the campus draw people through the central spine of the site, providing a connection to the river. The central spine, including two entry plazas, roof gardens, courtyards and unique streetscape elements encourages interaction between students, seamlessly integrating indoor and outdoor educational platforms, while pushing the boundaries of innovation.

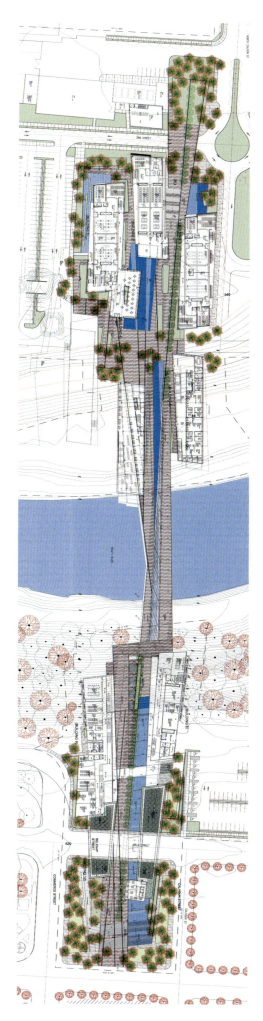

Master plan

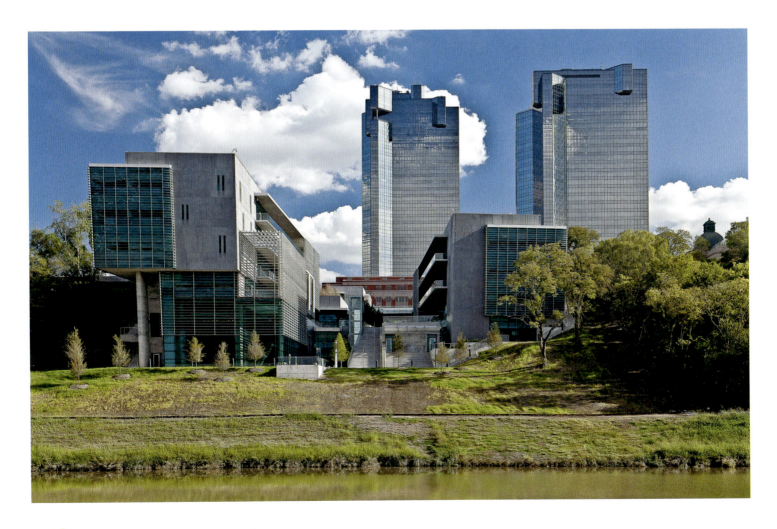

213 TARRANT COUNTY COLLEGE

217 TARRANT COUNTY COLLEGE

4

LANDSCAPE / GROUNDSCAPE FOR THE WORLD'S TALL AND TALLEST STRUCTURES

222	INTRODUCTION by Adrian Smith & Gordon Gill
	SELECTED PROJECTS
224	LG Twin Towers
228	Marinaside Crescent
230	LG Kangnam Tower
234	Roppongi 6-6 Urban Redevelopment
236	Tower Palace 1, 2, and 3
238	Zifeng Tower – Nanjing Greenland International Commercial Center
248	Lite-On Technology Headquarters
254	Pearl River Tower (Zero Energy Tower)
258	Burj Khalifa
278	Downtown Dubai
282	Suzhou Greenland Center
284	Nanchang Greenland Jiangxi Gaoxin
292	Nanchang Greenland Central Plaza
302	Minsheng Center
304	Jeddah Tower
306	Federation of Korean Industries Head Office
308	Chengdu Dongcun Greenland Tower
310	North Bund White Magnolia Plaza
318	Shanghai Tower
334	Burj 2020
336	Nanjing Greenland Pukou
338	Jinan Greenland CBD Super High-Rise
340	Cayan Tower
341	Mashreq Bank Headquarters
342	Chongqing A13 Jiangbeizui International Finance Center
343	Nanjing Hexi Yuzui Tower (Runmao Tower)
344	Downtown Dubai Opera District
352	Kula Belgrade
354	Liansheng Financial Center
358	Chengdu Tianfu New District High-Rise
362	Victoria Ward Waiea Tower
370	Wuhan Greenland Center
372	The Butterfly Tower
374	Georgia-Pender
376	Zhangjiang Science Center Parcel #56, #57, #58
378	Sky View 4, 5, 6 – The Address Residence

INTRODUCTION

By Adrian Smith, FAIA, Gordon Gill, FAIA. Founding Partners at Adrian Smith + Gordon Gill Architecture

For centuries, the role of landscape design has often been to define and uplift the human experience of built environments. Today, that role has expanded to include the nuanced understanding of the psychology of comfort, mobility, and environmental issues that are inextricably tied to landscape design and building design.

In this chapter, through his work at SWA, John Wong articulates and demonstrates how beautiful landscape experiences can enhance architectural design and improve upon the character of urban spaces. He explores the range of expressions for exterior spaces and interior spaces and has the breadth and depth of knowledge to apply his art to parks, buildings, and entire cities.

The landscape concepts herein respond to the culture, the aesthetic sensibilities, and the architecture while respecting local historical issues, sustainability goals, and the need to provide functional and attractive spaces.

Within the range of projects that John has engaged in with Adrian Smith + Gordon Gill Architecture (AS+GG) are supertall towers, parks, cities, and a host of venues that define cities and even countries around the world. Some of the most rewarding designs include establishing the arrival experience and grounding of supertall towers. These typologies respond to the skyline, the mid-scale of cities, and most importantly, the ground plane. It is always important to our firm that supertall towers meet the ground in a graceful manner; one that responds to the context and scale of pedestrians as they arrive and experience the project for the first or maybe their last time.

Adrian Smith has known and collaborated with John for many years both as Design Partner at AS+GG and previously at SOM Chicago. On each project he was instrumental in bringing to life the hardscape and softscape of many of these projects. The most impactful was the work he did for the Burj Khalifa in Dubai. John's work features patterns, textures, and water features that are exquisitely nuanced. His use of local plant materials helped define the public spaces in both beautiful and brilliant ways and are highly contextual with the architecture and the environment.

In many cases, as the projects demand greater integration of embodied carbon and universal accessibility, the art of landscape design is now infused with the science and data of comfort, water use, wind design, and thermal micro-climatic issues that result in timeless design.

Over the past thirty years of personal involvement on projects with John we have been provided with a lens into his work with his collaborative process where he successfully creates a range of expressions and experiences for users. The beauty and intelligence of these works lay the groundwork for a legacy of landscape design set within a deeper goal: simply to provide spaces of beauty and enjoyment for people.

John has accumulated an impressive portfolio of beautiful landscapes and place making; a tribute to his ability to successfully transcend fashion and create timeless spaces at all scales in a vast array of climatic and cultural conditions.

Specific projects are described in a variety of countries including the UAE, the USA, China, Saudi Arabia, South Korea, and Kazakhstan.

Each of these projects has their own identity, providing unique aspects of beauty while conserving energy and water and reducing CO2 and landfill waste. Of special note is the recent Expo 2020 design where John was not only responsible for the featured space in the Al Wasl Plaza landscape but also crafted the entire public realm of the Expo experience, which set the expectations of public realm experience for the Expo itself and now for the future of Expo City. This new city, designed in Dubai, has established a set of sustainable and public realm standards for the world to follow. A modern walkable city where cars are secondary and, once again, the human experience is paramount.

Opposite page Nanchang Greenland Central Plaza

LG Twin Towers
Seoul, Korea

The design team provided landscape architectural services and urban design consultation to the architects for development of a landscaped compound. The design depicts corporate identity and humanism for an office building complex sited on a major parade ground opposite the new governmental center in downtown Seoul.

The design includes twin high-rise towers for LG (Lucky Gold Star) with the center atrium to function as a public forum and media center. The plan features a public plaza with interior street and a bosque of shade trees to create the base setting for the tower complex. A major multimedia fountain with jets is centered to the front entry.

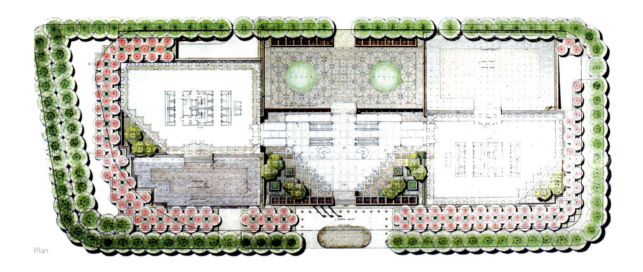

Plan

224   4. LANDSCAPE/GROUNDSCAPE FOR THE WORLD'S TALL AND TALLEST STRUCTURES

Marinaside Crescent
Vancouver, British Columbia, Canada

SWA provided urban design and overall conceptual landscape architectural design for this mixed-use project including condominium buildings with shops, restaurants and storefronts at street level, a waterfront promenade, a marina, parks, inner building courtyards, roof gardens and pedestrian-oriented pathways linking the Marinaside Crescent Road and surrounding streets. The design included four city blocks forming a crescent to a marina with pedestrian/bike promenade and a waterfront access drive behind linking the entire waterfront as part of a regional open space connection at False Creek. The residential towers are strategically placed to maximize and frame views to the water and allow additional views open to the back of the project site. Three to four story townhouses connect the towers and reinforce the crescent at the street with retail and shops at the side street and three open space corridors channel views and provide pedestrian connection to the waterfront and a waterfront park. The design goals also included privacy, and livability, and effective vehicular and non-vehicular movement throughout the site.

Plan

LG Kangnam Tower
Seoul, Korea

The design team provided schematic landscape design services for this new corporate high-rise headquarters for the Lucky Goldstar Group. The building is situated in an area of Seoul known as Kangnam, on the district's prestigious Teheranno Boulevard. The landscape design at the base of the tower is composed of four major spaces: the Sunken Pool Garden at the southwest corner, the Bamboo Garden Court on the northwest corner, the Arrival Plaza at the mid-level of the tower lobby, and the Art Hall Garden on the third level of the northeast corner.

Plan

Roppongi 6-6 Urban Redevelopment
Tokyo, Japa

The design team provided master landscape design for this 30,000-square-meter mixed-use redevelopment project in Tokyo's Roppongi area. The project includes a 50-story signature high-rise office building; a television studio; residential, commercial, and hotel uses; public plazas; and restoration of an historic Japanese garden. The Guggenheim Museum will also house a permanent collection of contemporary art in the roof penthouse of the office towers.

Plan

Tower Palace 1, 2, and 3
Seoul, Korea

Tower Palace (TP1, 2, and 3) represents three separate urban blocks, each with its own identity and use. The program for all three blocks proposed mixed-use development among the seven towers (one tower on TP3, two towers on TP2, and four Towers on TP1) encompassing retail, office, and residential spaces. Due to the complex nature of such a development, it was vital for the landscape to establish a coherent green framework responding to evolving urban conditions while acknowledging the duality of public and private spaces.

The design's broad landscape strategies strengthened the streetscape by establishing a double allée of ginkgos, and enhancing the connections between the different spaces through the use of paving and lighting furnishings. The landscape also creates a unifying structure for all three blocks while maintaining a distinct character for each. The private spaces' design is more playful, with open and intimate park and play spaces arranged in a manner that allows residents of all ages to feel a sense of ownership.

Zifeng Tower – Nanjing Greenland International Commercial Center
Nanjing, China

Nanjing Greenland International Commercial Center is a 12-acre urban high-rise site that encompasses existing parks and adjacent historic Drum Tower to the South. The 450-meter main tower, Zifeng Tower, and its concentric rings of mixed trees and linear water features is the focus of the overall site. Sidewalks are widened to include an urban parterre garden consisting of hedges, colorful perennial flowers, and seating, that increases the commercial vibrancy of the street and allows easy and convenient pedestrian movement between the ground floor retail stores and the adjacent streets.

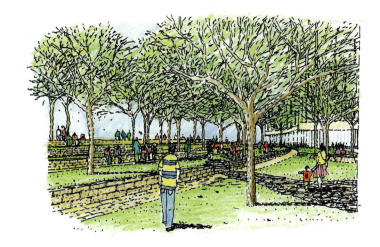
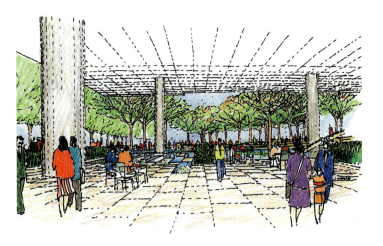

Plan

245　ZIFENG TOWER – NANJING GREENLAND INTERNATIONAL COMMERCIAL CENTER

Lite-On Technology Headquarters
Neihu Science Park

The overall concept for this major electronics company's headquarters is of a slender, 25-story tower rising above a sloped landscape podium that covers much of the site. The podium provides security, gardens, and a green roof while retaining stormwater for irrigation, and providing insulation for the public spaces below. As the garden slopes away from the tower, stepped water features create visual and aural interest. Halfway down, a light well opens to a courtyard below. Stepped fountains in the courtyard and a grove of Madagascar almond trees can be viewed from the cafeteria or from the pedestrian bridges on the podium above. The generous open space around the tower gives it distinction in a dense urban context, and plays a major role in accomplishing the owner's vision for completely "green" development. Conceived before LEED accreditation, this was the first green roof envisioned and built by a private party in this part of the continent.

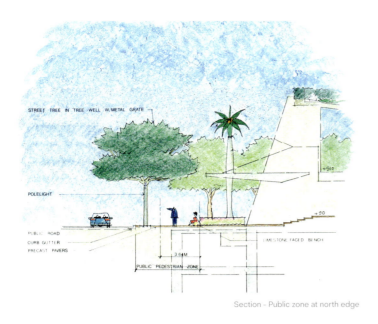

Section - Public zone at north edge

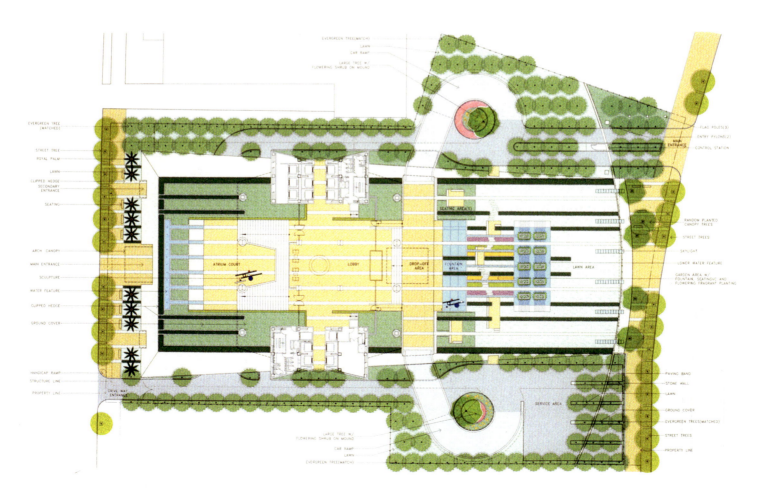

Landscape plan

251　LITE-ON TECHNOLOGY HEADQUARTERS

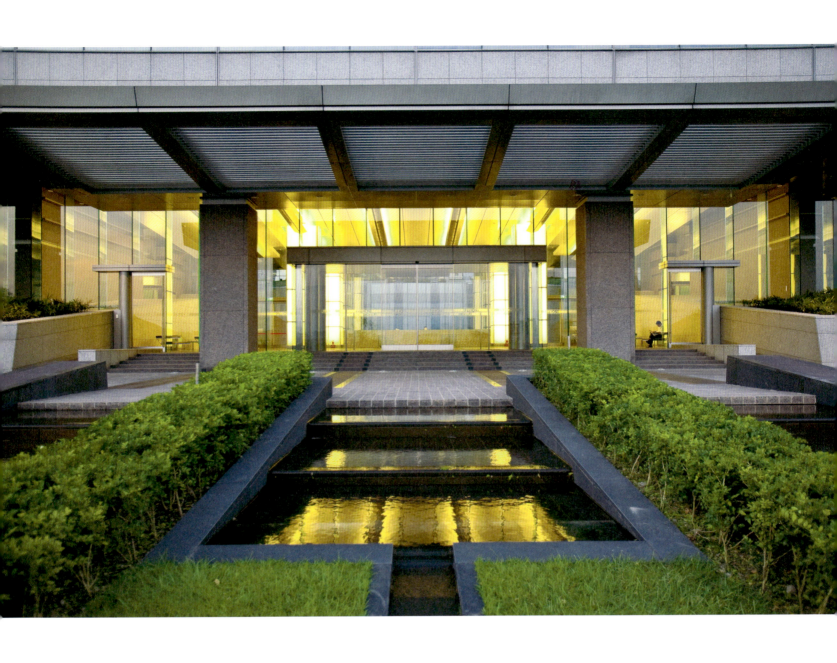

Pearl River Tower (Zero Energy Tower)
Guangzhou, China

This project is situated along the west side of the central axis of the new Guangzhou Development Park area. Its single tower standing at 70 stories, reaching a maximum height of 309.4 meters, represents the cutting edge in self-sustaining, high-performance, environmentally intelligent architecture. The project's landscape design reinforces principles of sustainability and zero-energy usage accomplished by the building's siting, architecture, and engineering. Along the street edges, a canopy of large shade trees provides natural cooling and gathering places, with benches provided in shaded areas. A linear planted "ribbon" along Jinsui Road intercepts the majority of drainage from the buildings. The landscape design also includes ponds at the east and west ends of the tower that serve both as storage basins for water cooling and as landscape features enhanced with water lilies and papyrus.

These landscape elements combine to reinforce the project's ambitious program of sustainability, function, and beauty; establish important public gathering places; and connect the project to the city's larger pedestrian and open space framework.

Plan

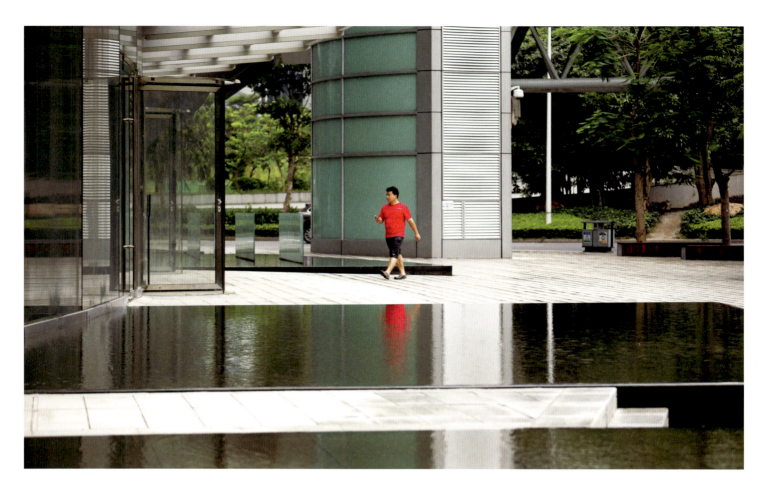

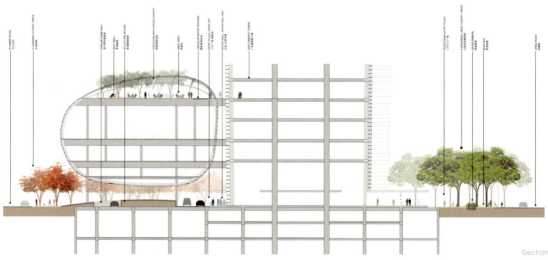

Section

256 4. LANDSCAPE/GROUNDSCAPE FOR THE WORLD'S TALL AND TALLEST STRUCTURES

Section

Burj Khalifa
Dubai, UAE

The design team provided landscape architectural services for Burj Khalifa Tower Park which covers eleven hectares of land and includes a lake-edge promenade, a functional island, a leisure forest grove, outdoor dining areas, and a children's play space. Spectacular stone paving patterns and six major water features welcome visitors. The landscape design of this mixed-use tower includes three areas that correspond to the tower's hotel, residential, and office spaces. A landscaped drop-off area is designed for each of the three sections of the building and gardens, with a lake and additional water features designed to draw people to outside activities and accompanying retail and restaurant spaces. The hot and humid outside air, combined with the chilled water-cooling system of Burj Khalifa Tower, results in a significant amount of condensation. The design allows 15 million annual gallons of condensed water to be collected, drained, and pumped into the site irrigation system for use on the tower's landscape plantings.

Plan

Main entry/water court arrival:
1. Palm tree grove at entry plaza
2. Water petals
3. Fog fountain
4. Special stone paving
5. Seasonal color
6. Entry signage

Tower garden zone:
7. Informal canopy flowering shade trees
8. Flowering shrubs & groundcover
9. Stone terrace walls
10. Palm-lined median road

Hotel entry arrival court:
11. Circular glass wall with lighting
12. Entry fountain
13. Central palm grove
14. Seasonal colors in radial pattern
15. Cobblestone driveway
16. Special stone paving & intricate banding
17. Special mosaic paving ring

Residential entry arrival court:
18. Circular stone texture wall
19. Entry fountain
20. Special flowering tree grove
21. Seasonal colors with palm circle
22. Special stone paving
23. Cobblestone driveway
24. Special mosaic paving ring
25. Visitor parking
26. Garden

Lake front recreation:
27. Grand viewing deck with special garden parterre
28. Water feature @ upper terrace and lower arrival
29. Special indigenous flowering shade trees
30. Informal seating
31. Shade canopy structure
32. Planes of reflecting water pool cascading with gravity flow
33. Sloped garden walks with flowering borders
34. Outdoor eating island incorporating major canopy
35. Landscape flowering/lawn parterres intersect with water
36. Flower gardens
37. Water fall at garage entry
38. Viewing lawn terrace
39. Water play area for children
40. Seating wall & stairs
41. Amphitheater
42. Bocce court
43. Viewing terrace
44. Palm-lined walkway
45. Waterfront seating & steps

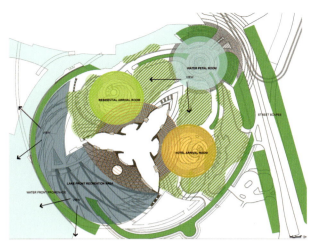

Tower park concept

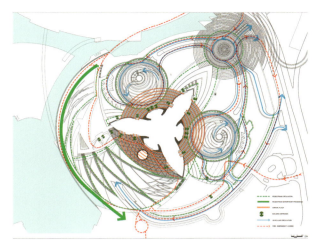

Tower park circulation

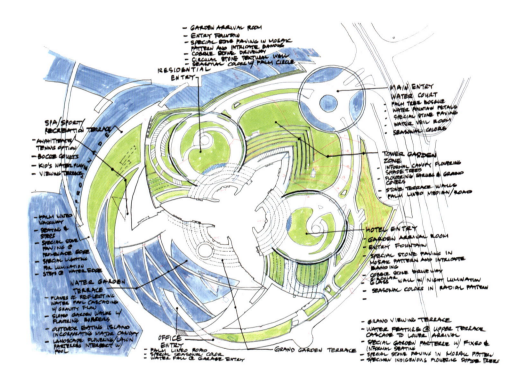

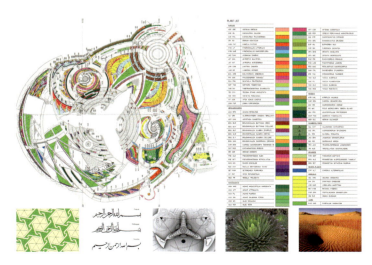

Planting design and Planting plan: The inspiration for the Burj Khalifa groundscape was the intricate and beautiful patterning found in the region's Islamic art, architecture, and gardens. Indigenous plant materials and local stone paving are woven across the ground plane in a complex geometric pattern reminiscent of the region's spider lilies as well as the formal gardens and mosques that spread throughout the gulf region.

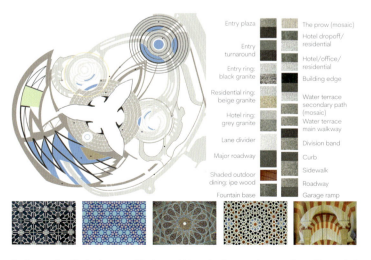

Hardscape plan: The landscape architects sought to make the groundscape – the setting against which this pinnacle of architectural and engineering achievement stands – as groundbreaking and awe-inspiring as the tower itself. The hardscape design references the geometry, patterning, and cultural influences of the region with interlocking or woven fabrics, textiles, and materials.

262   4. LANDSCAPE/GROUNDSCAPE FOR THE WORLD'S TALL AND TALLEST STRUCTURES

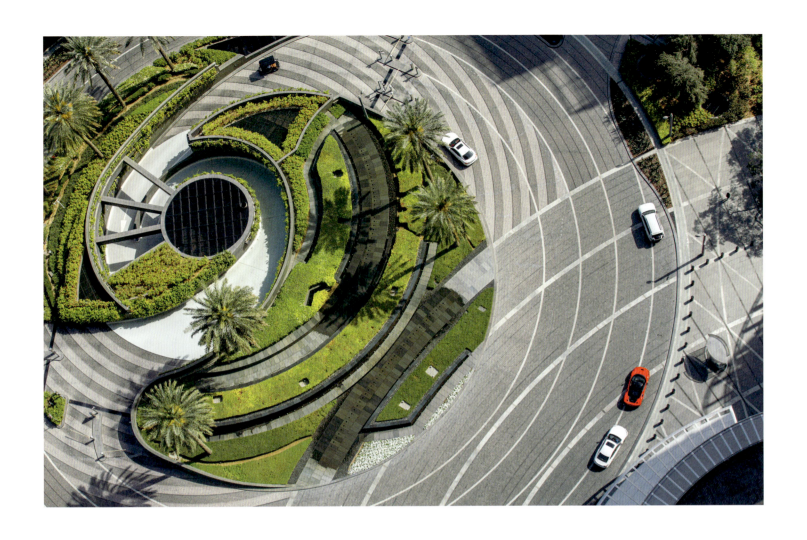

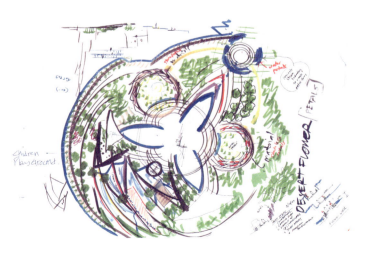

264   4. LANDSCAPE/GROUNDSCAPE FOR THE WORLD'S TALL AND TALLEST STRUCTURES

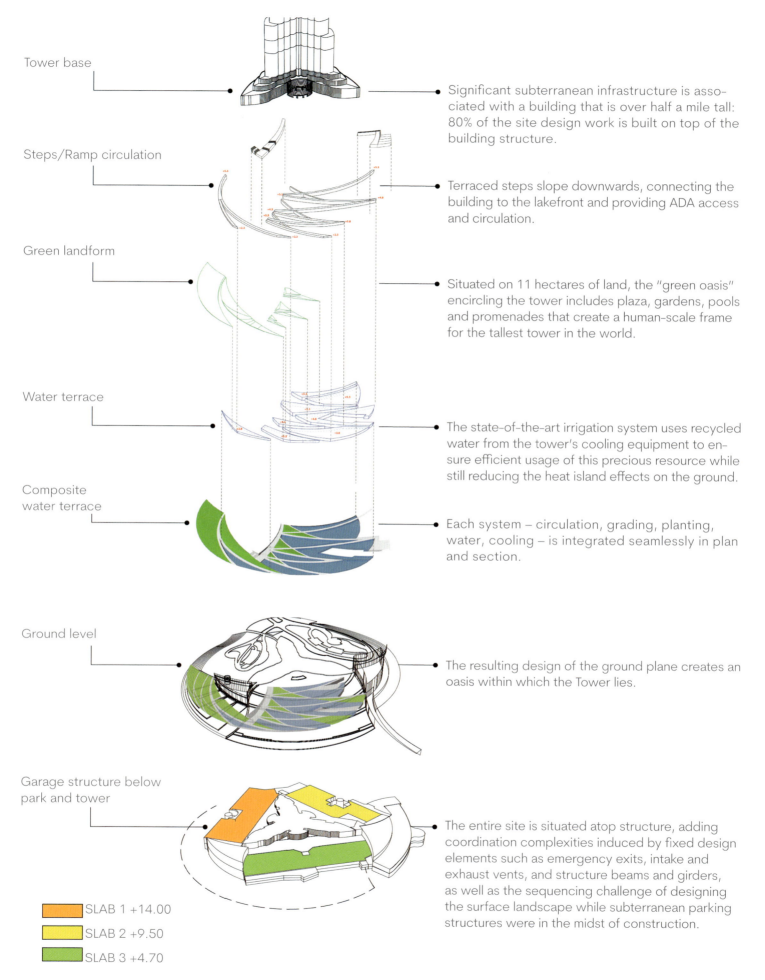

Structural diagram – Complexity and innovation: Surrounding the tower is a highly complex design knitting together a green oasis, multiple levels, water coolant and terracing, garage structuring, soil depth, load capacity, intake and exhaust, and entrance and circulation

Site section – Entry

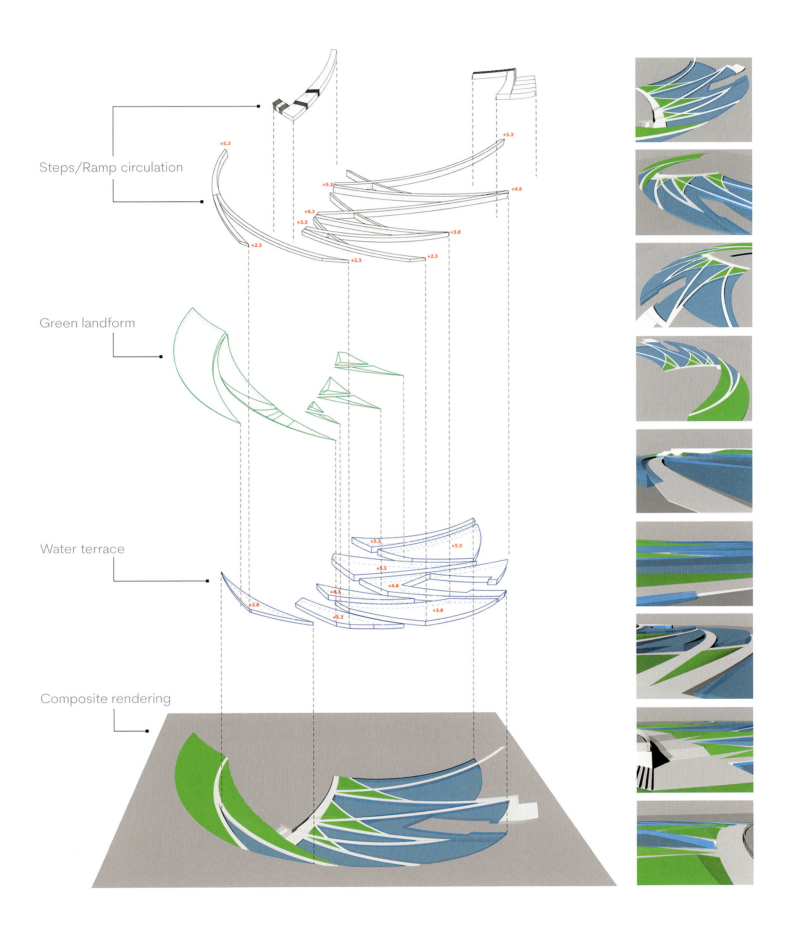

Structural diagram - Water terrace study

273　BURJ KHALIFA

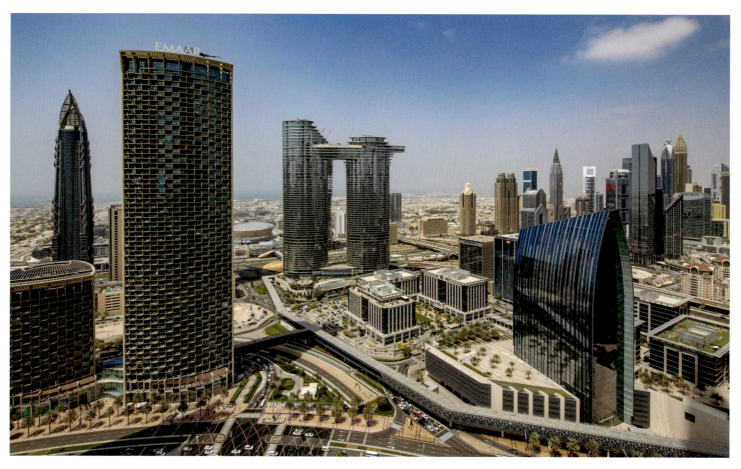

Downtown Dubai
Dubai, UAE

Downtown Burj Dubai – the area surrounding the Burj Khalifa Tower, the tallest man-made structure in the world – includes Burj Khalifa Tower Park and Sheikh Mohammed bin Rashid Boulevard, a 3.5-kilometer-long boulevard lined with luxury shops and cafes. The design for the boulevard includes a palm-lined greenway for shade, dynamic water features, and varied settings for public gatherings and celebrations.

Plan - At the center is the tower, surrounded by the tower park, lake, boulevard and urban district

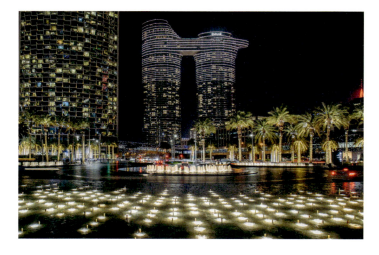

Plan

Suzhou Greenland Center
Suzhou, China

In the new urban center of Wujiang, Suzhou Greenland Center features a sculptural tower that offers residential and hotel living adjacent to a retail center. The design team developed the landscape design concept for the mixed-use complex to form the base for the high-rise tower. Sited prominently along Lake Taihu, in the Jiangsu province of China, the site is busy and active, and the first major development in the formerly agricultural area. At ground level of the iconic tower, separate lobbies ensure that each use can operate independently while the retail podium building features a main entrance on diagonal axis with the tower providing visual connectivity and creating a central multi-use plaza as the major public realm.

Nanchang Greenland Jiangxi Gaoxin
Nanchang, Jianxi, China

The landscape architectural design for Nanchang Greenland Gaoxin creates a landmark urban open space within Nanchang's new city center. In addition to providing clear definition of building entries and functions, the landscape supports a range of outdoor gathering areas and circulation routes to enhance visibility, access, and full use of the project's mixed-use program elements. The design of outdoor spaces and rooftops reflects the strong geometry of the signature tower and retail facade, with its triangular cladding that shades interior spaces and establishes a distinctive image and identity. This geometric module continues through the landscape in the patterning of trees, grass berms, and planter beds as well as special features of paving, site lighting, fountains and art placement.

Plan

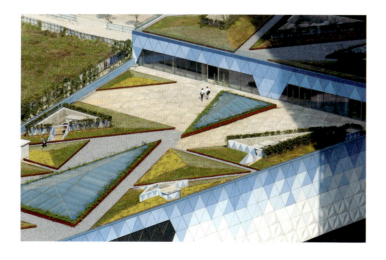

288   4. LANDSCAPE/GROUNDSCAPE FOR THE WORLD'S TALL AND TALLEST STRUCTURES

Nanchang Greenland Central Plaza
Nanchang, Jianxi, China

The landscape design for Greenland Central Plaza reinforces the project's bold vision: to create a window to the city, a focal point for the emerging Hong Gu Tan District and a connection between old and new. The landscape provides a vibrant retail environment with appealing, shaded outdoor spaces for pedestrians with the dramatic use of water, paving, and planting to integrate the towers and retail buildings into this important site. The residential block (Parcel B) is comprised of five residential high-rise towers, with one office building off to the northeast corner. To serve residents, the design establishes a central residential garden, children's playground, and senior garden all situated at either the center of, or adjacent to the circle of residential towers. A series of retail gardens serving workers, residents, and shoppers tie the office tower and residential block to the larger Central Plaza development. Several fountain features plus the geometric water feature in the center emphasize the overall concept of incorporating four parcels together by using water elements representing the Gan River.

Section

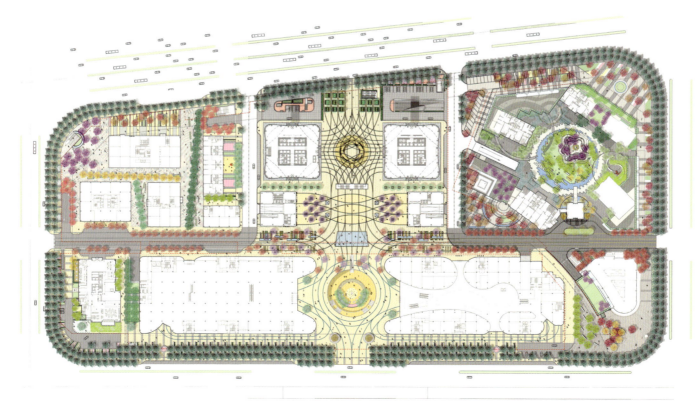

Landscape plan

294   4. LANDSCAPE/GROUNDSCAPE FOR THE WORLD'S TALL AND TALLEST STRUCTURES

295 NANCHANG GREENLAND CENTRAL PLAZA

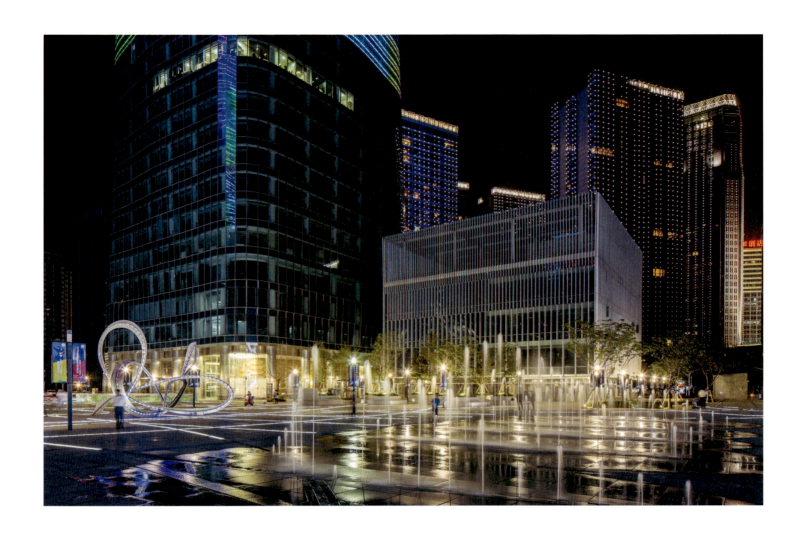

Plan

Minsheng Center
Shanghai, China

SWA's landscape design for Minsheng Center transforms 11 city blocks into a tapestry of park and green space of varying scales offering access to nature for residents, visitors, and workers alike. The reasons for integrating green space within the urban context are myriad: ecological benefits, clean air, sustainability, exceeding the green ratio and promoting health and happiness. Bordered by Old Shanghai and the Huangpu River, two historically significant buildings were retained in the new design to preserve their cultural significance and be adapted for reuse. The landscape celebrates the rich history of the city and the river that winds through it. Four main arteries run west to east: Park Walk, City Walk, Minsheng Walk, and Garden Walk. North to south arteries include the River Walk and the Cultural Corridor. These arteries are woven into the infrastructure of the site and promote cohesive links among areas of unique character.

Jeddah Tower
Jeddah, Saudi Arabia

The landscape architectural design for Jeddah Tower creates a landmark urban open space within Jeddah's new master planning for Kingdom City. In addition to supporting a clear functionality for the tower and the different levels of terraces, the design provides the dynamic composition of water, planting and paving, interweaving amenity and activity, and serves as an integrated base for the tower. Inspired by Jeddah's growth and cultural leadership, the landscape layers concentric to the tower reinforce the importance of the building and enhance the experience of the approach.

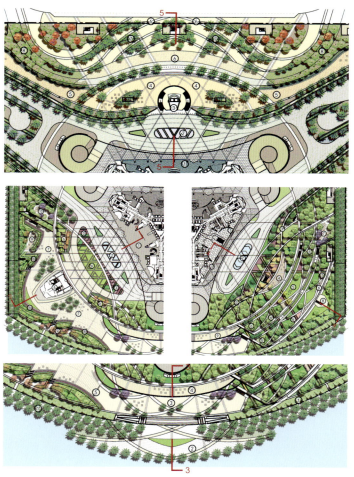

Illustrative plan

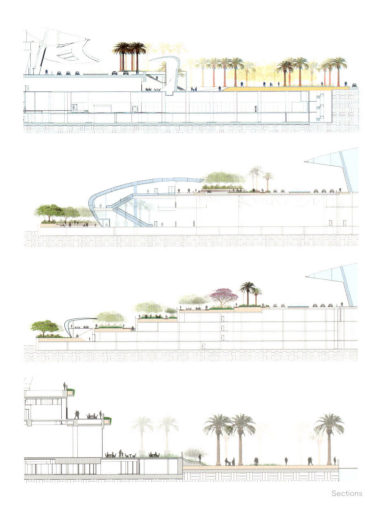

Sections

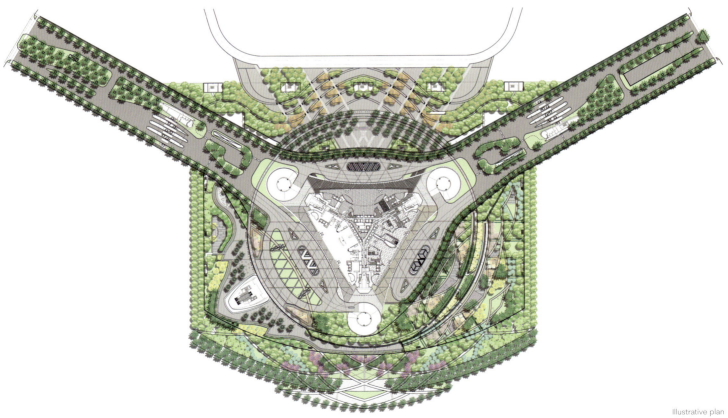

Illustrative plan

- ALBIZIA JULIBRISSIN – Silk Tree
- BOMBAX MALABARICUM – Kapok Tree
- BRACHYCHITON ACERIFOLIUS – Australian Flame Tree
- CASSIA NICOOSA – Pink Cassia
- CASSIA FISTULA – Golden Shower Tree
- CITRUS LIMON PONDEROSA – Ponderosa Lemon Tree
- CORDIA SEBESTENA – Geiger Tree
- DELONIX REGIA – Royal Poinciana
- HIBISCUS TILIACEUS – Sea Hibiscus
- PELTOPHORUM INERME – Yellow Flame Tree
- PLUMERIA OBTUSA – Singapore Frangipani
- TERMINALIA CATAPPA – Tropical Almond

Federation of Korean Industries Head Office
Seoul, Korea

Located in Seoul's well known Yeoido financial district, this urban infill project features a 50-story office tower and adjacent 4-story ground podium building, with a public plaza and sunken garden on the main public street and an arrival/drop off plaza to the rear. A reflecting pool and fountains connect the outdoor spaces while tree allées and groves extend the green park to the tower's base. The team's sustainable approach originated with a winning competition submission. SWA's landscape design establishes a variety of attractive outdoor spaces that incorporate functional requirements, provides important public gathering places, and connects the project to the city's larger pedestrian framework. A pond stores rainwater for reuse, and the lawn panel intercepts drainage from the paved plaza. Plant selection provides seasonal color and interest throughout the year.

1. Main plaza
2. Dropoff plaza
3. Fountain plaza
4. Overlook perennial garden
5. Sunken garden in lounge area
6. Visual garden in reflecting pool and planted islands
7. Lily pool/reflecting pool
8. Evergreen tree bosque w/lawn and seat wall
9. Street trees – ginkgo
10. Visual garden
11. Zelkova allee
12. Japanese black pine groves
13. Japanese cherry trees
14. Flag poles
15. Cooling tower
A. Property line
B. Setback line
C. Structure line below

Plan

306   4. LANDSCAPE/GROUNDSCAPE FOR THE WORLD'S TALL AND TALLEST STRUCTURES

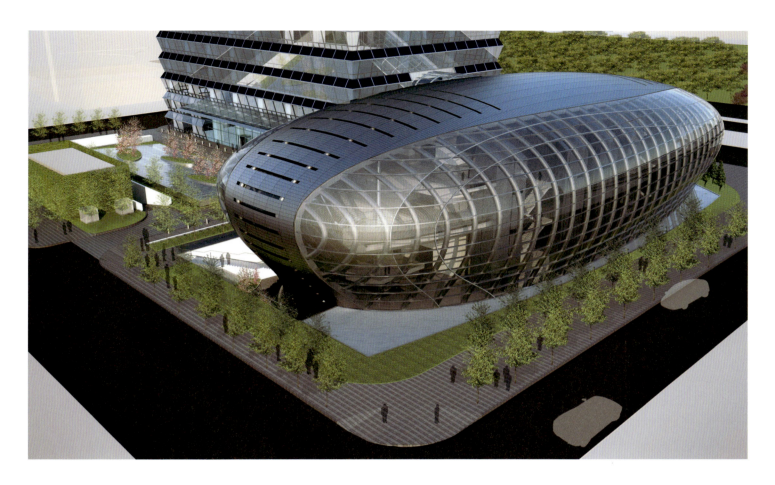

Site section

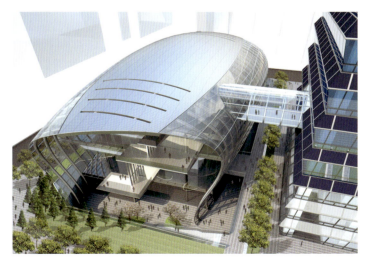

Plan

308 4. LANDSCAPE/GROUNDSCAPE FOR THE WORLD'S TALL AND TALLEST STRUCTURES

Chengdu Dongcun Greenland Tower
Chengdu, China

The landscape architectural design for this tower and podium complex complements the architecture with distinctive forms and multi-layered planting. The design for both the Tower Park and the podium roof garden makes use of a series of pyramidal berms that evoke the pattern of regional mountain topography and reflect the tower's crystalline geometry. These berms, with their gently sloping planes, serve to direct pedestrian and vehicular traffic through the Tower Park while offering sheltered outdoor spaces, accommodating grade transitions, and establishing a strong open space character that reflects enduring relationships of water, earth, building and sky.

North Bund White Magnolia Plaza
Shanghai, China

This 16.5-acre mixed-use development consists of high-rise towers consisting of a hotel, office, and retail space. Landscape components include civic plazas, integrated streetscapes, a podium-level pool and fountain, a sunken garden, rooftop terraces and gardens, observation decks, and an urban park. The concept of "sinuous fluidity" forms the basis for the landscape design, which takes cues from the building architecture as well as the geometries of unfolding Magnolia flower buds and fallen flower petals. The project renews green spaces within the North Bund district of Shanghai, employing eco-friendly technology including green roofs and facades to reduce carbon emissions, water consumption, and electrical demand.

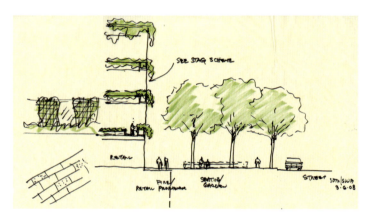

Plan

310   4. LANDSCAPE/GROUNDSCAPE FOR THE WORLD'S TALL AND TALLEST STRUCTURES

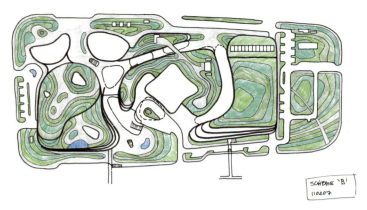
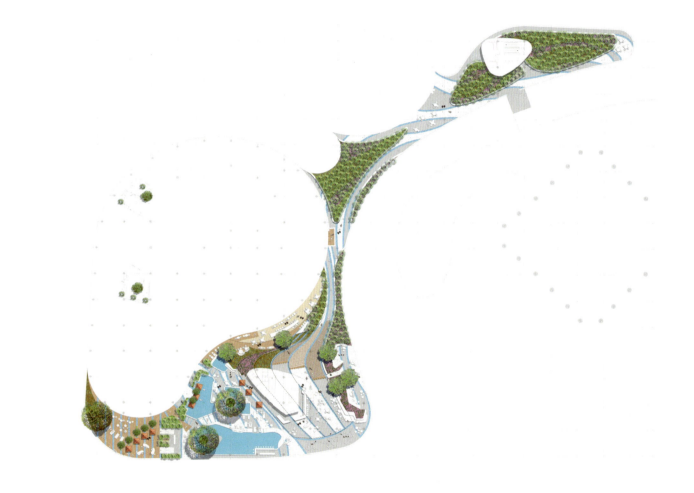

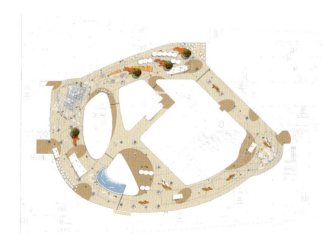

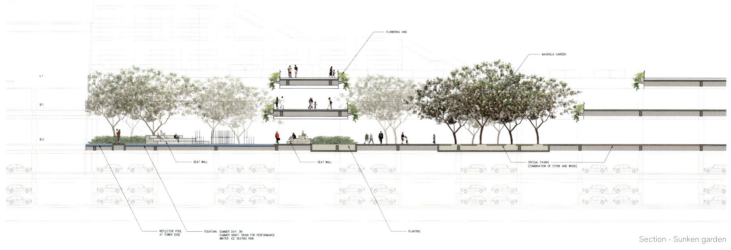

Section - Sunken garden

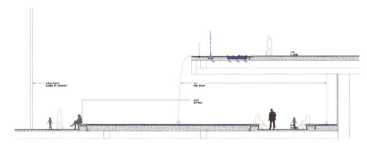

Section – Water feature details

317 NORTH BUND WHITE MAGNOLIA PLAZA

Shanghai Tower
Shanghai, China

At over 600 meters, Shanghai Tower is the tallest building in China. Its accompanying Tower Park is designed to complement the building's iconic form and function, connect the mixed-use project with its urban neighborhood, and provide a variety of beautiful settings for public gatherings and celebrations. Designed to satisfy LEED-Gold standards, it required 33 percent green cover—a unique challenge given the size of the building and amount of hardscape involved. The design team created an informal greenbelt and a park connecting to an adjoining property, yet 90 percent of the landscape is on-structure. Features include an event-center roof garden, a sunken garden with a bamboo island within a water pool, and dramatic sky gardens for each atrium that repeat plantings in a vertical pattern to draw the eye skyward and accentuate the tower's unique open-ended spiral form.

Plan

Construction observation – Team and John L. Wong

Tree planting plan

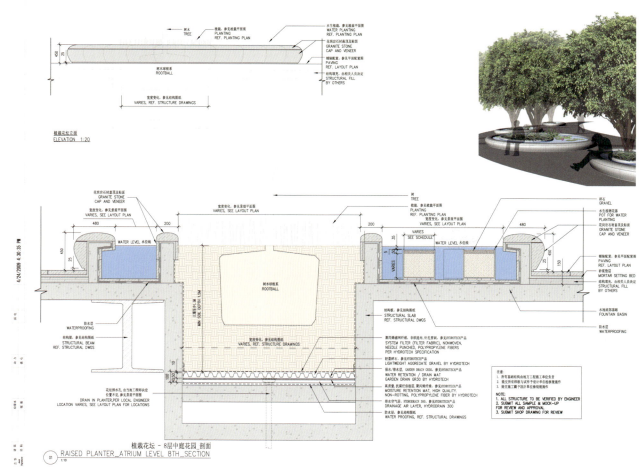

324 4. LANDSCAPE/GROUNDSCAPE FOR THE WORLD'S TALL AND TALLEST STRUCTURES

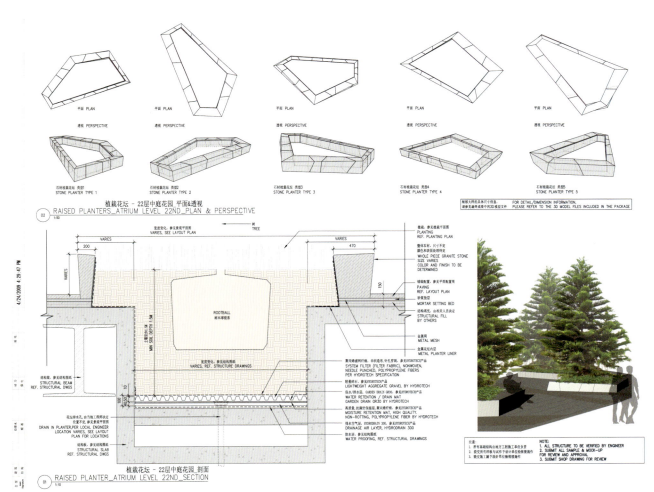

325 SHANGHAI TOWER

Section F - Sunken garden looking northeast

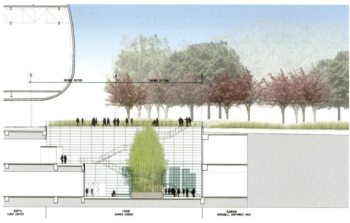

Section G - Sunken garden looking southwest

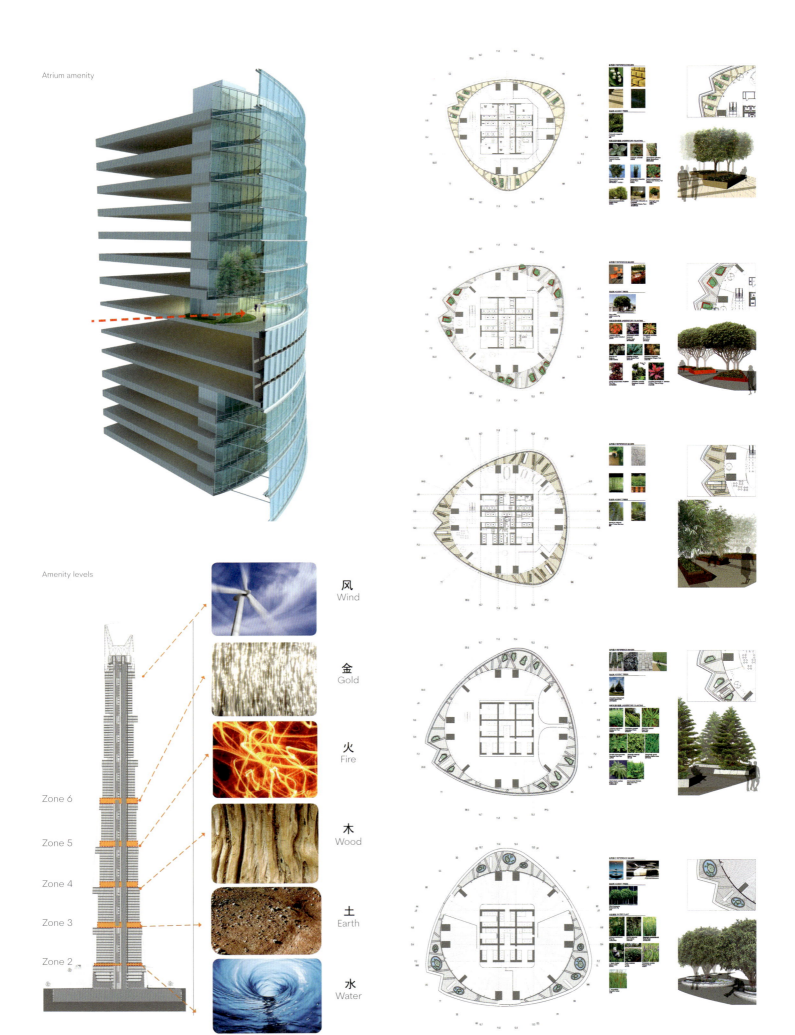

Burj 2020
Dubai, UAE

The Burj 2020 District is envisioned to be one of the most commercially viable, iconic, and visited places in the world. The design for the public realm treats the entire site as a park that establishes a signature identity for the development. At its heart is a multi-level plaza providing an unforgettable public space. Dispersed throughout the site are zones of elegant mixed-use activities featuring a 4 and 5-star hotel with conference center; four high-rise residences; an extensive, terraced retail/entertainment complex; and the landmark commercial tower. The key landscape principles included creating a world-class identity for Burj 2020; fashioning the central plaza as a large, flexible event space to "set the stage" for high-profile events; enriching an outstanding shopping experience by providing an array of exceptional spaces at various scales; maintaining a seamless design language throughout the site between architecture and landscape; and enhancing visual connections to the tower from all perspectives.

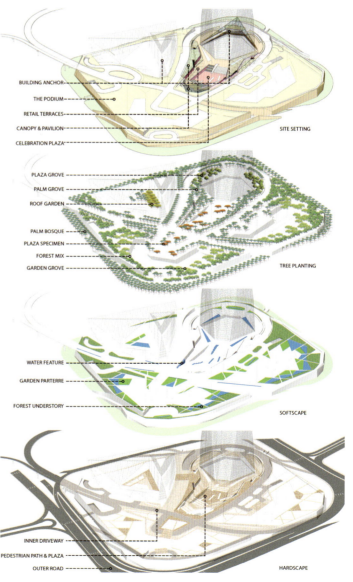

Lasndscape layers

Plan

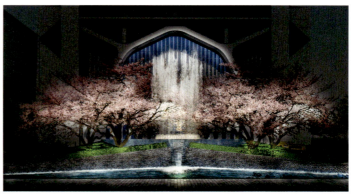

Nanjing Greenland Pukou
Nanjing, China

Located in Nanjing's Pukou district, the landscape design for this mixed-use supertower is inspired by the ancient city walls and gateways of Nanjing. The concept weaves the architectural fabric of ancient barriers with contemporary landscape elements such as a geometric-shaped water feature and graphic planting patterns in the retail promenade, hotel drop-off plaza, and roof garden. The overall design enhances accessibility to the site by creating a familiar tapestry for connecting with the historic culture of the site.

Combine plan

Jinan Greenland CBD Super High-Rise
Jinan, Shandong Province, China

At the nexus of the Jinan CBD at Greenland Shandong International Finance Center lies this Super High-Rise, towering like a mountain. It sits within the east-west axis between Wudingmaoling Mountain and Mashan Mountain and along the green north-south axis, where mountain meets forest. The site incorporates elements characteristic of Jinan – mountains, springs, and rock – telling the story of the transition from high mountain, like nearby Mount Tai, to the forest touching the city's edge. The primary material of the foothill site is stone, recalling a craggy mountain, and suggests the stepped-shape of the High-Rise and its geometric patterns. Planting areas also echo this craggy, staggered patterning.

Plan

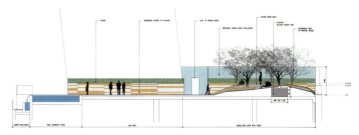

Cayan Tower
Dubai, UAE

Cayan Tower, formerly known as Marsa Dubai Infinity Tower, is a 73-story, approximately 110,000-square-meter residential tower sited at the Dubai Marina, EMAAR's three-kilometer-long canal-city neighborhood. The design team provided landscape design services for the roof garden and the main lobby entrance. The design applies a singular approach to solve multiple program requirements in a limited site area. Landscape design elements such as paving and fence patterns are derived from the building's architectural language, with a simple, continuous wood deck connecting all program areas. The sun deck transforms from a flat surface to undulating sloped planes with raised deck areas strategically sloped to maximize views and provide soil depth for tree planting.

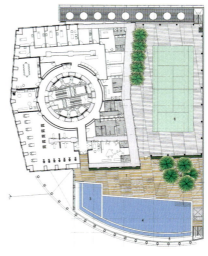

Plan

Plan - Ground level   Plan - Third level

Mashreq Bank Headquarters
Dubai, UAE

The Mashreq Bank Headquarters Tower in Dubai's Burj Khalifa District is a classic and iconic addition to the city's skyline. The comprehensive design considered context, climate, program, and site to develop an exciting, efficient and sustainable work environment. Landscape is featured on three levels. At the ground level a large water feature is a central focus of the front court, while a linear paving pattern welcomes visitors to the entrance. Date palms offer shade and a natural barrier along the main road. Level 5 offers child daycare service for employees. A terrace provides space for play, learning, and rest: a unique tower amenity of outdoor space for play and appreciation of the outdoors. Level 10 features an outdoor café and rest area for workers and serves as an iconic element of the building, offering an oasis in the urban tower environment.

Plan

Chongqing A13 Jiangbeizui International Finance Center
Chongqing, China

Located in the core CBD in Jiangbeizui, Chongqing – a district at the confluence of the Yangtze and Jialing rivers – this project's area includes a park, science and cultural attractions, business and residential towers, and shopping malls. The 470-meter high-rise tower will be the tallest tower in Chongqing, while a central podium will connect with three high-end residential towers at the remaining corners of the site. Based on the literal translation of Chongqing as "Double Celebration" and the traditionally auspicious connotations of "Double Happiness," the design concept is based on "Double Ripples," with one "ripple" sourcing from the tower (a center of business/leisure) and the other "ripple" from the podium (a lifestyle/high-end living center). Ground level design is focused on large-scale, inviting public spaces, welcoming drop-offs, and an active commercial shopping area. Due to Chongqing's subtropical monsoon climate, characterized by high summertime temperatures, material and color selections as well as shaded space design have been made to provide maximum comfort in the project's landscape. The design also replaces an existing lawn with a water feature to reflect the tower and become a landmark public amenity.

Plan

Nanjing Hexi Yuzui Tower (Runmao Tower)
Nanjing, China

The Nanjing Hexi Complex (Yuzui) Project landscape design aims to anchor the dominant design concept and narrative of the development by providing the main visual form and space for the landscape, and build upon the interrelationships of adjacent zones. The landscape responds to architectural features through various manipulations of form and space to create a dialogue between landscape and architecture, emphasizing the development's greater view corridor and main axis.

The design not only respects the architecture and makes the appearance of architecture more prominent, more importantly, it provides the site with iconic landscape features that offer users intimate outdoor spaces. In addition, it successfully achieves the goal of maximizing the site with multi-use roles in business, retail, and city life through well-rounded spatial arrangements, with careful considerations of form, operation, and planting design.

Downtown Dubai Opera District
Dubai, UAE

The Opera District is a stylish cultural destination in Downtown Dubai, in the vicinity of Burj Khalifa Tower, set to promote the arts, culture, ensure global exchange, promote local talent and serve as a vibrant events venue. The Opera District will feature luxury hotels, residential and serviced apartments, a retail plaza, waterfront promenades and recreational spaces and parks. At the heart of the Opera District is Dubai Opera, a venue for opera, theatre, concerts, art exhibitions, orchestra, film, sports events, and seasonal programs. The master landscape plan for this district creates a strong sense of place that defines gateways, squares and plazas.

Design is evocative of the elements that characterize the district as a destination (music and water) and differentiates each urban space with a distinct character. Situated in a harsh desert climate with brutal sandstorms and extreme desert temperatures, plant selection was key to the project's success. The design team identified and combined the best possible local, regional, and climate-friendly plants into a palette that matched plant species to specific requirements for drip irrigation, water quality, and soil amendments.

Plan

350   4. LANDSCAPE/GROUNDSCAPE FOR THE WORLD'S TALL AND TALLEST STRUCTURES

Above: master plan. Below: plan

Kula Belgrade
Belgrade, Serbia

The landscape of the St. Regis Belgrade will be a great public space at the nexus of several important roads as well as a future bike and pedestrian waterfront path. The landscape concept introduces a new central urban waterfront space at the heart of Kula Belgrade, inspired by the natural surroundings and the islands in the adjacent Sava River. The language of the river's water flow influenced the flowing paving patterns. The landscape will be a setting for this iconic tower that will celebrate the river and connect to the historic city. On the north side of the site, the landscape design creates a central, multi-use, seasonally adaptable civic space that is protected, yet opens views onto to the Sava River. At the center and south end of the site, the landscape will provide gracious entries for the hotel and residence, with garden areas interspersed with sculpture. The landscape design interfaces with the Belgrade Mall and the public promenade. Access for pedestrians integrates with the public promenade to the north and south, and bikes are introduced to the site from the promenade to the north.

Overall plan - Sketch

Liansheng Financial Center
Taiyuan, China

Liansheng Financial Center incorporates the curvilinear forms of the nearby river to create a vibrant urban setting for working, living, shopping, and civic life. The design provides a sustainable approach to capturing, reusing, and treating storm runoff, thereby improving water quality and supporting the health of the watershed and the river itself. Through elements of planting, paving, water, and movement, the resulting landscape expresses the larger natural setting, connecting river to city and unifying the dramatic and dynamic building forms that comprise Taiyuan's new mixed-use city center.

Plan - Sketch

Open to the Riverfront

357 LIANSHENG FINANCIAL CENTER

Mountain with nature is the golden mountain

Enchanted Village in the Valley concept

Chengdu Tianfu New District High-Rise
Chengdu, China

Situated within their district's most prominent location, these two sites host the tallest buildings in the southwest region of China – an office building, a hotel tower, and a service apartment tower – as well as two clusters of terraced retail buildings. The landscape, which utilizes sponge city strategies, native planting, and sustainably sourced materials, is designed to respond to all the site's opportunities and constraints, offering unique high-rise building landscapes that feature a series of choreographed pedestrian and vehicular experiences: gateway plazas, retail alleys, pedestrian spines, sunken courtyards, and upper terraces. The development's storyline celebrates Chengdu's rich cultural heritage and personality, while becoming the core cluster of Chengdu's new economy and strategic emerging industries.

Overall plan

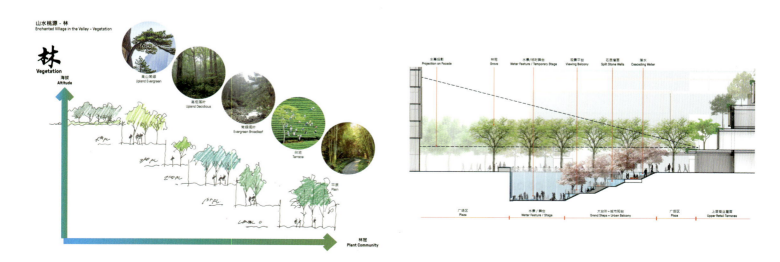

360 4. LANDSCAPE/GROUNDSCAPE FOR THE WORLD'S TALL AND TALLEST STRUCTURES

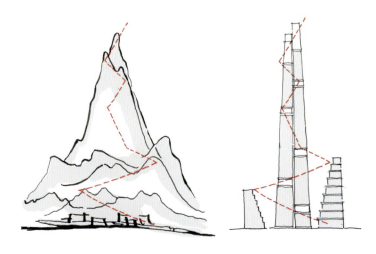

361　CHENGDU TIANFU NEW DISTRICT HIGH-RISE

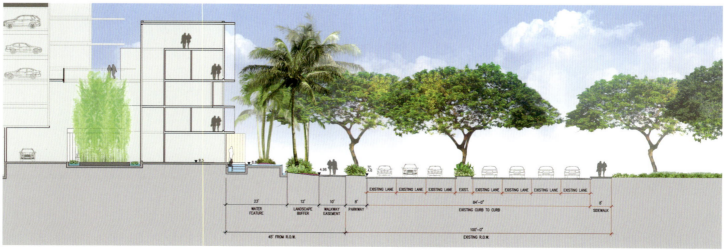

Section A Ala Moana Interim

Victoria Ward Waiea Tower
Honolulu, Hawaii

The 21-story condominium tower has a rooftop amenity area at level 5. Tropical gardens, barbecue areas, a swimming pool and spa provide outdoor areas for residents. New, tree-lined streets facilitate flow for pedestrians and cyclists, while plazas, public gardens, and open-air markets serve alongside new streets to facilitate movement between the mountains and the ocean.

Plan

East elevation at Kamakee

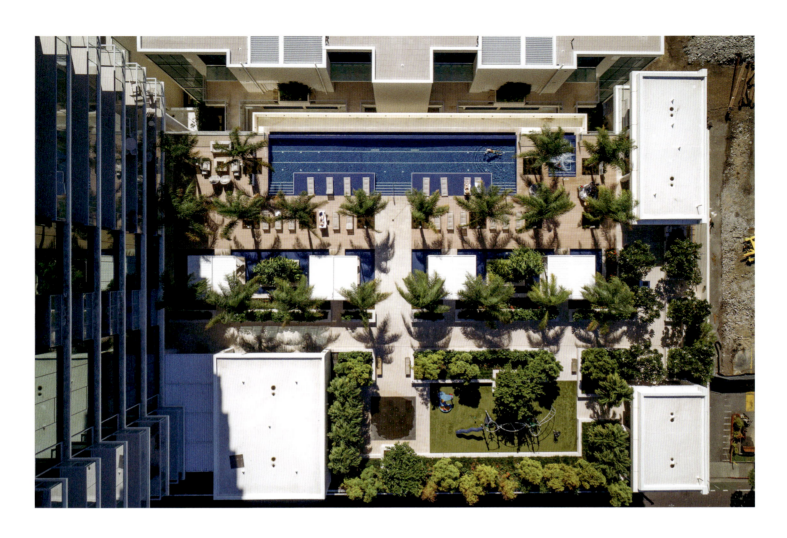

Section D thru Arrival Court South

Section Level 7 Amenity Deck

VICTORIA WARD WAIEA TOWER

Plan – Ammenity level

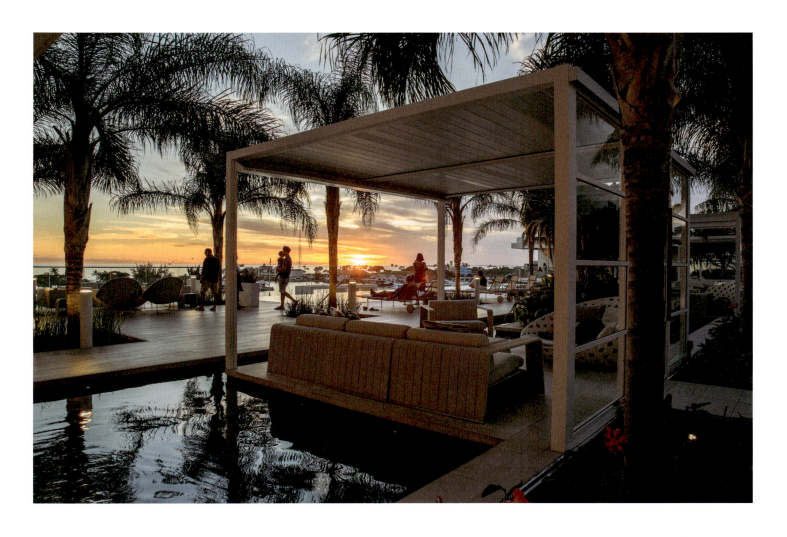

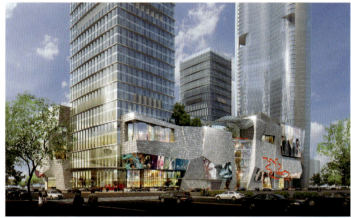

Wuhan Greenland Center
Wuhan, China

The landscape architectural design for Greenland Center creates a landmark urban open space within Wuhan's new International Financial district. In addition to supporting a clear functionality for both the tower and retail podium, the design offers a dynamic composition of water, planting and paving, interweaves amenities and activities, and serves as an integrated and strategic base to ground the architecture. The project was designed for LEED Silver certification.

Basemap

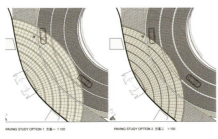

Section

The Butterfly Tower
Vancouver, BC, Canada

First Baptist Church is a mixed-use urban redevelopment project within Vancouver's downtown West End district that incorporates a new residential tower, affordable rental housing, an expansion of the church facilities, a new daycare center, a swimming pool, homeless meal services and emergency shelter, teen and counseling services, and other education and training resources. Additionally, it provides two semi-public spaces adjacent to the renovated church courtyard at Burrard and the new Nelson plaza at the base of the residential tower. The landscape design ties together the downtown and the West End districts, creating a new focal point for the city of Vancouver along its northwest-southeast axis. The landscape design for Nelson Plaza mirrors the design of the facade of the residential tower; a pattern of curvilinear bands gives form both to the planted areas inside the plaza and to the custom designed benches. The landscape of the plaza "flows" into the public realm, opening the space to the pedestrian traffic. Similarly, the remodeled church courtyard opens onto the Burrard streetscape. A system of steps and water runnels leads visitors into the space of the courtyard, providing secondary access to the church facilities.

Plan

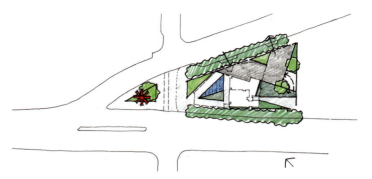

Georgia-Pender
Vancouver B. C., Canada

The site's striking location at the convergence of West Georgia and Pender Streets heralds a new landmark gateway building. The architect creates a tall, slim, wedge-shaped, sculptural form on a unique flat-iron site. With a restricted parcel size, the tower extends high above the ground plane to create an outdoor "urban room" that minimizes the tower footprint at grade, maximizes open spaces, and creates a landscaped setting that provides views of the site from all vantage points.

The landscape approach creates a seamless integration of landscape and architectural design through triangular patterns that respond to the tower form and the site setting. The main plaza integrates and enhances flag plaza at the tip to complete the triangular setting. The unique public "urban room" creates a daytime/nighttime open-air focal point in a cathedral-high space under the tower. A grand water feature animates the space while public seating creates a strong, unified setting at this key intersection. The landscape concept strengthens the public realm at this highly visible triangular space at the western gateway to downtown Vancouver.

Plan

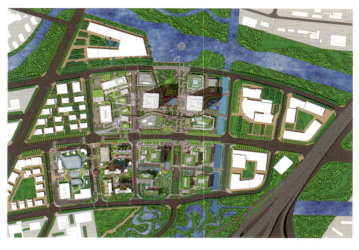 

Zhangjiang Science Center Parcel #56, #57, #58
Shanghai, China

Located in the core of Zhangjiang Science City, south of the "Science Gate" twin towers, Parcels 57 and 58 host a high-end retail shopping mall and an office building.

The landscape design, which leverages Sponge City strategies and a native planting palette, aims to break out of the traditional enclosed shopping center typology in favor of a "journey of discovery" concept. The design creates a connected and diverse experience from a sunken courtyard to a roof garden, offering a multi-dimensional indoor/outdoor retail and entertainment destination characterized by a sense of discovery and wonder.

Parcel 58 hosts high-end housing for innovation talent. The inspiration for "Woodland Creek Living" derives from the creek walk that connects parcel 75 to adjacent parcels. The water runs from a forested and contemplative environment to the "Creek Living" mixed-use area, establishing peace and serenity in an urban environment.

Sky View 4, 5, 6 – The Address Residence
Dubai, UAE

The landscape architectural design for Sky View creates a lush and beautiful setting for the various attractions and activities of this exciting new mixed-use venue. On all levels, the design's elegant planting, paving and water elements emphasize views to Burj Khalifa and downtown, inviting guests to gather, linger and explore. Echoing the concentric rings of sand that define the desert landscape east of the city, the design for two towers distinguishes itself with a series of appealing mixed-use spaces that largely focus inward. The landscape architecture announces and underscores this internal gesture throughout the site. The garden-like character of the landscape, combined with indigenous planting and dramatic paving and water features, creates appeal for residents and visitors alike.

Landscape plan

Section

385　SKY VIEW 4, 5, 6 – THE ADDRESS RESIDENCE

387 SKY VIEW 4, 5, 6 – THE ADDRESS RESIDENCE

5

DESIGN RESPONSES FOR GREATER RESILIENCY

390	**INTRODUCTION by James K.M. Cheng**
	SELECTED PROJECTS
392	Suzhou Center
408	Guthrie Green and Tulsa Arts District Streetscape & Arkansas River Concept Development
418	UC Davis West Village
424	Ko Olina Master Plan
428	University of Chicago Booth Center
436	XIQU Center
444	Grosvenor Ambleside
446	Amazing Brentwood
454	EXPO 2020

INTRODUCTION
By James K. M. Cheng, Founding Principal at James KM Cheng Architects Inc.

John and I first met on the Orientation Day at the Graduate School of Design at Harvard University. He came over with several other students from Berkeley to introduce themselves. We got along right away as we have very similar backgrounds. We both had our bachelor degree from the West Coast, him from Berkeley, me from University of Washinton and we are both first generation immigrant sons of Chinese descent and had lived in San Francisco. Hence, we share a love of Chinese food and that eventually proved to be the connection as we would often take breaks from the studio and go to Boston's Chinatown for late-night snacks. The only difference now is that John has graduated from Chinatown Moon Palace food to Michelin Star restaurants.

John and I both had similar professional experiences, we both had worked before going to graduate school, he joined Sasaki Walker in Sausalito, California and I worked in San Francisco for Bull, Field, Volkmann and Stockwell, and later for Arthur Erickson in Vancouver, Canada. It used to be said that west coast designers design from the heart and east coast designers design from the head. In other words, we were considered the west coast romantics and they the east coast intellectuals. Both John and I were schooled in the west and were curious about what the east had to offer to round out our education.

John was pursuing his Master in Landscape Architecture in Urban Design and I was in the Master of Architecture program. On weekends, a group of us from the west coast would visit the landmark projects around the GSD and John would ask to come along. At first, we were quite curious why a landscape architect would want to hang around a bunch of architects visiting buildings. Then we realized that just like us who had prior working experiences, we were more interested in Why and What than the How. For me, I was trying to find my own definition of what architecture is; why does the building have to be either an object "on" the landscape or "of" the landscape. Why can't it be "with" the landscape?

In those days, around 1976, there was no internet, no Facebook or YouTube and travel was difficult and expensive. We relied on the print and lecture circuit for information. Naturally, the focus of the design world at that time was much less broad geographically and mostly concentrated on works in the US around New York and the Ivy League schools. On the west coast it was post "Sea Ranch", "Design with Nature" and Christopher Alexander's "Pattern Language". On the east coast, the work of the New York Five inspired by Corbusier's white period was the rage in architectural schools and in the architectural press. Jerzy Sultan and Richard Meier held court in the GSD design studios and professors and architects from all over the world came. Those were heady days.

We visited "old" classics by Le Corbusier, Gropius, Mies, Alto, TAC, Rudolf, Kahn and Pei as well as the "new" controversial icons by White architects, Meier, Graves, Eisenman and Gwathmey. But we also visited New England towns like Cape Cod, and cities like Boston, Philadelphia, and New York. Perhaps because of our background and perspective, we were less swept up in the polemics of the time. After each weekend visit, we would have long evening discussions about what we saw and how we responded and why. Generally, we felt that the polemics alone did not satisfy all our questions. Something was missing but we could not quite put our fingers on it.

John and I were particularly interested in the siting of buildings in their context rather than the buildings themselves. Invariably, we wanted to understand how the buildings and their context interacted. Intuitively, we wanted to understand the relationship of building and site (environmental), users and program (Culture and Social Interaction), and economics. We would visit buildings that blew us away in magazine photos only to be totally disappointed by the Context, or the state of disrepair of the buildings. We started to talk about how People, Culture, Social Norms, Economics, Climate Change and, most importantly, Time would ultimately determine the success or failure of these projects. It was a conversation that we never finished while we were at Harvard, and it continues with each project that we do separately or together. We did not have a name for it then, but now we do, we call it Resiliency.

After graduation from Harvard, John and I took different paths. He went back to join and subsequently led many SWA projects all over the world and I went back to Vancouver to begin my own architectural career. We said at the time, as most graduates do, "let's keep in touch and try to find some projects to work on together." It turned into a prophecy and the collaborations continue to this day.

As Vancouver grew, so did my practice. Instead of doing merely single buildings, we started to design complexes of multiple buildings that grew into precincts, neighborhoods, and then sections of downtown. As Vancouver's reputation grew, we started to attract attention from all over the world and clients from China, Singapore, Hong Kong China, Dallas, Seattle, Las Vegas and Hawaii. With each project we had to deal with a lot of the same questions that we raised on those study trips. We had to learn to deal with cultural differences, variation in social norms, ethnic diversity, climate change and sustainable design. With larger projects in different parts of the world we had to deal with transforming auto-oriented suburban malls into modern day transit-oriented developments; transforming former dilapidated single use neighborhoods into mixed-use power centers while incorporating preventive and sustainable measures to sea level rise and climate change. We learned to include employment opportunities in our designs and perform urban repairs. These were the things we were questioning at Harvard but were not able to clearly grasp at the time.

It is rather fortunate that John and I were able to connect over time whenever one of these projects required collaboration of architecture and landscape to create a holistic environment and those opportunities allow us to expand our travels together to Europe and Asia. It is fitting that after all these years, we have been able to visit Berlin, southern France, Amsterdam and many more locations, to sit in the gardens of Japanese temples, and all the while to continue our unfinished Harvard discussions and ponder the next frontiers of urban design.

Above Xiqu Center

Section - Main axis croppped

Section - Surface parking

392   5. DESIGN RESPONSES FOR GREATER RESILIENCY

Landscape plan - Ground level

Suzhou Center
Suzhou, China

Suzhou Center is a landmark urban space within the Suzhou CBD. The project embodies the spirit of Suzhou as a gateway at the intersection of old and new culture; it will help Suzhou become a garden city, combining high-density development and ecological conservation.

The urban landscape of the CBD will be seamlessly linked to the public waterfront open spaces, creating a unique environment in which natural greenery is in harmony with the urban setting. The design provides outdoor recreational spaces of various levels and types to facilitate interaction and communication among people as well as between people and the environment, and to create an urban center that serves residents and visitors alike. By incorporating state-of-the-art sustainability measures, Suzhou Center will be a paragon of responsible urban development.

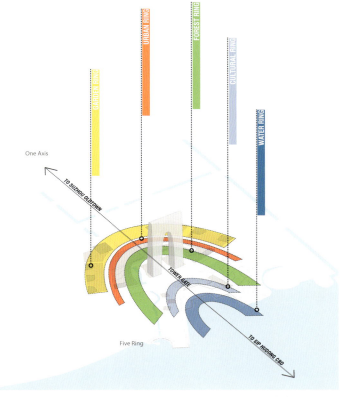

Multiple connections

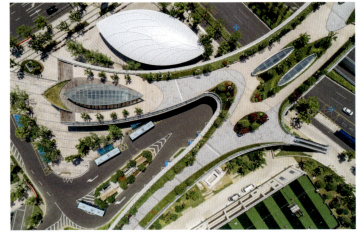

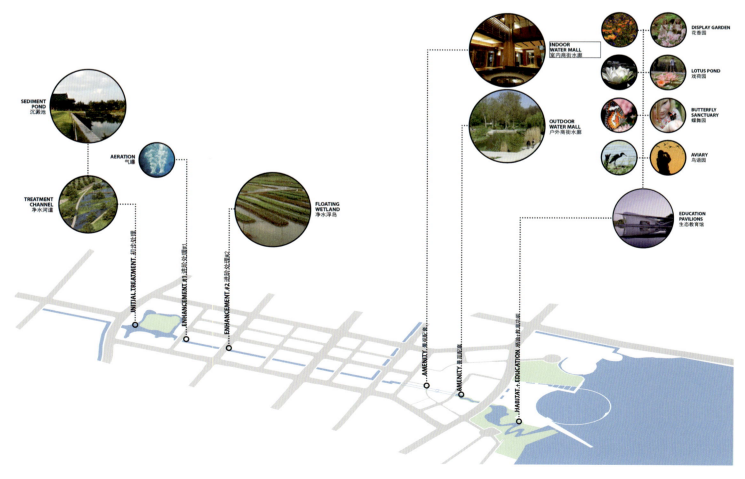

400　5. DESIGN RESPONSES FOR GREATER RESILIENCY

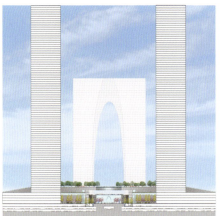
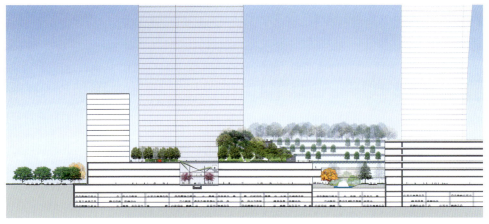

Sections

401　SUZHOU CENTER

402   5. DESIGN RESPONSES FOR GREATER RESILIENCY

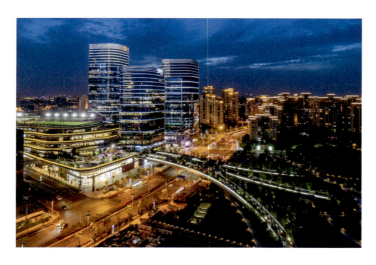

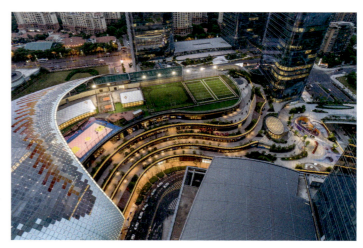

Guthrie Green and Tulsa Arts District Streetscape
Tulsa, Oklahoma

Guthrie Green transforms a 2.7-acre former truck loading facility into a lively new urban park offering gardens, interactive fountains, a lawn amphitheater, an outdoor stage with vine-covered "green rooms," and an 11,200-square foot cafe pavilion. Located in the heart of Tulsa's emerging Brady Arts District, the project offers an outdoor "living room" for the district's artists, urban professionals, students, families and visitors. The design supports a strong connection to nearby buildings and destinations including a new TV station, museum spaces, artist studios, a local historic theater, and the ONEOK Ballpark. Sustainable design approaches included installing a ground-source heat pump system under the park. Supported by public-private funding as well as ARRA and State Energy grants, the grid of 500-foot deep wells provides heating and cooling for non-profit tenants in nearby buildings, offsetting the need for traditional energy sources. The park's grid layout of gardens and paths reflect the geothermal well field hidden below, while fountains express the seeping, misting and jetting characteristics of water. Guthrie Green's lawn, gardens, and stage pavilions support a robust program of performances, films, public markets, exercise classes, and exhibits.

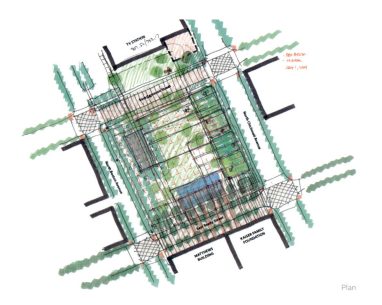

Plan

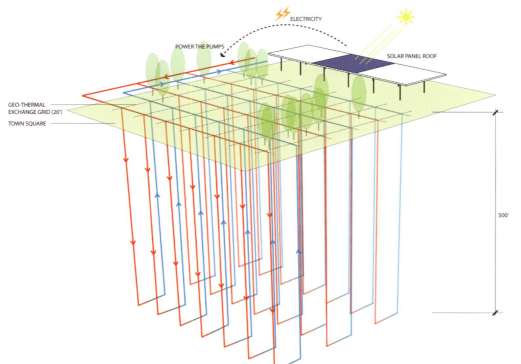

Geothermal Well Field:
- 120 Wells drilled to 500 feet, generating 600 tons of heating/air conditioning
- Energy distributed to users via underground piping systems
- Developed with $2.5 Million arra energy demand reduction grant and $200,000 odeq brownfield development grant
- Feeds heat pumps in Tulsa paper company and visual arts center

Other green features:
- Bioswales
- Led lighting
- Photovoltaic cells on pavilion

Designed and equipped for:
- Cinema
- Festivals
- Markets

411 GUTHRIE GREEN AND TULSA ARTS DISTRICT STREETSCAPE

Section A-A

Section B-B

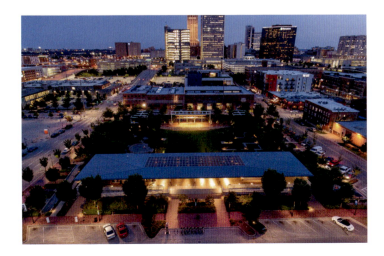

UC Davis West Village
Davis, California

The University of California initiated West Village as a campus expansion project to provide much-needed housing for students, faculty, and staff. SWA's Implementation Plan and landscape design build on core principles of housing affordability, environmental responsiveness, and quality of place to create the largest planned Zero Net Energy Community in the United States. Landscape weaves together new buildings, integrates site drainage into a hierarchy of parks, sports fields, and trails, and creates a green framework for livable and healthy neighborhoods, with bicycles as the primary mode of connection. The village includes mixed-use commercial/office spaces with housing above; site infrastructure and facilities including a village square, neighborhood parks, greenbelts, paseos, drainage features and ponds, bikeways and bus routes, and habitat; education facilities including a pre-school/day care facility, a community college, and a satellite high school; and recreation fields for university-wide recreation and intramural sports. Stormwater detention and retention ponds; permeable paving; photovoltaic panels; solar thermal collectors; and passive cooling of building and pavements are among the community's additional "green" elements.

Landscape plan - Ground level

420   5. DESIGN RESPONSES FOR GREATER RESILIENCY

Plan

Ko Olina Master Plan
Oahu, Hawaii

The Master Plan seeks to re-envision an entitled development plan for Ko Olina accentuating aspects of the existing culture and heritage of the area that will focus on sustainability, food production, education and experience as key ideas.

Green design elements include walkable mixed use buildings, stormwater management, connections to transit, educational components, an integrated nursery, and gardens with agriculture and aquaculture components.

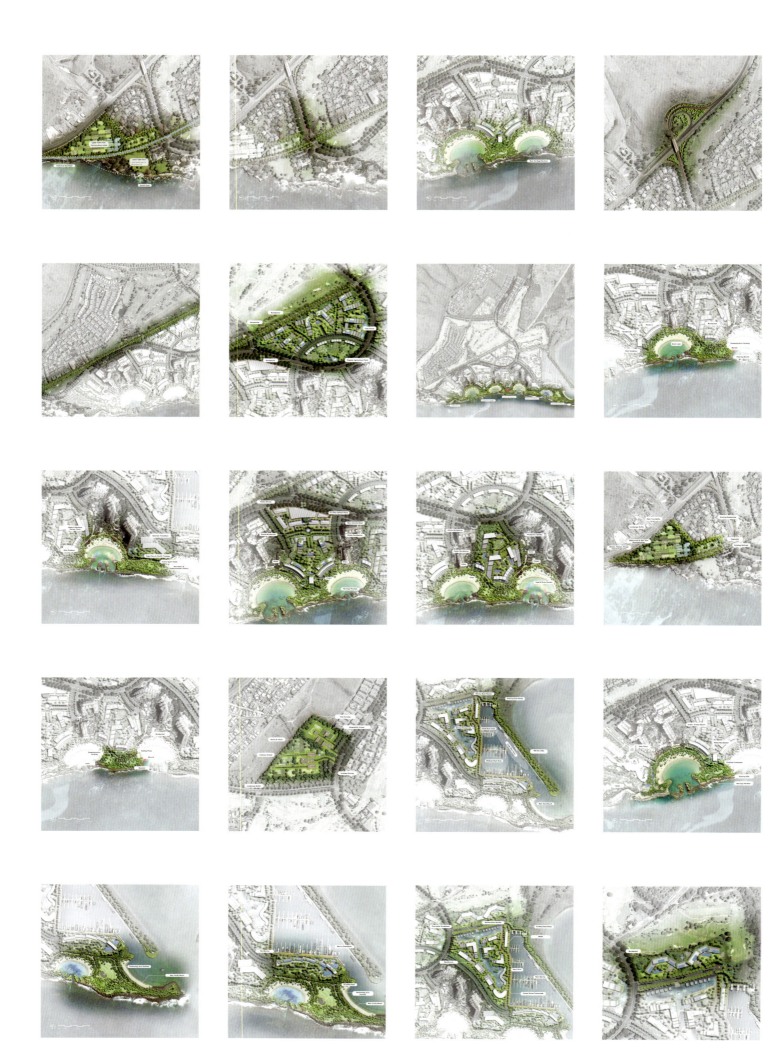

426   5. DESIGN RESPONSES FOR GREATER RESILIENCY

University of Chicago Booth Center
Hong Kong, China

The Booth Center activates and regenerates a spectacular, historic hillside site, injecting it with new purpose while revealing its origins as a former military fortress and prison. At first glance, this new campus for the University of Chicago on the outskirts of Hong Kong, China reads as a bold architectural gesture – but it is the approach to the landscape that gave rise to its form and footprint. The design team was required to preserve the site's trees and to reveal the ruins of its former structures, all the while fulfilling the new program. The project's landscape architecture finds expression not in what is introduced, but in what is strategically retained. Leading with landscape, the new campus pays quiet homage to the site's former military use, while advancing education as a lofty and natural succession. The design delineates four primary outdoor spaces: a Grand Entry Plaza; a Heritage Court, with a bosque of specimen trees; a View Terrace oriented toward the water; and a Flame Tree Promontory, consisting of a wooden deck surrounding an existing tree on advantageous high ground. Pathways through the site beckon visitors and students on an inspired exploration of the site and its transformation.

Plan

433 UNIVERSITY OF CHICAGO BOOTH CENTER

434   5. DESIGN RESPONSES FOR GREATER RESILIENCY

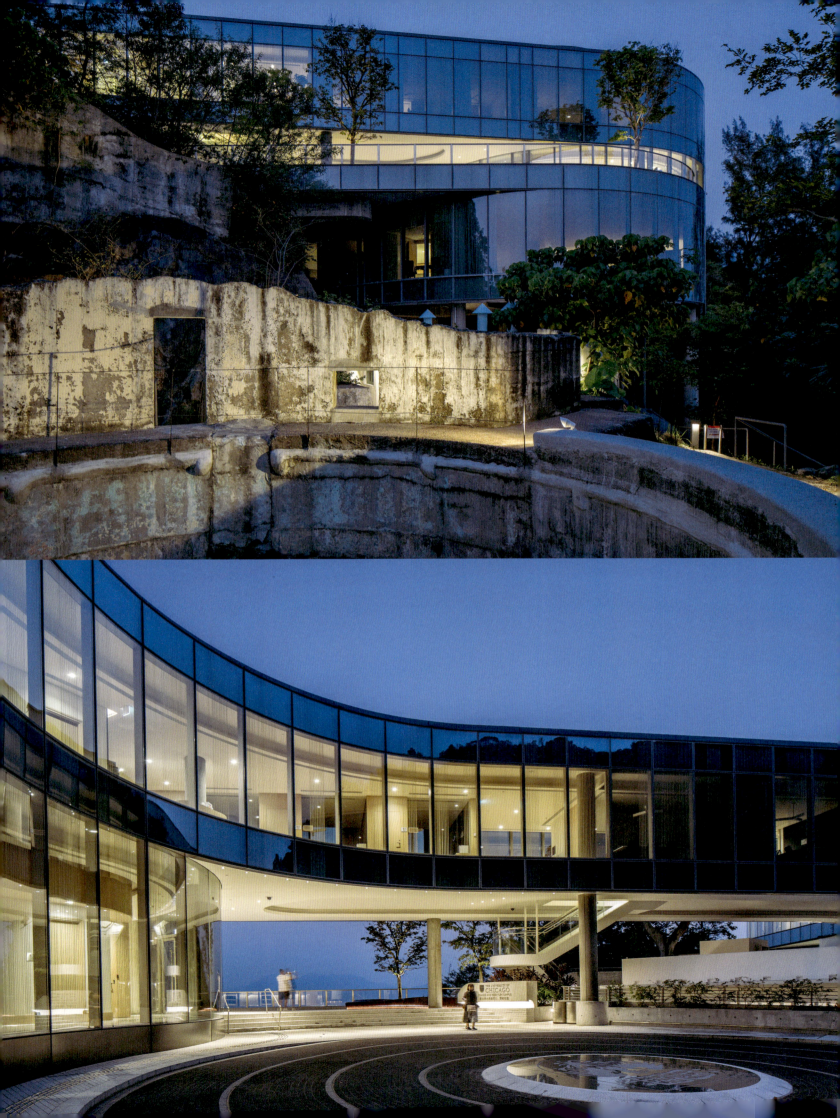

XIQU Center
Hong Kong, China

Xiqu Center's theater and performance spaces, intended to celebrate traditional Cantonese opera, are the first manifestation of the potential of the West Kowloon Cultural District (WKCD), a vital new cultural precinct that has come about as the result of many years of conceptualization and planning. The Center's design is a journey of transition from an urban site to a cultural landscape. From the courtyard to the main theater, patrons travel by escalators through vertical landscapes, building a sense of wonder, anticipation, and excitement. Inspired by the concept of flow, or qi, the landscape and theater experience are closely intertwined with majestic views of Victoria Harbor. The exterior facade is three-dimensionally curved, with arched openings strategically located at all four corners to form urban corridors that direct the flow of pedestrians at multiple levels from the neighboring transportation and commercial hub into the Center and the Cultural District.

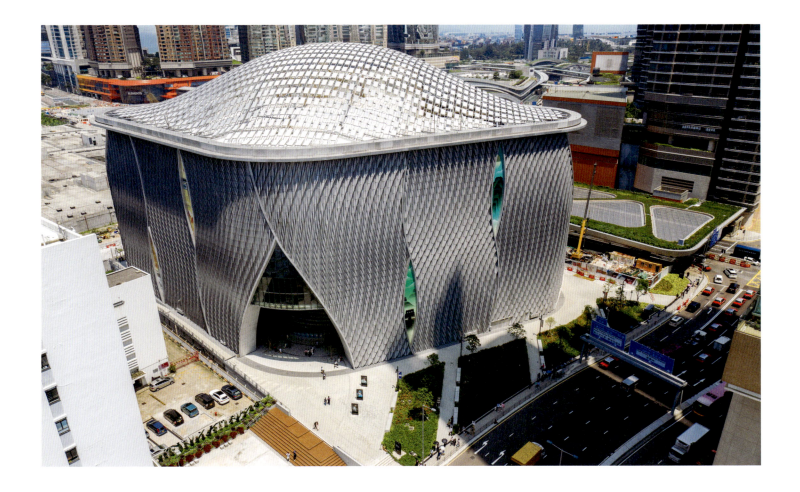

Landscape plan – Ground level

437

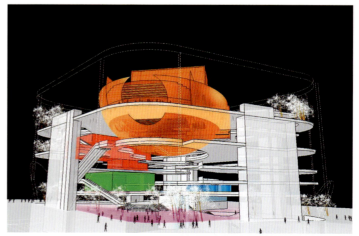

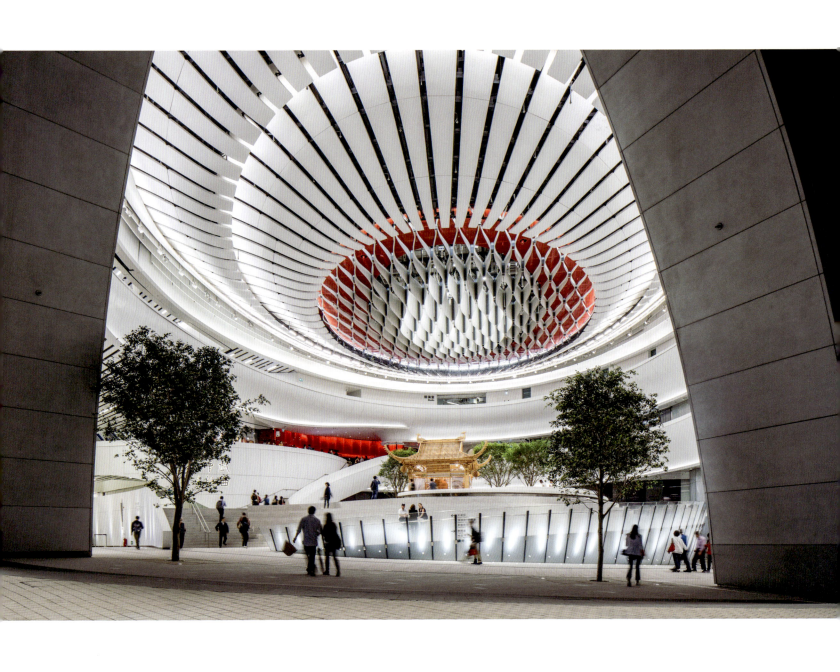

439 XIQU CENTER

442   5. DESIGN RESPONSES FOR GREATER RESILIENCY

Grosvenor Ambleside
West Vancouver, British Columbia, Canada

The landscape improvements for this new mixed-use development integrate and enhance the streetscape improvement measures the city of West Vancouver is currently implementing, providing a vibrant and pedestrian-friendly landscape along the entire perimeter of the site. A continuous planting of maple trees creates a unified street edge and provides continuity with the existing tree canopies along Marine Drive. The central Galleria offers an appealing new location for cafes, seating, and social gathering. An overhead canopy provides shelter extending beyond the building edge. Sustainable elements throughout the project include the use of permeable paving and a series of linear landscape panels that serve as rain gardens.

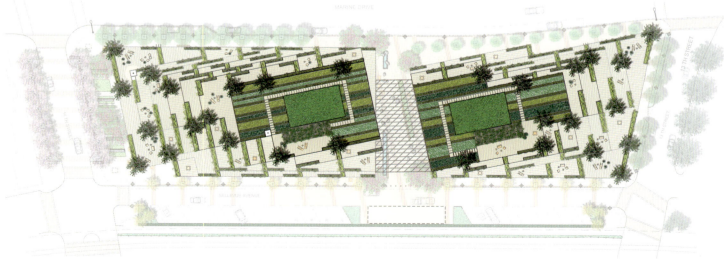

Landscape plan – Roof

Amazing Brentwood
Burnaby, BC, Canada

The Amazing Brentwood Town Centre Development Plan transformed an existing suburban style shopping mall into a mixed-use, transit-oriented community. Reasserting itself as the nucleus of the Brentwood Town Centre, the site accommodates 2,000–4,000 high-, medium-, and low-rise residential units. After developing the project's master plan, the design team was engaged to design the project's public realm and to expand its role from a shopping destination into an integrated, sustainable, urban community. With key connectivity to main vehicular arteries and a high-speed train line, the new development functions as a major hub for the region, featuring 12 residential towers, extensive new retail, and public spaces, including urban plazas, streetscapes, and public facilities. The design focuses on creating a continuum of urban landscape spaces, with a particular focus on pedestrian circulation and the establishment of several smaller, more intimate public spaces. Continuity of paving materials and streetscape treatments provide a seamless transition from one area to the other. A new plaza sits at the core of the new development, and ties together the existing mall with the new towers and retail spaces.

Plan

Plan

1. Town center plaza
2. Vessel – planter for specimen tree
3. Town center main water feature
4. Stone benches
5. East mew
6. West mew
7. Sky train connection at +167.0
8. Elevator
9. Stair connection to level below
10. Bike parking
11. Brentwood + Halifax corner plaza
12. Raised pedestrian connection to existing mall
13. Existing mall
14. Bus stop

450   5. DESIGN RESPONSES FOR GREATER RESILIENCY

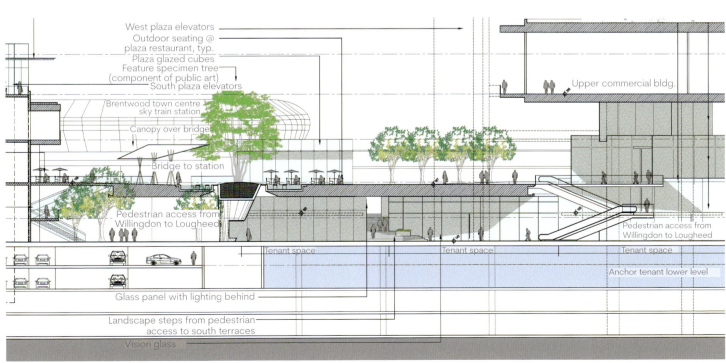

Section

453　AMAZING BRENTWOOD

Expo 2020
Dubai, UAE

The 1,083-acre grounds of Expo 2020, held in Dubai, UAE, establishes a shared space for celebration and learning for millions of international visitors. The public realm is designed to mitigate extreme climate conditions and to provide experiential connectivity and wayfinding, sensory delight and distinctive place-making.

Designing outdoor landscape spaces for the Expo 2020 event has presented significant challenges especially for those spaces that will stay in place beyond the world's fair and will be continuously open to the public.

This submission focuses on the public realm including the central garden at Al Wasl (the Expo's theme structure and centerpiece), the 0.8-mile long loop boulevard that allows visitors to stroll from one section of the Expo to the other, the main welcoming entry plaza and four parks – each of a different character.

The focus on mitigating the harsh temperatures and providing a more comfortable and stimulating experience of the outdoor public realm was key to the success of this project.

Context

Diagram

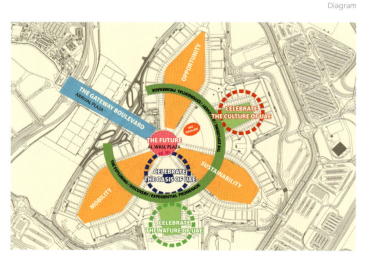

Metro Welcome Plaza

The Main Arrival Plaza will be turned into the Legacy plaza when Expo 2020 closes. Re-usable materials and products are used and sustainability and longevity are the main considerations of the design. The transition of this Expo arrival plaza to a legacy plaza only requires minimal construction. Trees in a grove are planted in boxes for future convenience. Pavings are reusable as they are placed in the sand temporarily. Planters will be incorporated into the future design phase for aesthetics and to improve space quality. Flags of all the participating nations form the central arrival plaza with alleés of flowering natives shading the main procession to Al Wasl plaza.

Plan

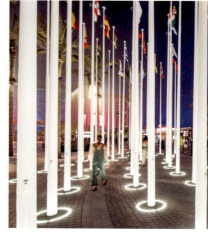

Al Wasl Plaza

The landscape design for Al Wasl plaza provides a lush, flexible, and unique urban open space in the context of Dubai. The gardens of the plaza offer elements of interest for people of all ages which, in the spirit of the name (Al Wasl means connection), provide opportunities for people to connect, experience public events together, and enjoy a diverse landscape experience. The plaza is a true urban oasis, where nature becomes a catalyst for human interaction. Under the shelter of the trellis, much like inside a tent in an oasis, people will gather, meet, rest, and play. The Al Wasl garden, the central hub of the expo, is protected by a 65-meter-high domed trellis that was designed in close collaboration with the project architects AS + GG. The trellis structure, infilled with fabric panels, shields visitors from the sun, allows air to move freely and provides a projection surface for outdoor entertainment. The landscape design of Al Wasl reflects and integrates the dome's design. Seven water features were designed to enrich the experience of the landscape, each with a different treatment of the water, and provide respite and entertainment to the visitors. A central fountain mirrors the oculus of the dome, and complements the central stage of the garden. Finally, a combination of exotic and native plants display a diverse array of colors and textures.

458   5. DESIGN RESPONSES FOR GREATER RESILIENCY

Plan – Legacy

Isometric – Rooms

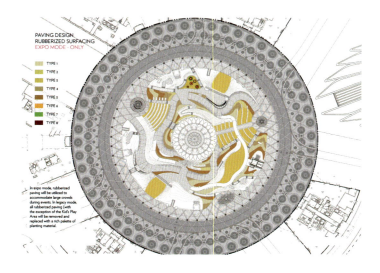
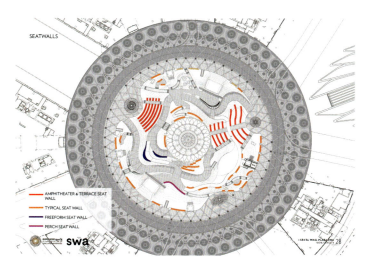
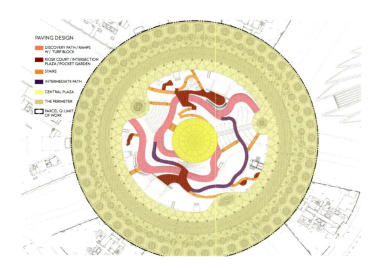
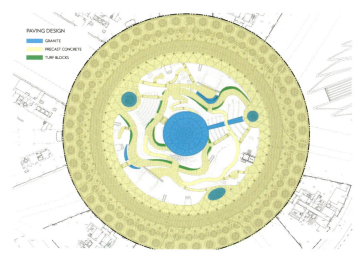
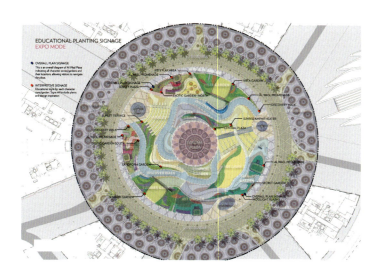
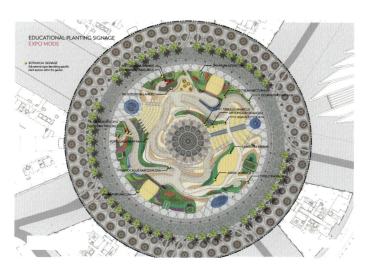

460   5. DESIGN RESPONSES FOR GREATER RESILIENCY

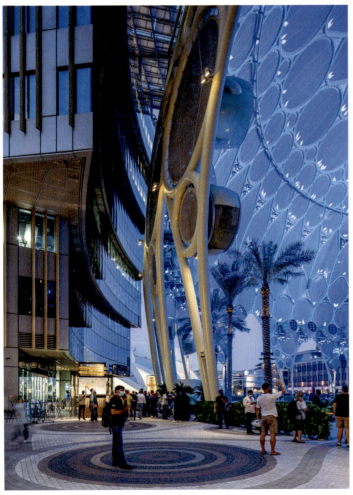
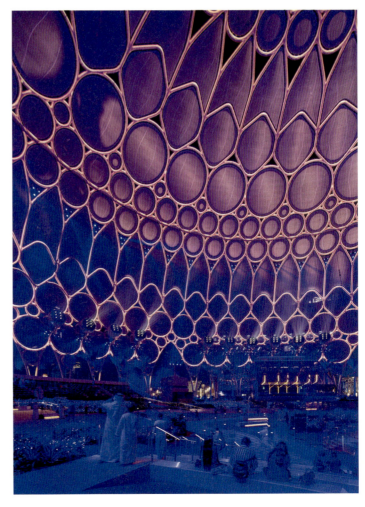

Oasis – "Surreal"

As visitors leave Al Wasl they enter the "Urban Oasis". This park is designed as an oasis, a traditional environment where people find respite from the hostile climate of the desert, where goods are traded and crops are grown thanks to the abundance of water. The design reflects these functions with a souk market and a spectacular water feature (home to "Surreal", a signature fountain) at the center of the area.

Jubilee Park

Jubilee Park is inspired by wadi, seasonal rivers that are formed in the desert through periods of intense storms and give rise to a rich palette of vegetation that often survives through the dry months. Wadis bring life to the desert creating, along their path, green oases allowing plants to bloom.

Paving patterns in Jubilee Park serve as a metaphor for the wadi, with their color, patterns and sinuous curves representing the flow of water in the landscape. Here the wadi pathway meanders through the site to create distinct landscaped spaces: it follows the edges of the large performance space at the center of the park, and continues on to the main arrival plaza adjacent to the loop boulevard. Here we find some of the park's main features including restaurant and snack facilities, the kiosks of the souk market and the observation tower.

A swath of date palms follows the edges of the wadi path and connects the main arrival plaza to the outdoor event stage at the opposite side of the park.

The vegetation selected for this park closely reflects the character of the native, UAE desert flora. Drought tolerant, native and adapted species are mixed with a variety of soft grasses and seasonal planting species.

AL Forsan Park

While the Jubilee Park is inspired by Dubai's distinctive natural beauty, the Al Forsan Park takes its cues from culture.

Nested between the Opportunity and the Sustainability Thematic Districts, on the two sides, and the UAE pavilion to the south, the Al Forsan Park is a green hub for different cultural and social experiences.

Design inspiration comes from the mosaic, an art form found throughout the Islamic world. Al Forsan Park is inspired – physically and programmatically – by this art form, forging a series of spaces that bring together different programs, themes and age groups. Here, individual spaces converge like a mosaic of colorful tiles in a coherent design characterized by abstract, repetitive geometric patterns. The park can be read as a metaphor of the UAE, a historic crossroads of people and cultures, and a nation of seven emirates, together, each with its distinct identity.

Inside the park, each "mosaic space" is also designed to meet different needs of various age groups, from engaging interactive displays to showcase and activate the Expo experience to the more somatic spaces such as restaurants, snack facilities and resting areas for visitors to relax.

Ghayath Trail & Art Park

Located between the iconic UAE pavilion and North Park, Expo Art Park allows visitors to experience a selection of fine art pieces representing four culturally significant "desert heroes". Art displays will be set amid vibrant and varied gardens, plazas, and desert landscapes featuring UAE native and adaptive plant species, majlis seating nooks, climbable stone mounds, a central fire pit, and other interactive elements. These garden "rooms" will deliver a unique setting for visitors to experience the colors, forms, and textures of art and nature at once. The exhibit space will be designed to accommodate a flexible range of different events throughout the Expo. Furthermore, a portion of the site includes gardens showcasing culture from other parts of the world, bringing an international flavor to the Art Park experience.

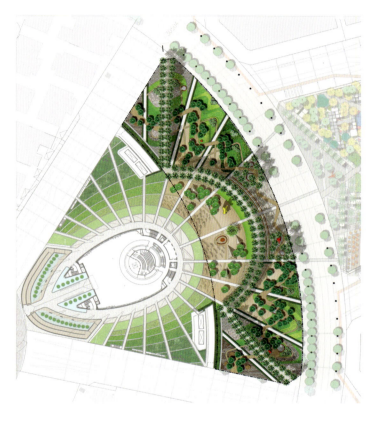

Inner Loop

The proposed design of the Expo Loop Promenade aims to create a shady, elegant streetscape that will serve as the main spine of the Expo site. This pedestrian-friendly green artery will provide respite for the Expo's venues and attractions, as well as the planned post-Expo urban development of the area. The design celebrates native species with fully grown Ghaf trees a species that has strong ties to the environment and the culture of the UAE. The trees are planted both in-ground and, where utilities do not allow this, in large boxes integrated with the furniture of the streetscape. A large trellis structure provides additional shade to the visitors of the Expo through a system of canopies that mimic the shapes of birds. The canopies will enhance the experience of the promenade, sheltering visitors from the intense sun.

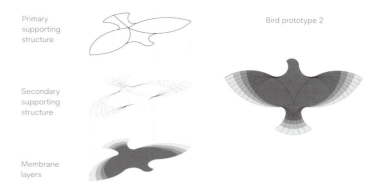

Shade structure - Bird design development - Stage 3 progress 20%

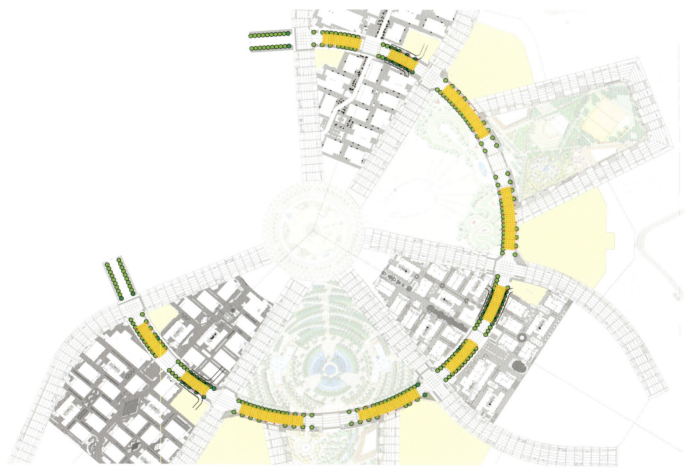

Inner Loop layer 3 with parks

470   5. DESIGN RESPONSES FOR GREATER RESILIENCY

6

RECENT WORKS AND ONGOING CHALLENGES / OPPORTUNITIES

476	**INTRODUCTION by John L. Wong**
	SELECTED PROJECTS
478	Shanghai International Dance Center
486	Ko Olina Four Seasons
494	Bank of China Hainan
496	Shimao Shenzhen International Center
500	Shijiazhuang CBD Park
502	Bank of China FTZ
506	Project C
510	Durres Waterfront Master Plan

INTRODUCTION
By John L. Wong

One of the greatest challenges of our time has been the rapid changing of our environment due to climate change, sea level rise, and social inequity. A central goal for all of us is to create environmental resiliency within our projects. The landscape architecture field is in an excellent position to lead the response and turn the tide through our design thinking, action, advocacy, and teaching. By intentionally approaching each project with ideas and tools that support a more sustainable and livable world, we have the opportunity to make a positive impact on the environment. It remains to be seen how effective we can be in tackling this responsibility, but I believe we have the training, skills, and knowledge to lead the way.

The projects illustrated in this chapter demonstrate the complexity of bringing together the myriad elements of urban design and planning, architecture, engineering, infrastructure, and cultural and regional context responses through the particular intervention of landscape architecture within the public realm and open space design. The Shanghai International Dance Center, Victoria Ward Master Plan - Ward Center, Shimao Shenzhen International Center, Shijiazhuang CBD Park and Office, Bank of China FTZ and Project C all demonstrate a major effort to create a more resilient "Place" that marries the above elements while navigating the burgeoning challenges of urban renewal and transformation.

Opposite page Ko Olina Four Seasons

Plan

Shanghai International Dance Center
Shanghai, China

The Shanghai International Dance Center is designed as the transcendent synthesis of dance and architecture. The interwoven buildings and landscape have been choreographed to capture the fluid movement, grace, and vitality of dance. This world-class facility promotes all forms of dance, expanding the cultural reputation of Shanghai and creating and attracting top international performers and choreographers. The landscape design reinforces the graceful, curving forms of the building architecture while defining clear outdoor spaces and connections that link the various program areas. Interwoven landscape elements such as benches, planting hedges, allées of trees, and pedestrian walkways create interesting views and dynamic experiences.

The landscape design preserves the existing park, with its numerous trees, while adding significant tree canopy to offset the heat island effect. Extensive planted areas exceed the minimum required ratio for green space, providing for effective onsite filtration of stormwater and groundwater recharge. Roof gardens help to absorb and slow storm water while assisting with building insulation, and plant material selection is well-suited to the city's climate and ecology.

Section

Section

Section

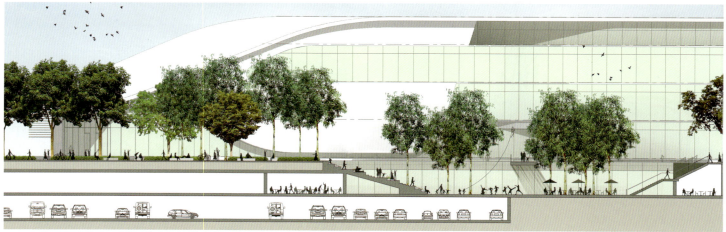

484   6. RECENT WORKS AND ONGOING CHALLENGES/OPPORTUNITIES

Master plan

Ko Olina Four Seasons
Oahu, Hawaii

The Four Seasons Hotel redevelopment and new residences by Toyo Ito Associates is the first flagship project intended to raise the profile of Ko Olina as a world-class, sustainable resort destination rooted in local Hawaiian culture.

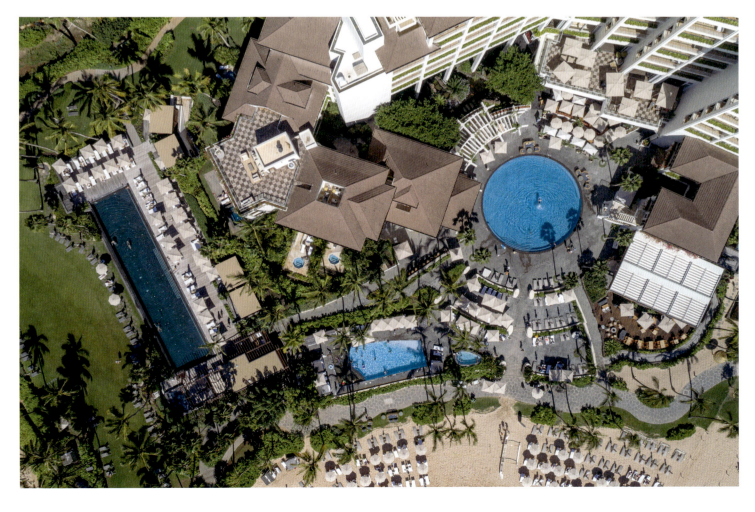

Bank of China Hainan
Jiangdong New Area, Haikou, China

Located on the coast to the east of Haikou City, the Jiangdong New Area sits between prominent rivers and alongside pristine beaches. The Bank of China is shaping up to be a central building at the heart of this development, which is poised to be the ecological central business district (CBD) of Haikou. Inspired by the natural beauty of the island, the landscape offers an immersive tropical experience. Native flora cascades from the street level to the lower building entrances of a museum, hotel, conference center, and the banking office. A series of terraces and water features activate the landscape and blend with the architectural language of elegance and transparency in an artistic, urban realization of a tropical beachfront garden city.

Plan

Shimao Shenzhen International Center
Shenzhen, China

Programmed to be active and lively and set within a pristine pedestrian garden, the public realm of this project connects the new plan to existing venues, thus ultimately defining the tower site as the culmination of all energy and activity throughout the entire district. This connection will be a continuation of the public space system already in place at the center of the existing sport venues to the south. Lush vegetation will combine with walkways, al fresco dining areas, exercise plazas, and retail shops. Landscaping and culture amenities will be the connective urban tissue that unites all the buildings within the development and draws the public's eye to the towering icon. The tower evokes the form of a sprinter set in motion, or a swimmer poised on the starting block, or a gymnast in flight: all expressing the beauty of dynamic motion.

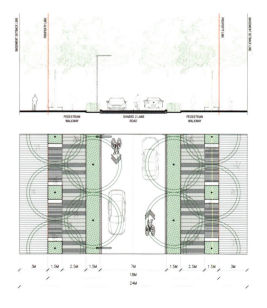
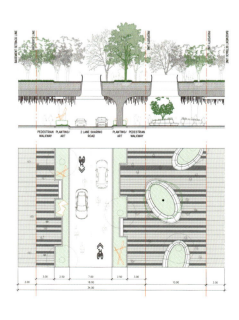
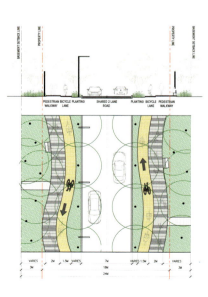

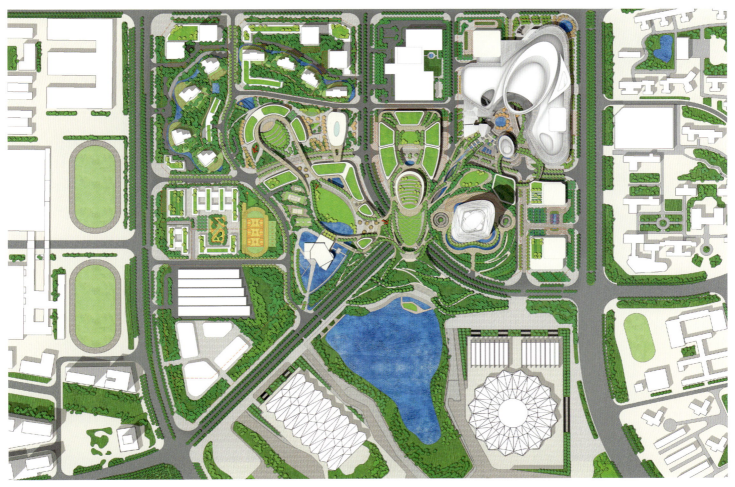

道路体验性 - 文化大道
STREET HIERARCHY AND IDENTITY - CULTURE WALK A

道路体验性 - 文化大道
STREET HIERARCHY AND IDENTITY - CULTURE WALK B1

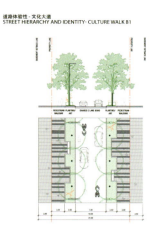
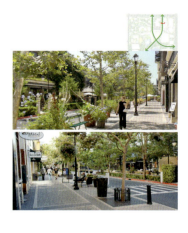

道路体验性 - 体验大道
STREET HIERARCHY AND IDENTITY - EXPERIENTIAL WALK D

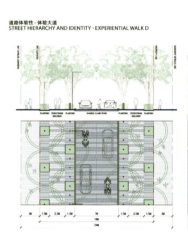

道路体验性 - 休闲大道
STREET HIERARCHY AND IDENTITY - LEISURE WALK

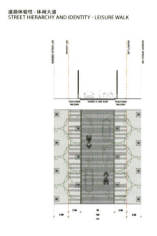
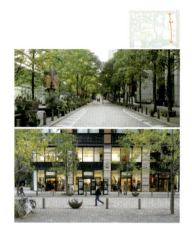

道路体验性 - 体验大道
STREET HIERARCHY AND IDENTITY - EXPERIENTIAL WALK E

道路体验性 - 城市大道
STREET HIERARCHY AND IDENTITY - CITY WALK

道路体验性 - 空中公园
STREET HIERARCHY AND IDENTITY - SKY PARK STRUCTURAL LAYER

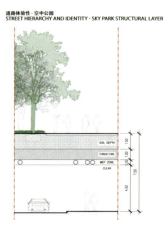

道路体验性 - 体验大道
STREET HIERARCHY AND IDENTITY - EXPERIENTIAL WALK C1

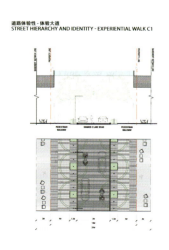

鸟瞰 AERIAL VIEW

高架公园景观 SKY PARK VIEW

SHIMAO SHENZHEN INTERNATIONAL CENTER

Shijiazhuang CBD Park
Shijiazhuang, China

This project seeks to reclaim the historic center of Shijiazhuang from industrial development and restore it as an active area for commerce, exchange, and finance, while also providing an active green space that acts as a calming transitional buffer to adjacent residential districts. The proposed park reflects the many facets that make Shijiazhuang unique, taking cues from the local topography, cultural beliefs, historic urban and industrial past, and the city's essential rail connections. The central park design features dynamic pedestrian experiences, including various three-meter-wide walking paths, a tree-lined promenade, and jogging loops connecting the park to the upper-level outdoor terrace of the Sports Center on the site. The park uses a Sponge City design framework. The overall "Treasure Bowl" topography of the on-structure park lends itself to an effective system of stormwater management. The landform concept of the park is based on the traditional Chinese "Treasure Bowl," symbolic of magic and good fortune. The auspices of good fortune are combined with environmental benefits, with the bowl shape serving to catch life-sustaining water. The park rewards the city with good fortune and health in return for having been designed with a focus on resiliency and environmental sustainability.

Plan with trees

Site plan

Bank of China FTZ
Shanghai, China

Located on the iconic Dishui Lake in Eastern Shanghai's Free Trade Zone, the landscape of the Bank of China brings together land and water to celebrate the prominent location and towering buildings. The 11-hectare rectangular island rests at the edge of a perfectly circular lake at the terminus of a major urban axis and cultural corridor. The landscape draws inspiration from the land and the bank towers and embraces the symmetry along the east-west axis. There is a poetic relationship between the buildings and landscape: the towers rise above the lake and sit on a retail podium surrounded by a landscape plinth, which is comprised of unique gardens, collectively contributing to the overall landscape setting. A series of gardens and plazas include 360-degree waterfront views and a complete promenade that surrounds and complements the angular geometry of the architecture. A web of walkways, paving patterns, and sloped and stepped terraces achieve continuity in the design, while various water features throughout provide interest and a calming, welcoming experience of the park on the island.

人类 | 生物 | 绿色空间　Human / Animal / Green space

Open spaces with diverse characteristics provide ecological services for the urban outdoor environment, improving biodiversity as they connect to the main waterfront ring park. Within the salinity spray environment, salt tolerant plant species have been carefully selected to survive in this specific context and improve the long term environment of the project. The grove of trees and shrubs mitigates salt water intrusion and maintains the PH balance and moisture in the soil. These green area developments provide home & habitat patches and migration corridors for animals such as birds, pollinators, and amphibian species.

盐碱景观治理　Landscape Treatment in Salinity Condition

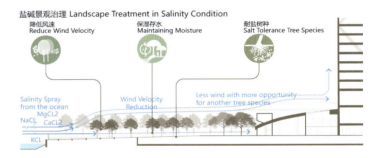

Green infrastructure - Urban biodiversity & Co-habitation

经济技术指标
Economic and technical indicators

建筑占地面积：28389平方米
Building floor area
建筑密度：25.60%
Building density
容积率：1.6
Volume ratio
建筑层数：39层
Number of building floors
建筑高度：194.24米
Building height
地上停车位：188+8 个
Above-ground parking spaces

绿地面积：55469 平方米
Green area
绿地率：50.02%
Green space ratio

蓝色+绿色基础设施
Blue & Green Infrastructure

Green Buffer 绿色屏障
Filtrates polluted air from outside & reduce wind velocity for outdoor comfort

喷泉水景 Water Feature
Provides moisture to reduce temperature during the summer and creates dynamic space for activities

Green Roof 绿色屋顶
Reduces runoff velocity and captures rain water while providing an insulation for building to reduce temperature and energy consumption

Plaza 广场
Specialized materials use the Solar Reflectance Index (SRI) to reduce the heat consumption

Raingarden 雨水花园
Retain water for infiltration process and maintain moisture in soil & reduce water consumption for irrigation process

Salt Tolerance Species 耐盐植被
The salt tolerance tree species maintains the balance of salt and fresh groundwater and also PH level in the soil

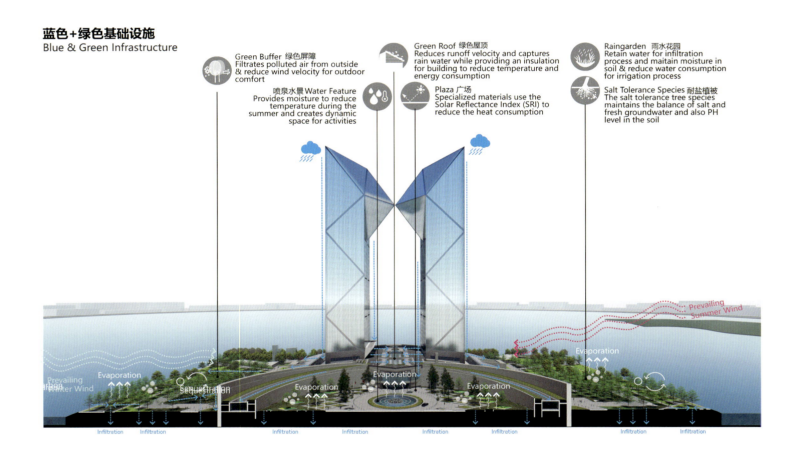

行人友好 + 满足多元需求的项目
Pedestrian Friendly & Programs for Everyone

步行网络以及满足多元需求的项目
Pedestrian Network & Programs for Everyone

The project highlights the pedestrian network that connects to the central loop park and is separated from the vehicular circulation by a planting strip and bollard. The configuration creates a safe and comfortable walking experience for the project. The pedestrian experience is further prioritized by providing plazas or nodes with facilities to gather or relax from any location within the site. From the various public space programs, the project promotes equitable opportunities to service a broad spectrum of the public's physical and mental health needs. The green spaces system supports active and passive programs, health and wellness programs, and social gathering programs to provide an enriching and beneficial environment for many different types of workers and visitors.

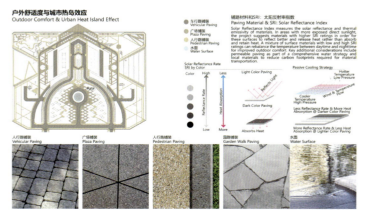

户外舒适度与城市热岛效应
Outdoor Comfort & Urban Heat Island Effect

铺路材料和SRI: 太阳反射率指数
Paving Material & SRI: Solar Reflectance Index

Solar Reflectance Index measures the solar reflectance and thermal emissivity of materials. In areas with more exposed direct sunlight, the project suggests materials with higher SRI ratings in order for these surfaces to reflect better and release heat rather than absorb and retain heat. A mixture of surface materials with low and high SRI ratings can rebalance the temperature between daytime and nighttime for improved outdoor comfort. Key additional considerations include permeable paving as part of a comprehensive water strategy and local materials to reduce carbon footprints required for material transportation.

户外舒适度与城市热岛效应
Outdoor Comfort & Urban Heat Island Effect

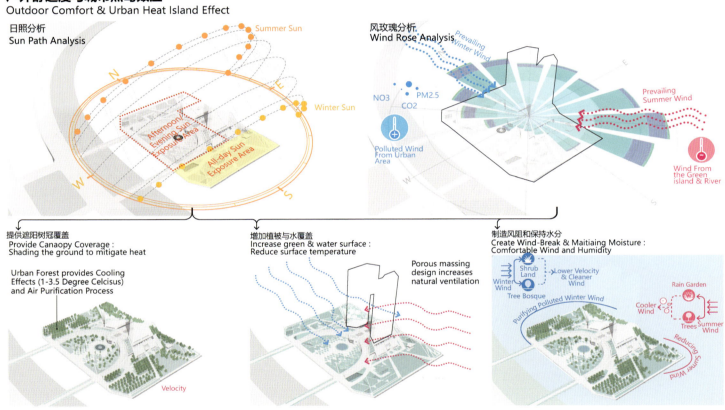

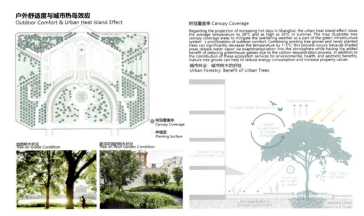

Project C
Bangkok, Thailand

The C Project is a new urban hub in the suburban Rangsit District of northern Bangkok. With convenient access to a rail station and an expressway, the site occupies a key location within an increasingly interconnected urban transportation network. The project will include major retail, residential, R & D, office, medical, hospitality, and education uses serving the township. Strong urban design and a heavily programmed open space framework organize the site. The design team designed the landscape of the project's public realm in close partnership with the lead master planning architect. The park and open space strategy includes preservation of key existing tree groves and natural areas, large gathering and event spaces, flexible sports facilities, organic farms, gardens and nurseries, an interconnected trail and bike network, and an extensive canal system throughout the 120-hectare site. With the entire region subject to periodic flooding, the water retention and storage strategy is a critical design element of the project's long term success.

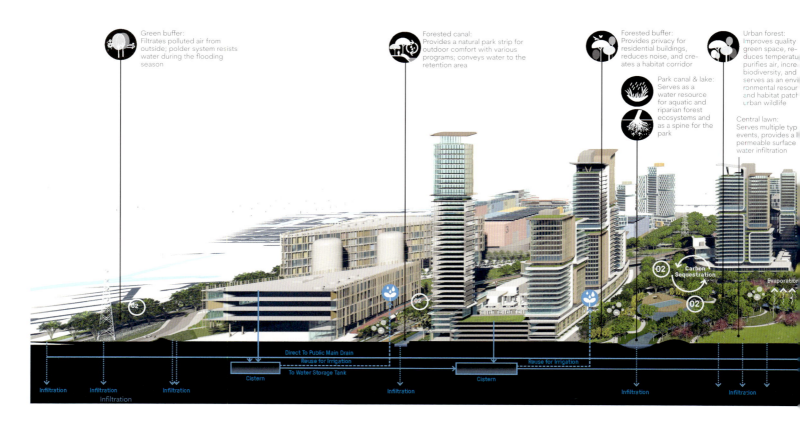

Sustainability strategies – Sustainable concept & Site transect

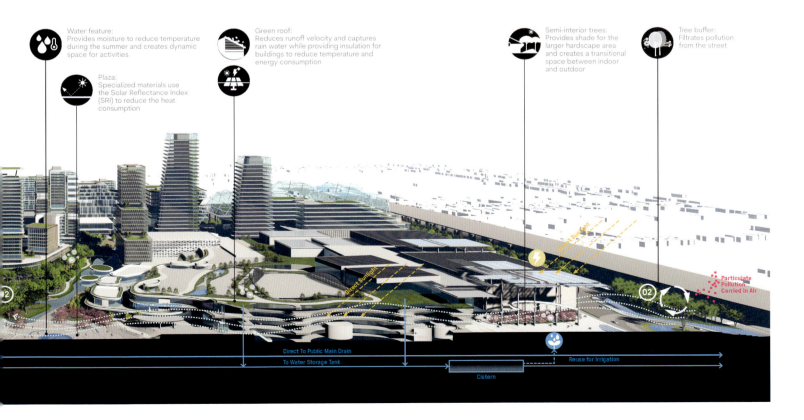

Water feature:
Provides moisture to reduce temperature during the summer and creates dynamic space for activities

Plaza:
Specialized materials use the Solar Reflectance Index (SRI) to reduce the heat consumption

Green roof:
Reduces runoff velocity and captures rain water while providing insulation for buildings to reduce temperature and energy consumption

Semi-interior trees:
Provides shade for the larger hardscape area and creates a transitional space between indoor and outdoor

Tree buffer:
Filtrates pollution from the street

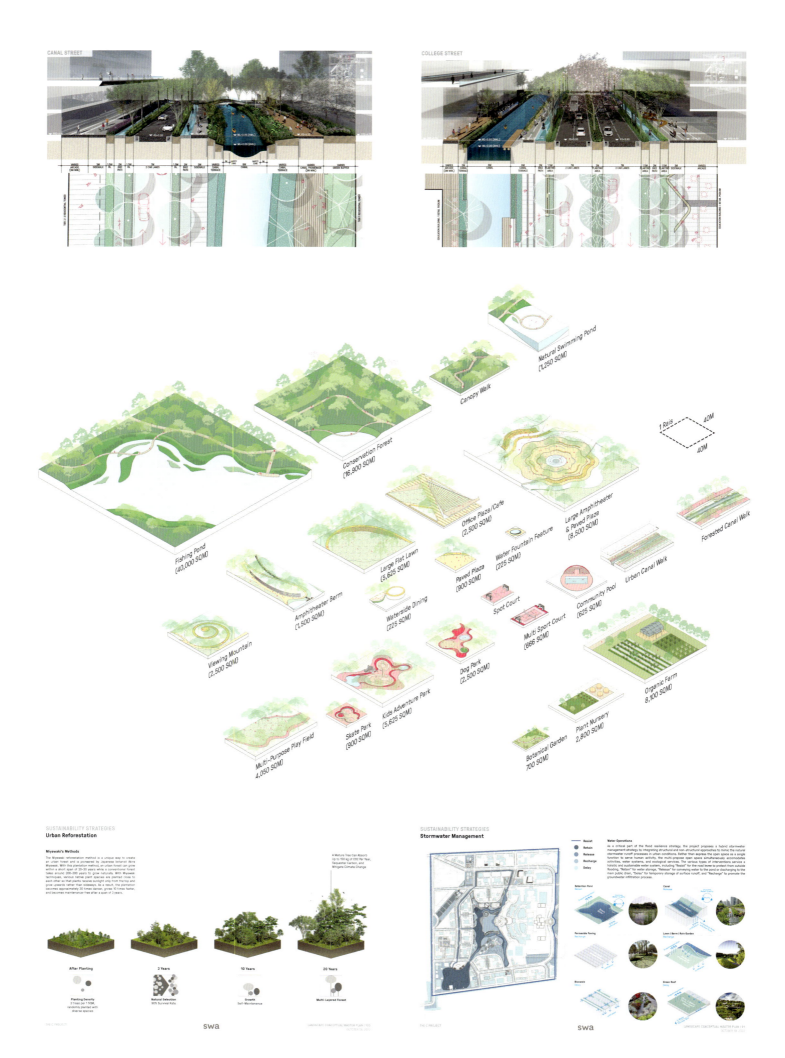

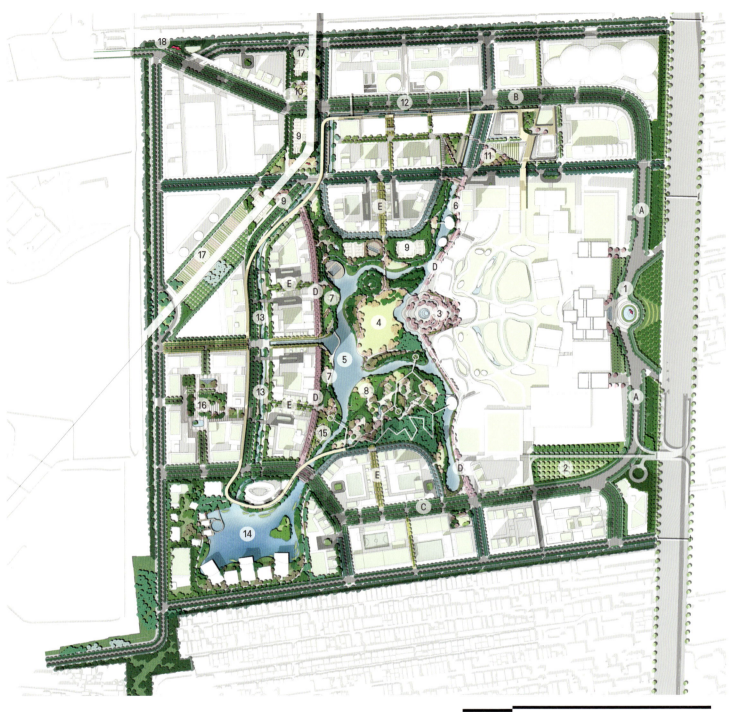

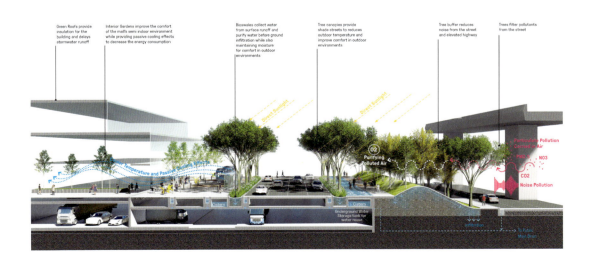

Plan

1. Entry plaza
2. Flyover entry plaza
3. Central plaza & amphitheater
4. Central lawn
5. Central canal & lake
6. Waterfront dining promenade
7. Urban recreation area
8. Urban recreation family zone
9. Urban recreation sport zone
10. Creative park
11. Office plaza
12. Canal walk @ retail street
13. Forested canal walk
14. Nature preserrved area/lake
15. Arboretum
16. Inner court
17. Urban farm & nursery
18. Art object/sculpture

Major street:
A. Retail street
B. College street
C. Hospital street
D. Parkway boulevard
E. Urban paseo

Plan

Durres Waterfront Master Plan
Durres, Albania

This project transformed the waterfront of the city of Durres from an obsolete shipping dockyard to a vibrant waterfront commercial and residential public realm. By leveraging unique natural and cultural assets and working closely with multi-disciplinary consultants, the city and the public, the design team imagined alternative configurations that address the needs of placemaking, commerce, and leisure. The team explored the traditional street scales of the "old city" and adapted this special character and experience to contemporary uses for pedestrians.

Durres Waterfront Development will act as a continuous catalyst that connects the old and new urban space while accommodating the significant pedestrian flow between them. This is a key urban concept and approach that serves both the neighborhood and visitors worldwide.

Isometric view of Beachfront Promenade Planter Seatwall

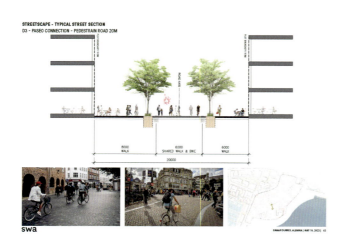

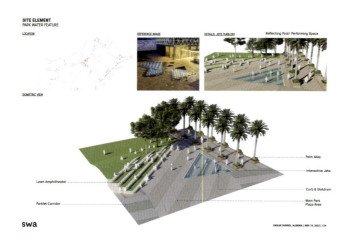

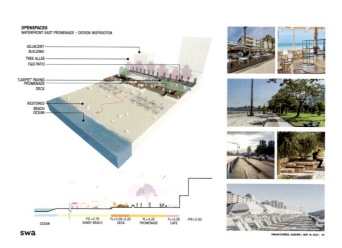

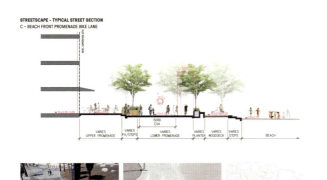
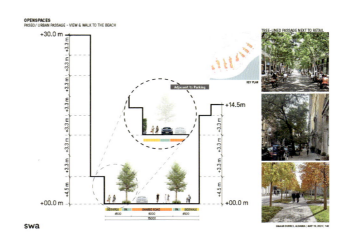
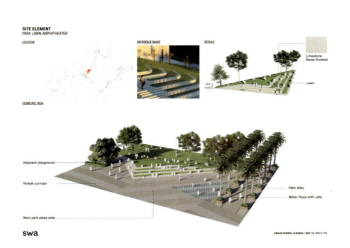
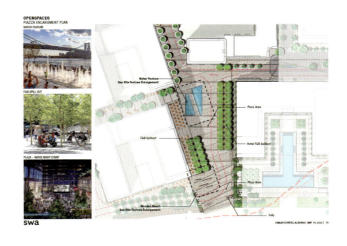

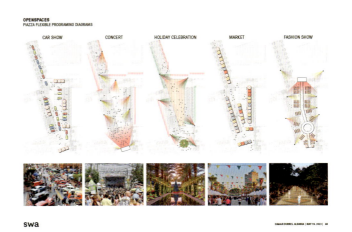

DURRES WATERFRONT MASTER PLAN

7
RESIDENTIAL GARDENS

506   **INTRODUCTION by John L. Wong**

SELECTED PROJECTS
- **518**   83 Dalvey Road
- **522**   Dermody Farms
- **524**   Cantor Residence
- **530**   Zakin Residence
- **536**   Robson Residence
- **544**   The Ranch
- **550**   Vineyard Residence

INTRODUCTION
By John L. Wong

Garden design has been an enduring interest of mine over the course of the past 50 years. Experimenting with design expression in the garden setting offers an invaluable contribution to the modern city landscape and the larger order of modern urban design. I find that work with a single individual or couple and often with the rest of the family is the most rewarding. There is a better chance of successfully applying new ideas in this context than in public projects that face limiting restrictions in code, program, budget, and politics and therefore require a different approach to creative problem-solving.

I design one or two gardens every year. I typically do not market my services for residential garden projects but the demand is always there. Many of these gardens are the homes of clients for whom I am designing commercial projects while some come through word of mouth and recommendations. The design process for these sites is intriguing because the conversation usually goes into great depth regarding program, requirements, and personal needs. The work is demanding and the reward is very satisfying since many of these residential garden clients have become close friends. These private garden projects are interrelated to the portfolio of commercial and public works presented in this publication and reflect my continuous search for design solutions that create "Exceptional Environments."

Opposite page Leahy Residence

83 Dalvey Road
Singapore, Republic of Singapore

This prominent site in the upper node of an established residential neighborhood enclave has open views to downtown Singapore and surrounding neighborhoods within the botanic garden district. The design recreates the grand villa tradition inspired by 18th-century French Chateaux and early 20th-century American interpretations of formal residences. The landscape is designed around a series of garden rooms and terraces on a sloping site with a formal entry court, estate drive, arrival court, art court, water lily pool garden, grand lawn, infinity pool, fruit orchard, vegetable and herb garden, east and west parterre gardens, moon garden, secret garden, flowering trellis, palm garden, and pavilions connected by water and fountains. Using mostly native and indigenous plants, the design captures the tropical flora of the region and highlights a unique collection of outdoor art.

Plan

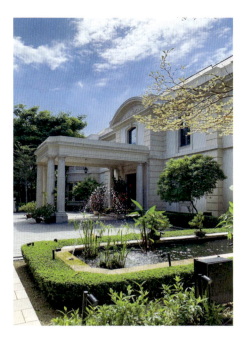

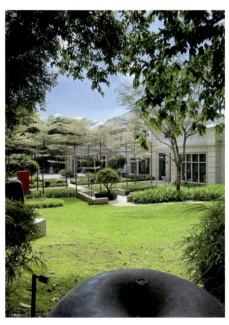

Dermody Farms
Reno, Nevada

Master planning and design for this residential estate were done with careful consideration for the land and its surroundings. Planting, water elements, walls and fences, and other landscape elements were used to provide lasting quality for the residential environment and enhancement of the project site.

Plan

Cantor Residence
La Belle Vie, Bel Air, California

The residence, sited in an established neighborhood in Southern California, is of French limestone with traditional, classic period architectural details. The landscape and garden were designed to respect and complement the formal layout of the main house and to provide a setting for the display of the owners' private collection of bronze sculptures by Rodin. The design also includes a series of garden rooms, a pool house, and a formal entry court. Limestone, bronze, wood lattice and Mediterranean plant palettes were the main elements used for the exterior.

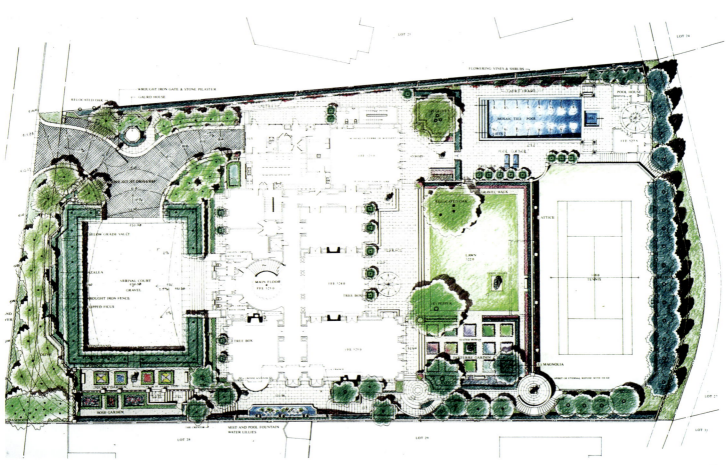

Plan

Plan

Zakin Residence
Napa Valley, California

The Zakin Residence is a private estate located in the hills of Napa Valley, California. Comprising 150 acres, the land is 70 percent wooded and steeply sloped with a small creek transecting a portion of the site.

The program for the landscape design included a small family vineyard, a multi-use field, flower gardens, fountains, terraces, a koi pond, swimming pool and spa, tennis courts, courtyards, a helicopter-pad and guest parking. The design condenses the program within an efficient area to minimize impact on the natural landscape. Native grasses, trees, and the natural landforms will dominate the site and integrate these new interventions.

534   7. RESIDENTIAL GARDENS

Robson Residence
Monte Sereno, California

This stunning 1.5-acre single-family residence evokes the spirit and character of a Provence-region farmhouse, guided by goals for environmental sustainability and the highest level of craft. Strong indoor/outdoor connections were forged using intimate verandas, covered outdoor terraces, and doors and windows that open to shaded pathways, verdant gardens, and expansive views. An evocative loggia incorporates outdoor seating around a fireplace for summer dining and entertaining.

The home was sited into the landscape by reusing flat portions of the landscape, and cut and fill were carefully balanced to avoid any import or export of material. About a third of the lot was preserved as a steep, vegetated ravine, and the remaining land was populated with water-conserving native grasses and plantings. SWA also used recycled, reclaimed, and locally available materials, and the hardscape was designed to be permeable for groundwater recharge.

Plan

Conceptual master plan

The Ranch
Northern California

The design team provided a master plan and landscape architectural services for a weekend compound with a collection of site-specific art pieces to be commissioned by the owner. The initial piece is by Beverly Peppers in the form of a stone pyramid for a music venue. Additional pieces include the artwork of Jaume Plensa, Anish Kapoor, Roxy Paine, and others. The master plan and design made provisions for a series of outdoor gardens for entertainment, recreation, organic fruit and vegetable growing, and art installation. Three special structures are included in the master plan: an art installation site to house a private collection of photographs, a guest house, and a gallery for a collection of small art pieces. Program elements have expanded to include a new barn for entertaining, great lawn, orchard, pizza oven, and terraced spaces to take advantage of the majestic site and surrounding open space.

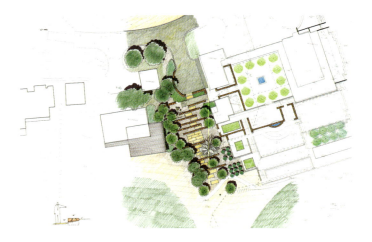

Overall plan

Plan

Vineyard Residence
Sonoma, California

Nestled against a natural rock outcropping, the estate and vineyard commands a panoramic view over the town of Sonoma with extended views to San Francisco. This wine country residence features dominant roof forms and tight integration of interior and exterior spaces allowing for year-long enjoyment of its remarkable location. The entry sequence follows a ranch road to an auto court and spectacular views beyond. A series of outdoor rooms have been created that are a natural extension of the building, utilizing native rock to reshape the hillside and curate a backdrop that is a counterpoint to the expansive views. The existing oaks and hillside vegetation were carefully retained to preserve the natural character of the site while allowing for a vegetable garden and fruiting olive trees referencing the agricultural heritage of the area. An allée of Red Maple trees provide a shaded refuge on this promontory overlooking the valley.

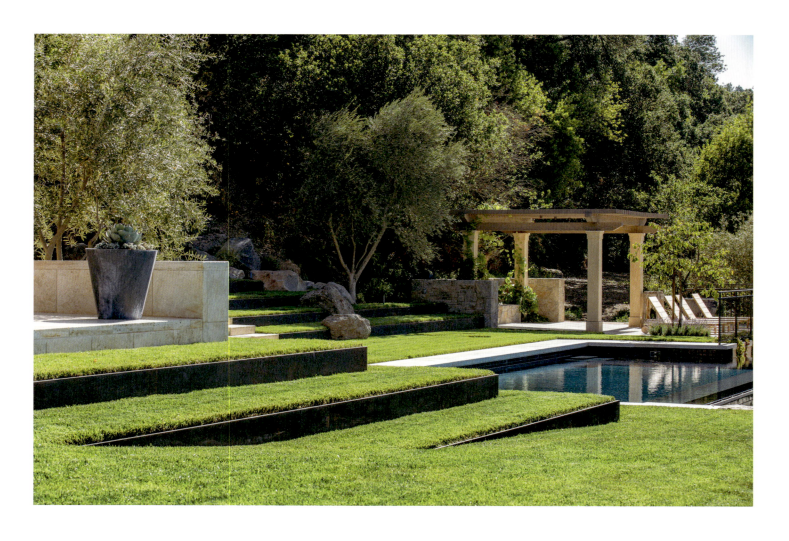

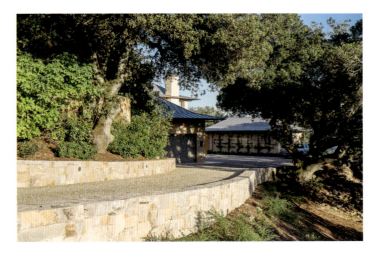

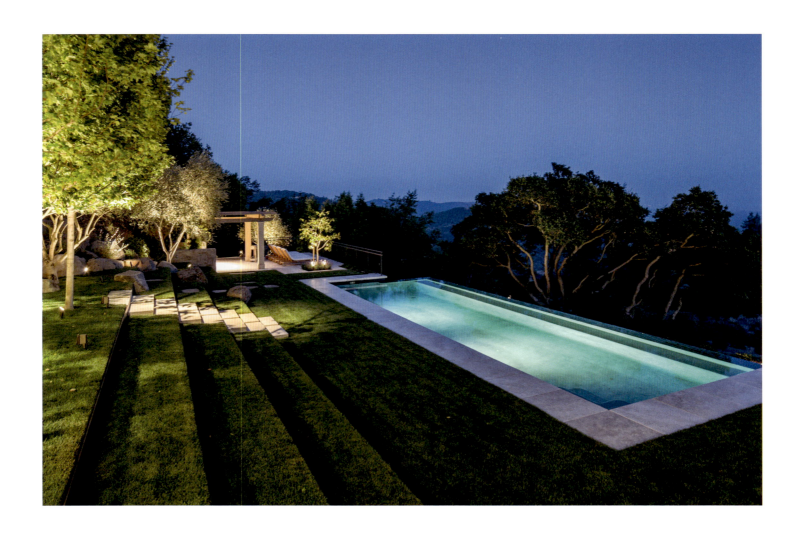

Section

7. RESIDENTIAL GARDENS

Section

INTERVIEW

By James Moore McCown with John L. Wong

James Moore McCown: Hello John. Thanks for taking the time to talk to me. I'd like to start with your early years in Hong Kong, China and your family's eventual emigration to the U.S.

John L. Wong: I was born in Hong Kong, China 1951. My parents were both college trained educators. My father taught English in a high school. My mother was a teacher as well and became a superintendent for a grammar school.

My family had emigrated to Hong Kong, China from mainland China. At that time, Hong Kong was a British colony, and so my parents thought we would be better protected under the British.

JM: Was Hong Kong, China a boom town or was it just a sleepy outpost of the British Empire?

JW: Hong Kong, China was a boom town when my parents first got there. The city was already considered one of the densest in the world. Because of the strong influx of people from China, the local authority went through a major urban expansion. Most of the growth in the city took place on the north side of the island, where we lived.

Across the water, the mainland side was also relatively dense and going through a major urban renewal. The last time I returned to the island, which was about 30 years ago, those buildings were replaced with single slim tall residential towers up to 40, 50, 60 stories. Now, most of the growth in the island takes place in the mainland side.

JM: Those tall buildings must have had an impact on you, a precursor to your "An Entire City in Vertical Form."

JW: Yes, it was quite incredible because the only direction to build was vertically, so the city was a very dense metropolis.

JM: What language did you speak at home?

JW: Cantonese, which I still speak today. Hong Kong, China is 100% Cantonese. Mostly when you're in the Southern region of China from Guangzhou to Kowloon to Hong Kong, China, they're all Cantonese speaking.

JM: So there must be some place in Hong Kong, China that had particular relevance for you. Some sort of woods, park, or building. What resonates for you to this day?

JW: The idea of open space is very important to me because it makes a dense place very livable. Hong Kong, China is mostly an urban metropolis. The city grew over the years and expanded into the mountains. Following the significant growth in the city center, we spent a great deal of time as kids in the mountains and Victoria Park, which is the largest park in Hong Kong, China and equivalent to 1/20th the size of New York's Central Park.

JM: Would you describe the neighborhood you grew up in as solidly middle class?

JW: Yes. The wealthy typically lived near the mountain base with the tall towers. However, most of the buildings were located in the dense flat areas and were considered middle-class enclaves.

JM: Where did you settle in the United States?

JW: I was ten years old when we emigrated to the U.S. We were a family of five: my mom, my dad, my brother, my sister, and myself. I'm the youngest. We sailed by ship from Hong Kong, China to Tokyo to Hawaii and finally to San Francisco.

From the time I first set foot in San Francisco until now, I find the city to be very pleasant. San Francisco has very strong neighborhoods and distinctive populations, like Nob Hill, Russian Hill, North Beach and Pacific Heights, due to its geography.

JM: What neighborhood did you live in?

JW: We lived near Nob Hill right next to Chinatown. We were able to find an apartment about a mile up on the hill. It was very easy living.

At the time the city's growth was concentrated in the Financial District. San Francisco neighborhoods have never been strong at growth. Most of the physical growth is in renovation but the scale, the density, stays the same. San Francisco is unique due to three things. First is the water, which surrounds us on three sides. You have the ocean, the bay, and the inner bay. Second is the weather – mostly moderate. The third thing is the varied neighborhoods.

JM: You spent a couple of years at community college and then went to UC Berkeley.

JW: Yes. In those days Berkeley got the enrollment of their students from City College and a couple of other junior colleges in the Bay Area and the City College tuition was free.

I took a mechanical drawing class at City College of San Francisco. My first exposure to architecture began with drafting. I went from drawing nuts and bolts to lettering all the way to drawing houses. I was told I had a "good hand." I was able to communicate ideas and think three dimensionally, which continued to improve as time passed.

My parents always said there's a lot of opportunity in this country but you need a good education because they were from an educated background. The reason they moved to the United States was not for them – they were trying to create better opportunities for their children. Hong Kong, China was a very competitive city for higher education. With a population of 3 million, countless kids wanted to attend the University, but there were limited slots. So your chances of getting in required that you were either very rich, had connections, or were very smart. My parents knew that no matter how bright we were, we may not be able to make it to college, which would lead to working in a second-class or not high paying job. Coming to the United States opened up opportunities for me. My parents imprinted upon us that a good education is the way up and the way out.

JM: Let's talk about your mentor Peter Walker. How did you meet him?

JW: At Berkeley we'd always have guest lecturers – some of the most prominent designers then in practice. One of the lecturers was Pete Walker. I sat in and he was talking about his firm in Sausalito called Sasaki Walker Associates or SWA.

That's when I first learned about "landscape architecture." I talked to Pete afterward and said to him, how does one get into your field? He said you needed a degree in landscape architecture. So I went down the hall and inquired further about the program. It was very easy to switch from architecture to landscape architecture. At the end of my third year Pete also told me that SWA had started a summer program in Sausalito and he encouraged me to apply. I got accepted and that opened the path to bring me into the firm.

In 1974 I graduated from Berkeley with a Bachelor of Arts in Landscape Architecture, with honors, and Sasaki Walker offered me a full-time job. So I took it. However, nine months into my new job, there was a major market crash.

JM: I remember that terrible mid-'70s recession.

JW: Sasaki Walker went from 80 people down to 30 and I was one of the casualties. I was introduced to a Southern California firm called Pod that was run by three Harvard graduates and doing a lot of design work for the Irvine Company. Pod was an aspiring firm that wanted to be like Sasaki Walker and I went to work for them for two years.

At that time, all the partners at Sasaki Walker, as well as many senior associates had gone to the Harvard Graduate School of Design. Of the 80 people, I would say 30 of them were Harvard graduates. So it was a Harvard connection that drew us together.

JM: So you applied to Harvard and got accepted.

JW: Yes and it was also the same time that Pete took the Chairmanship at Harvard. It had been something that he really wanted to do. Pete was very much involved in teaching but he also wanted to continue to practice landscape architecture. So he didn't want to separate the two.

JM: All right. And you were made a partner at the East Coast version of SWA?

JW: Yes, the office was in Cambridge and it was the SWA Group East. Pete was a very prominent design figure. He would develop and come up with the idea and bring jobs into the firm and then there a group of very talented designers and project managers provided support and development for all the design work.

Later in 1981, I won the Rome Prize from the American Academy in Rome and went to Rome because Pete said you ought to go to Rome to open my eyes and learn new stuff. Even while I was working in 1978, he said I ought to go to France and see some of André Le Nôtre's work – one of the most influential landscape architects of the 17th century. Le Nôtre is one of my heroes.

And so, in 1982 during my fellowship, I travelled a great deal in Italy and in Europe and went to see the work of André Le Nôtre. I think he did maybe hundreds of gardens in France but I went to see the most notable ones. It was almost like a kid visiting a candy store for the first time.

JM: All right. So talk to me about when you started talking about Chicago and Skidmore, Owings & Merrill.

JW: Bruce Graham of SOM's Chicago office was one of Pete's clients. At that time, Bruce was considered one of the most influential architects in terms of his connections to major projects due to the growth of the late '70s and throughout the '80s that generated banks, headquarter buildings, and high rises. Earlier on, Pete had collaborated on a couple of projects with Bruce and one influential one was the Upjohn headquarters in Kalamazoo, Michigan and the other one was Weyerhaeuser Headquarters in Seattle, Washington.

JM: I just want to situate this economically because we had the terrible recession of 1982, but then in 1983, 1984, the economy really started to pick up steam and a lot of building was taking place. And that was kind of the beginning of the boom here in the United States. But there was sort of a very slow boom in the Middle East and in Asia, right?

JW: There was a Middle East focus at the time, except it was very early in their development because the countries in this region were building these military cities, educational facilities and large communities.

JM: And when did you return to the West Coast?

JW: In 1985. I got married in 1984, and my wife went to Rhode Island School of Design (RISD) at that time to get her degree in Interior Architecture. She said the weather in the East Coast is too tough - let's move back to the West Coast.

JM: China and Japan were starting to rumble in terms of a market, especially China. And I want to hear about your identity as someone from Hong Kong, China who began to

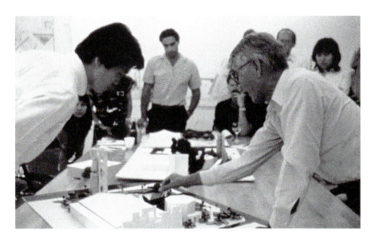

First row SWA Group East, Boston, Massachusetts, office picture; John L. Wong. at the office in Sausalito, California. **Second row** Summer Student Program 2022, photograph by David Lloyd; Design collaboration works. **Third row** Summer Student Program 2022, Site Tour, photograph by Bill Tatham; John L. Wong & Hideo Sasaki. **Fourth row** Construction field review for Rosewood Hotel, Sand Hills Road; The project team at the start of the Expo 2020 Al Wasl Plaza Construction.

do more work in China, the Far East, and in the Middle East. How did your background form that? By this point, you had achieved a lot in landscape architecture but were now beginning to foray into overseas markets.

JW: Being an Asian, educated and trained in the US and having collaborated with some of the best architects and designers at the time was a unique combination and I was able to bring a fresh new design perspective and sensitivity to these growing countries. The growth of the market occurred in three to four major periods. There was 1985 to1995, which was the Japan heyday. Then after that there was Korea. They kind of overlapped in 1992 to about 1999. Then there was a 30-year run with China until say last year when things took a major downturn because of the pandemic and because of the slow growth as China went from 6.5% in GDP to like 2.1% (now China's GDP is slowly coming back up again).

JM: It was a 30-year run. That's amazing.

JW: I won't give up on China. I think they're going to have another uptick. And then the fourth period that I would say is the Middle East, which is comprised of the UAE, United Arab Emirates, and the subsequent neighboring countries Oman, Kuwait, the Kingdom of Saudi Arabia, Qatar, and now Egypt.

JM: I think this is a very important juncture because you're beginning to work in three Asian countries and I want to hear how your Asian background informed your work here.

JW: I think of the work as going from Japan, then to Korea, then to China, and then to the Middle East. Those first three Asian countries became the Asian Tigers and wanted to be very international. I was able to bring my design sensibility and experience to that part of the world given the background and training that I had to that point.

JM: Think of SOM's Gordon Bunshaft as the Chase Man. He did a beautiful sunken Japanese garden at Chase Manhattan Plaza in downtown New York. There's a real affinity between that Asian landscape sensibility and modernism, don't you think?

JW: That's right. I think we try to recreate and I call it an abstraction. I remember in the fall of 1982, I came back to Boston after spending a year in Rome, and the first thing Pete Walker told me was to get rid of all the stuff that I just learned. He said what you want to do is understand it and abstract those ideas and make them into forms and design that you would do. I think Pete basically told me, "Don't throw away the learned vocabulary but understand how to abstract it, express it and solve the problem."

JM: There's an analogy between Le Nôtre who was very disciplined, very geometric, and the Asian landscape sensibility, which is very... Well, I don't know what you'd call it. Very sensitive. Very, very geometric.

JW: The Asian design sensibility is about poetry, consisting of the ability to tap into intuitive qualities of delight, beauty and cultural resonance. I think Le Nôtre's work was geometric and grand in the way he manipulated the visual ground plane. Nobody could do that better than Le Nôtre. And I think he learned that from Vignola, one of the early influential architects of the Italian Renaissance. I'm sure Le Nôtre went to see some of the best landscape design in Italy, where it's very hilly and therefore the gardens are much more intimate and smaller scale. But Le Nôtre learned how the Italians manipulate the ground plane to control nature and create a geometric setting for the building for the person who commissioned the design, be it a king, a pope, or some other powerful individual. They wanted a physical manifestation of their power and wealth.

JM: Let's talk about Stanford where you've done so much work.

JW: In 1982, I was doing a project at Stanford that was part of Pete Walker's design for a fountain and a plaza at the new library. I was drawing the plaza that Pete Walker and James Reeves designed and that was my first exposure to Stanford. David Neuman, an extremely talented individual, had just been hired as the campus architect.

JM: What in a nutshell, was the idea? Was it all around a central plaza?

JW: The fountain was the central focal feature for the plaza and it opens up the main entrance for the new library. Stanford's campus is really about axial relationships. The axis between the main quad, north/south and east/west with the two adjacent schools all interconnected. The other important site aspect is that it has axes also relating to the peninsula, which is where the train station is in Palo Alto. And in the old days, that's how people came in. And then there was a whole procession going up to the main center and from there connecting to the hills. So those axes are view corridors. They are connective elements for students, faculty and visitors. They are also outdoor gathering places. Some of those ideas got lost because some architect came in and added a building that blocked it. So David wanted to reinvigorate the original principles of the vision of Charles Allerton Coolidge and Frederick Law Olmsted. While working with campus facilities and with David, at times some of these projects were donor funded and the donor always has his or her choice of designer. We were able to convince them that we were the right individuals and the right firm to work with. So we successfully grew from a few projects into dozens of projects at one time.

JM: You took the Olmsted plan and made it relevant to the present day in other parts of the campus. How did you do that?

JW: The key thing to understand there is that the buildings are not the main players. The main heart of the project is really about open space, public realm and connections.

JM: Let's talk about your sense of how to succeed in the diverse landscape architecture career that you've had.

JW: There are four essential elements that provide a foundation for a good project: Client, Program, Site, and Budget. Of the four, I would say the Site is probably the most important. The Site informs us about the place, the culture and the overall physical relationship to the proposed intervention.

You need to develop a good grasp of all four elements by asking a lot of questions and engaging in active listening.

JM: Say more about the budget.

JW: The budget I think is probably the least important thing. I've done projects where we had a limitless budget. That doesn't mean it's going to be the best project. I find that some of the best projects I've done had a tiny budget and when we were pushed against a wall, we were able to come up with the best idea. The budget in essence answers the question "can you get this project built?"

JM: I want to hear your reflections on tall buildings. Ada Louise Huxtable's book *The Tall Building, Artistically Reconsidered* offers an energetic defense of cities and a brilliant consideration of the skyscraper as art, as business, and as the product of political speculation. There's this idea about the tall building being ecologically responsible and being efficient by not using too much land. What are your thoughts about the tall building in general?

JW: I'm for tall buildings. But I also understand the impact of a tall structure. If it's not designed well, it's problematic. You can ruin the skyline or if you design a very poor performance building that requires a lot of energy, it will affect the long-term cost to operate. I believe in sustainable, ecologically designed buildings that meet certain performance criteria by using very little energy and yet providing maximum comfort and a spatial experience for the user.

The tall building makes a lot of sense in terms of efficient use of land, which I discuss in my article "The Entire City in Vertical Form." It is very economic if you do it in the right way where one concentrates a lot of energy and people in a very small area of land. And if you locate people in a central place with transportation, they have access to bikes, green corridors, open space parks, and recreation. Tall buildings allow people to live, work, and recreate in a footprint that uses the least land possible.

And hopefully the rest of the land is preserved for open space, conservation, and agricultural use. The world needs more concentrated areas with wonderful environments for people to work and to live.

JM: Frank Lloyd Wright claimed to hate tall buildings, but he designed a mile-high skyscraper for Chicago.

JW: That's right. In a way. Had that building been built it literally would have been a city within a city. I mean, it was a hotel. It was a residence. It was an office building. Now Adrian Smith has designed the world's first kilometer-high building, Jeddah Tower, and I am excited to be doing its landscape architecture. This is a classic example of what I call "an entire city in vertical form."

JM: Right. It brings up an important point. Whenever you talk about these landscapes that you've created at the Burj Khalifa or at the Jeddah Tower, you use the term park. But are these really parks that are open to everyone or are they privatized?

JW: It's a hybrid, both public and private. We designed it so that it benefits the user, the owner, and the community, but also it benefits the public. So the public can come to the hotel. They can enjoy the park and can enjoy a portion of it. On the ground plane, the Burj Khalifa was designed in the shape of three leaves to form three separate entrances. One entrance is for the hotel and office use. One is for residential use. And then the third one is a plaza that we designed as a terrace that related to a lake. You will see in many of my projects that I take some cues from the architect in terms of the material, the geometry, and the shape of the structure and sometimes apply that onto the ground plane. At Burj Khalifa, we created a park as the base for the tower. The park at the hotel portion is all public. Now, to answer your question, are we actually creating a park? The way it works is that the hotel portion is all public. The office area is semi-public. And then the residential area is for the people who live there. They have their own private park.

JM: Okay, let's pivot to talking about resiliency. We've been talking about tall buildings, but have yet to discuss the implications of tall buildings on the shore. It's less of an issue in the United Arab Emirates because they're farther from the sea. But in San Francisco and Shanghai, rising sea levels are a very urgent issue.

JW: That's why we need to be very smart about designing projects that are adaptive and have a direct positive impact on our environment. For instance, take Manhattan, which has a major concentration of urbanization. However, by mid-century or maybe the end of the century, the southern portion will be under water. That's a major challenge and concern we need to address. One single project is not going to solve the problem, but in new cities and towns we need to be more careful with site selection and craft more resilient responses into the long-term effect. A Green City, typically, reflects more affluence, a better living environment, and a more middle-class population. So I think landscape architecture can lead the charge to solve a lot of these problems. We can plant more trees, provide more greenery, increase efficiency and open space, and reduce hardscape – if we create more green infrastructure, it will lead to a higher standard of living.

JM: I want to talk about individual clients and single-family homes that you've done. How did these commissions come about? For instance, the Cantors are a very high-profile couple. They have this huge collection of Rodins. Did you design the garden for their home around the artworks?

JW: Their base company is Cantor Fitzgerald and they manage financial services. I was working on the museum and they brought me in to look at the garden and that's how it started. In turn they introduced me to other clients and that's how most of these individual projects came about. I don't market my services on single family homes. What I do is 1 or 2 gardens a year because I think they are very interesting and demanding. You have to listen closely to what the client is looking for and likes and respond to their needs and requirements. I always find it intriguing because the home garden design allows you to experiment with new ideas and also to get to know the client in a way that you normally don't in a commercial situation. And many of my clients became close friends.

Iris Cantor took me to a storage warehouse in LA. She said, "John, I want you to take a look at some of these art pieces and place them in the garden." I went in there to find a huge collection and pieces of the artwork in full scale and maquettes! "Just choose whichever one you want to use, you can use it." You get these opportunities you normally don't get and it becomes a unique challenge.

JM: That's amazing. What are other keys to success besides client, program, site, and budget?

JW: For client development you need to develop good and long-term relationships. I started with Pete Walker, then with Bruce Graham, and then many of his partners. And then there are other designers like Adrian Smith and Gordon Gill who went to work for SOM and left. We became good friends and continue to collaborate together. And Bing Thom, a talented architect whose works contributed to this book and he was introduced to me through James Cheng, who was a fellow architecture graduate at Harvard and a life-long collaborator and close friend.

JM: Who are your other architectural heroes?

JW: I have many favorites, but 1 or 2 come to mind in particular. I have always liked I.M. Pei. I find his buildings to be timeless; they're very Asian influenced but also have a unique architectural presence and of course. Louis Kahn. It's hard to pick a favorite architect, although I also have always admired

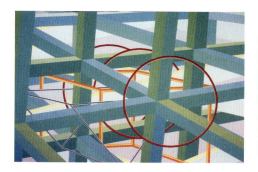  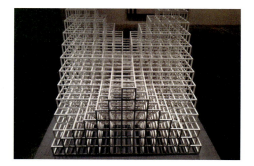

First row Inspirational Artists to my work: Al Held (left), Frank Stella (center), Sol LeWitt (right). **Second row** Andre LeNotre, Vaux Le Vicomte and Sceaux; American Academy in Rome, Italy; Cartoon landscape architect.

a firm like SOM. I like Adrian Smith and many of the firm's partners. The buildings that Adrian and Gordon Gill design are very rigorous: well proportioned, well detailed, well designed, and well built. And I think that it's very important to do design work at that level.

JM: Tell me more about where you live and work. You work in Sausalito, which is a very bucolic kind of place. Where do you live?

JW: I live in San Francisco on the north edge of the city in a unique neighborhood that is very close to the bay. My house is adjacent to the Presidio, which is a national park now, and overlooks the Golden Gate National Recreation area, the whole north, and the Bay. I'm a stone's throw from the beach and nature. And I like that I live close to a neighborhood where I can buy all kinds of things including special cooking ingredients and eat at some of the most tasty and unique restaurants in the city.

JM: What's the name of your neighborhood?

JW: Seacliff. I designed my house with my friend Michael Chan. I like that I live in an urban neighborhood and work just across the Bay in Sausalito, a beautiful town. My commute across the Golden Gate Bridge every day is about nine minutes. So it's ideal.

JM: Do you have any closing thoughts to share?

JW: Most people live in cities today and urbanization will continue at their edges. As we exit a global pandemic, people are rediscovering the importance of outdoor spaces and the public realm. Some cities are closing streets to car traffic and allowing a pedestrian right of way. It's an inexpensive way to get people outside safely and it enables them to connect to urban parks and key neighborhood destinations. In New York, it would be great if you could close a street for most of the day, say 9 a.m. to 8 p.m., to allow a pedestrian thoroughfare from Battery Park to the Bronx. It would open up a different way of experiencing the city and civic leaders/urban planners could do it tomorrow at very little cost.

"Thinking outside the box" is really about observing the world with fresh eyes, finding connections you haven't thought of before, and solving emerging and important issues like climate change, environmental resilience, and social equity. If you aspire to be a landscape architect, be a modern version of a "Renaissance" person. It's valuable to have broad knowledge of the humanities and the sciences and not just design.

JM: Vitruvius said an architect should learn something about everything.

JW: Yes, exactly. You have to. And landscape architects by training also have knowledge of the natural sciences and economics, plus other disciplines. We are trained to think very broadly and are the ones who have the best opportunity to design a more responsible and resilient world. We need support from patrons, cities, and the public. We need to have a stronger idea and voice to take charge on small to medium to large projects where we can provide a point of view that would help address challenges related to sea level rise, climate change, and so forth. I do think that that we can do that and by no means are we the only ones. But, within a professional design consultancy, landscape architects in some ways have the best opportunities to make a major impact. And having the opportunity also presents you with a challenge in itself.

JM: How do you go about creating projects that do good?

JW: You start by putting ideas on paper . . . and then you translate those ideas into advocacy. I think we all need to go to the public and tell them about the important work we do and demonstrate this through projects that can provide examples for others to follow. And then the last thing would be to apply these learnings toward education. That's why I'm always interested in teaching. I think one should both practice and teach. Teaching doesn't have to take place in a school setting. It could be in your studio. When you see my list of collaborators, these are people with whom I collaborate, learn from, and design. It is a continual two-way street of exchanging wisdom and ideas in the quest to design "Exceptional Environment".

ACKNOWLEDGMENTS
By John L. Wong

The Selected Works of Landscape Architect John L. Wong – From Private to Public Ground, From Small to Tall represents a body of work that has been a life's career in the making. The projects illustrated in the book grew from collaborative relationships with diverse clients, landscape architects, architects, engineers, and allied industry professionals. I wish to thank every individual on the project teams who has contributed to the designs and projects that this publication showcases and explores in depth.

I want to extend my deep appreciation to the SWA Group Principals who have continually inspired me with their support, guidance and critique over the years. I am grateful to all of my colleagues and friends at SWA Group along with the numerous clients, consultants, and craftsmen I have crossed paths with for their creativity, talent, hard work, responsiveness, and resilience in the enduring quest to create exceptional environments. I am indebted to them all.

I would also like to express my heartfelt thanks to the SWA creative team who worked on the graphic materials, photography, research, writing, and editing to produce this comprehensive and unique publication:
- Photography: David Lloyd, Tom Fox, Bill Tatham, Gerry Campbell, Dixi Carrillo, Tom Lamb, Jonnu Singleton.
- Text, Project Description, Project Research: Heidi Engelbrechten, Liz Batchelder, Glenn Jones, Yang Zhang.

I feel immense gratitude for the following individuals who have generously offered their mentorship, collaboration, inspiration and, most importantly, friendship, through the years: Peter E. Walker, Kalvin Platt, William Callaway, James Reeves, David J. Neuman, Adrian Smith, Gordon Gill, James K M Cheng, Bing Thom, Michael C. F. Chan, Peter Wong and many others. I am privileged that some of these distinguished individuals have also provided the Foreword and Introductions for this monograph. I am very fortunate to have had the opportunity to learn from and be strengthened by their creative talents and words of wisdom.

A special acknowledgement to ORO Oscar Riera Ojeda Publishers Limited – Oscar Riera Ojeda, Juan Sarrabayrouse, Lucía Bauzá, Carrie Tang and the ORO team for the book design and layout and to James McCown for engaging in an in-depth conversation about my design works. They all helped to translate this idea from concept into reality.

And finally, I feel especially grateful for the unfailing love, patience and support from my family during all these years: they have allowed me to do what I love and enjoy. Whether I was commuting down the peninsula to Stanford, Palo Alto or flying West, East, and everywhere in between, I am forever indebted to my family for supporting me on my creative pursuits. First, I want to thank my parents who made tremendous sacrifices in coming to the United States to pursue a new life, which gave me the opportunity to learn and thrive. Thank you to my wife Milky, my first line of support, and my two daughters Alyson and Nicole. Without your sacrifices and support, none of this would have been possible.

Thank you all!

John L. Wong
August 1, 2023, San Francisco

Opposite page Zifeng Tower - Nanjing Greenland International Commercial Center

APPENDIX

Photography Credits

- David Lloyd

- Tom Fox

- Bill Tatham

- Gerry Campbell

- Dixi Carrillo

- Tom Lamb

- Jonnu Singleton

- Alan Ward: 190 Marlborough St, John L. Wong

- J Widjaja: 83 Dalvey Road

- Christian Horan: Ko Olina, Four Seasons

- Stephen Li: Grosvenor Ambleside

- Jason O'Rear: Expo 2020 Projects

Project Credits

83 Dalvey Road
Singapore
Project Team: John L. Wong, Shih-Ying Chuang
Client: Owner Name Withheld
Architect: Richard Manion Architecture, Inc.
Local Landscape Architect: Nyee Phoe Flower Garden Pte Ltd

190 Marlborough St.
Boston, Massachusetts
Project Team: Peter Walker, Martha Schwartz, John L. Wong
Client & Architect: Peter Walker

400 S. Hope Street
Los Angeles, California
Project Team: John L. Wong, Richard Law, Richard Thomas, Donald Tompkins
Client: O'Melveny & Meyers LLP
Architect: Welton Becket Architects

Amazing Brentwood Town Center
Burnaby, British Columbia, Canada
Project Team: John L. Wong, Min Young Choi, Anya Domlesky, Tyler Eash, Patrick Haesloop, William Hall, Natalie Harper, Erica Huang, Yoonju Kametani, Caroline Kim, Jinwook Lee, Jia Li, Ronald Lim, Sergio Lima, Hilda Lin, John Loomis, Shaun Loomis, Catherine McDonald, Anna Park, Mandana Parvinian, Caroline Templeton, Travis Theobald, Amity Winters
Client: SHAPE Properties
Architect: James KM Cheng, Architects, Ltd.
Local Landscape Architect: Durante Kreuk Ltd.

Bank of China FTZ
Shanghai, China
Project Team: John L. Wong, Julie Canter, Minyoung Choi, Ron Cubbage, Vincent Hsu, John Loomis, Mandana Parvinian, Xinye Shen, Monica Streeper, Vaan Surajuras, Amanda Tom, Zihan Zhu
Client: Bank of China
Architect: Pei Partnership Architects
Local Architect: CADG China Architecture Design & Research Group

Bank of China Hainan
Jiangdon New Area, Haikou, China
Project Team: John L. Wong, Julie Canter, Peter Clark, Ron Cubbage, Zi Gu, Jing Li, Sergio Lima, John Loomis, Mandana Parvinian, Monica Streeper, Amanda Ton
Client: Bank of China
Architect: Pei Partnership Architects
Local Architect: CADG China Architecture Design & Research Group

B Bentley School
Lafayette, California
Project Team: John L. Wong, Claudia Kath, Conard Lindgren, John Loomis, Valerie Maillet, Maureen Simmons
Client: Bentley School
Architect: ELS Architects

Boca Raton Hotel & Beach Club
Boca Raton, Florida
Project Team: John L. Wong, Peter Walker, William Clark, Kalvin Platt, Danny Powell, James G. Reeves
Architect: Killingsworth Brady Architects

Boston Piers 1, 2, 3
Boston, Massachusetts
Project Team: John L. Wong, Peter Walker, Tom Adams, Michael Sardina
Client: BRA

Bunker Hill
Los Angeles, California
Project Team: John L. Wong, Peter Walker, Tom Adams, Richard Law, James Lee, Michael Sardina
Client: AC Martin

Burj 2020 District
Dubai, United Arab Emirates
Project Team: John L. Wong, Minyoung Choi, Zhongwei Li, Ronald Lim, Sergio Lima, Ayaka Matthews, Anna Park, Mandana Parvinian, Travis Theobald, Zhaojie Wu, Chuhan Zhang, Yang Zhang
Client: DMCC- Dubai Multi Commodities Center
Architect: Adrian Smith + Gordon Gill Architecture

Burj Khalifa Tower Park
Dubai, United Arab Emirates
Project Team: John L. Wong, Gerdo Aquino, Chih-Wei Chang, Shih-Ying Chiang, Gerald DeDios, Chistiane Dreisbusch, David Gal, Michael Herrin, Minhui Li, Yoonju Kametani, Pei-Ching Kao, Caroline Kim, Benjamin Knoll, Huiqing Kuang, Todd Larudee, Han Song Lee, Hui-Li Lee, Sergio Lima, Chih-Wei Lin, John Loomis, Sheradyn Mikul, Ross Nadeau, Joseph Newton, Michael Odum, Mandana Parvinian, Sarah Peck, Annabelle Rebar, Eric Story, Kathy Sun, Travis Theobald, Leah Thompson, Zhaojie Wu, Ying Zeng
Client: EMAAR Properties, PJSC
Architect: Skidmore, Owings & Merrill LLP

Burnaby Civic Square & Library
Burnaby, British Columbia, Canada
Project Team: John L. Wong, John Loomis, Maureen Simmons
Client: Corporation of District of Burnaby
Architect: James KM Cheng Architects
Local Landscape Architect: Durante Kreuk Ltd.

Burnett Park
Fort Worth, Texas
Project Team: John L Wong, Peter Walker, Tom Adams, Duncan Alford, Michael Sardina
Client: Tandy Foundation

Butterfly Tower (The)
Vancouver, British Columbia, Canada
Project Team: John L. Wong, Minyoung Choi, Natalie Harper, Jia Li, Ronald Lim, Sergio Lima, Shaun Loomis, Trent Matthias, Adam Novack, Alyssa Olson, Yang Zhang
Client: Westbank Corp.
Architect: Revery Architecture (formally Bing Thom architects)

Cantor, La Belle Vie Residence
Bel Air, California
Project Team: John L. Wong, Rene Bihan, William Blossom, Jill Ann Gropp, James Lee, John Loomis, Nancy Noble, Maureen Simmons
Client: Cantor Fitzgerald
Architect: Michael C.F. Chan and Associates

Cayan Tower
Dubai, United Arab Emirates
Project Team: John L. Wong, Hui-Li Lee, Hansong Lee, Sergio Lima
Client & Architect: Skidmore, Owings & Merrill LLP

Charles Square
Cambridge, Massachusetts
Project Team: John L. Wong, Peter Walker, Tom Adams, Duncan Alford, Michael Sardina
Client: Cambridge Seven, Carpenter Company

Chengdu Dongcun Greenland Tower
Chengdu, China
Project Team: John L. Wong, Po-Shan Chang, Minyoung Choi, Christiane Dreisbusch, Pei-Ching Kao, Jinwook lee, John Loomis, Anna Park, Yi Qu
Client: Greenland Holdings Corp.
Architect: Adrian Smith + Gordon Gill Architecture

Chengdu Tianfu New District High Rise
Chengdu, China
Project Team: John L. Wong, Thomas Balsley, Zi Gu, Steven Lee, Brandon Cappellari, Chen Hu, Vincent Hsu, Grace Prem, Phoebe Xiao Cheng, Jing Li, Ron Cubbage
Client: Zhonghai Group
Architect: Kohn Pedersen Fox

Citicorp Plaza
Los Angeles, California
Project Team: John L. Wong, Peter Walker, Tom Adams, Duncan Alford, Michael Sardina, Jack Sullivan
Client: Skidmore, Owings & Merrill LLP
Client: Oxford Properties
Architects: Skidmore, Owings & Merrill LLP

Chongqing A13 Jiangbeizui Int'l Center
Chongqing, China
Project Team: John L. Wong, Minyoung Choi, Vincent Hsu, Yuting Jiang, Ayaka Matthews, Mandana Parvinian, Yuzhou Shao, Ao Zhang, Xiao Wen Zhang, Yang Zhang
Client: Chingqing Sunac Hua Cheng Real-estate Development Co., Ltd.
Architect: Adrian Smith + Gordon Gill Architecture and Tongii University Consultants

Copley Square Competition
Boston, Massachusetts
Project Team: John L. Wong, Robert McCaughey
Client: Copley Square, NEA

Dermody Farms
Reno, Nevada
Project Team: John L. Wong, Rene Bihan, John Loomis, Maureen Simmons
Client: Paula Dermody
Architect: Backen Arrigoni & Ross, Inc.

Disney World Properties
Orlando, Florida
Project Team: John L. Wong, Peter Walker, Tom Adams, Kalvin Platt, Michael Sardina
Client: Disney Arvida Company

Downtown Dubai
Dubai, United Arab Emirates
Project Team: John L. Wong, Gerdo Aquino, Chih-Wei Chang, Shih-Ying Chiang, Gerald DeDios, Chistiane Dreisbusch, David Gal, Michael Herrin, Minhui Li, Yoonju Kametani, Pei-Ching Kao, Caroline Kim, Benjamin Knoll, Huiqing Kuang, Todd Larudee, Han Song Lee, Hui-Li Lee, Sergio Lima, Chih-Wei Lin, John Loomis, Sheradyn Mikul, Ross Nadeau, Joseph Newton, Michael Odum, Mandana Parvinian, Sarah Peck, Annabelle Rebar, Eric Story, Kathy Sun, Travis Theobald, Leah Thompson, Zhaojie Wu, Ying Zeng,
Client: EMAAR Properties PJSC
Architect: Skidmore Owings & Merrill LLP, Emaar Design Studios

Durres Waterfront Master Plan
Durres, Albania
Project Team: John L. Wong, Nora Chen, Phoebe Xiao Cheng, Abdallah Labib, Vaan Surajuras
Client: Eagle Hills Real Estate Development/ EMAAR Misr/ Symphony Investment LLC
Architect: EMAAR Design Studios; Atelier 4

Expo 2020 Projects
Dubai, United Arab Emirates
Project Team: John L. Wong, Junpei Asai, Brandon Cappellari, Minyoung Choi, Patrick Haesloop, Natalie Harper, Siyu Hou, Chen Hu, Yuting Jiang, Shigeo Kawasaki, Xiaoyin Kuang, Steven Lee, Jing Li, Ronald Lim, Sergio Lima, Carson Lindley, John Loomis, Shaun Loomis, Xiaomeng Ma, Kelly Mathiesen, Ayaka Matthews, Pavel Petrov, Eva Phe, Yi Qu, Kari Sorensen, Rick Story, Ying Tan, Jie Xu, Ao Zhang, Xiaowen Zhang, Yang Zhang, Hangqing Zhao, Jie Zhao
Client: Expo 202 Dubai, AS + GG
Architect: Adrian Smith + Gordon Gill Architecture
Collaborators: Crystal Fountains, E Construct, Ojanen- Chiou Architects LLP, Ovi Inc., Parsons International Ltd., Werner Sobek, Wet Design, Vagan, Thornton Tomasett, Asif Khan Ltd.

Fantasy Pointe at Nasu Highland Park
Nasu, Japan
Project Team: John L. Wong, Sara Anning, Suvarna Apte, Gerdo Aquino, Arthur Bartenstein, Jeffrey Bergfeld, Rene Bihan, Claire Bobrow, Bradley Burke, Camela Canzonieri, Kimberly Capham, Brennan Cox, Christine Eaton, Leah Greenblat, Jill Ann Gropp, Ying-Yu Hung, Roy Imamura, Akiko Ishii, Masato Kametani, Haven Kiers, Toshihiko Kitayama, Jill Kuper, Barry Landry, Sergio Lima, John Loomis, Clifton Lowe, Kui-Chi Ma, Justiniano Mendoza, Nancy Noble, Joseph Nootbaar, Larry Pearson, Emily Pierce, Kalvin Platt, Larry Reed, Edward Rodriquez, Isis Schwartz, Marureen Simmons, Eric Story, Dan Tuttle, Corazon Unana, Yitan Wang, Mitch Waufle, Chien Wu, Merrick Zirtzman
Client: Towa Nasu Resort company, Ltd
Architect: ED2 International, Architects & Planners

Federation of Korean Industries Head Office
Seoul, Korea
Project Team: John L. Wong, Chih-Wei Chang, Pei-Ching Kao, Chih-Wei Lin, John Loomis, Amity Winters
Client & Architect: Adrian Smith + Gordon Gill Architecture

Georgia/Pender
Vancouver, British Columbia, Canada
Project Team: John L. Wong, Patrick Haesloop, Sergio Lima, Travis Theobald, Shuyang Wang, Yang Zhang
Client & Architect: James KM Cheng Architects

Grosvenor Ambleside
West Vancouver, British Columbia, Canada
Project Team: John L. Wong, Josselyn Ivanov, Yoonju Kametani, Pei-Ching Kao, Chunjin Li, Sergio Lima, Cendra Ramirez, Travis Theobald, Amity Winters
Client: Grovesnor Americas
Architect: James KM Cheng Architects
Local Landscape Architect: Durante Kreuk Ltd.

Guthrie Green and Tulsa Arts District Streetscape
Tulsa, Oklahoma
Project Team: John L. Wong, Nathaniel Behrends, Conway Chang, Nancy Coulter, Alfred DeWitt, Michael Herrin, Minhui Li, Sergio Lima, Mandana Parvinian, Bokyung Rhee, Elizabeth Shreeve, Eric Story, Caroline Templeton, Amity Winters
Client: Goerge Kaiser Family Foundation
Architect: Bing Thom Architects, KKT Architects

Jeddah Tower (Formerly Kingdom Tower)
Jeddah Kingdom of Saudi Arabia
Project Team: John L. Wong, Chih-Wei Chang, Erica Huang, Sergio Lima, Joseph Newton, Yi Qu
Client: Jeddah Economic Company
Architect: Adrian Smith + Gordon Gill Architecture

Jinan Greenland CBD Super High-rise
Jinan, Shandong Province, China
Project Team: John L. Wong, Minyoung Choi, Vincent Hsu, Yuting Jiang, Ronald Lim, Ayaka Matthews, Eva Phe, Yi Qu, Shuyang Wang, Ao Zhang, Xiaowen Zhang, Yang Zhang
Client: Greenland Jinan
Architect: Skidmore, Owings & Merrill LLP

Ko Olina Master Plan
Oahu, Hawaii
Project Team: John L. Wong, Minyoung Choi, Anya Domlesky, Marco Esposito, Taizo Horikawa, Erica Huang, William Hynes, Caroline Kim, Jia Li, Sun Li, Ronald Lim, Wenwen Lu, Anna Park, Haoyang Wang, Yang Zhang
Client: Westbank Corp.
Architect: James KM Cheng Architects

Ko Olina, Four Seasons
Oahu, Hawaii
Project Team: John L. Wong, Minyoung Choi, Anya Domlesky, Marco Esposito, Taizo Horikawa, Erica Huang, William Hynes, Caroline Kim, Jia Li, Sun Li, Ronald Lim, Wenwen Lu, Anna Park, Haoyang Wang, Yang Zhang
Client: The Resort Group; Westbank Corp.
Architect: James KM Cheng Architects; Toyo Ito @ Associates, Architects; Group 70

Korea World Trade Center
Seoul, Korea
Project Team: John L. Wong, Herman Chein, Jill Ann Gropp, Jill Kuper, John Loomis, Cara Manzo, Larry Reed, Maureen Simmons
Client: KITA – Korea World Trade Association
Architect: Skidmore Owings & Merrill LLP

Kula Belgrade
Belgrade, Serbia
Project Team: John L. Wong, Minyoung Choi, Anya Domlesky, Patrick Haesloop, Taizo Horikawa, Zhongwei Li, Ronald Lim, Sergio Lima, Shaun Loomis, Mandana Parvinian, Eric Story, Travis Theobald, Jie Xu, Yang Zhang
Client: Eagle Hill/ EMAAR Properties
Architect: Skidmore Owings & Merrill LLP

Lawrence Livermore National Lab DPRF-NTTC Buildings
Livermore, California
Project Team: John L. Wong, William Blossom, Eddie Chau, Jill Ann Gropp, John Loomis, Nancy Noble, Maureen Simmons
Client: Lawrence Livermore National Laboratory
Architect: ED2 International Architects, Fredrickson Architects

LG Beijing
Beijing, China
Project Team: John L. Wong, Tom Adams, Claire Bobrow, Herman Chein, Jill Ann Gropp, Akiko Ishii, Andrezej Karwacki, Jill Kuper, John Loomis, Cara Manzo, Larry Reed, Maureen Simmons
Client: L. G. Beijing
Architect: Skidmore, Owings & Merrill LLP

LG Kangnam Tower
Kangnam, Seoul, Korea
Project Team: John L. Wong, Herman Chein, Roy Imamura, Marueen Simmons
Client: Lucky Goldstar Group
Architect: Skidmore Owings & Merrill LLP
Local Architect: Chang-Jo Architects

LG Twin Towers
Seoul, Korea
Project Team: John L. Wong, Peter Walker, tom Adams, Michael Sardina
Client: LG Group
Architect: Skidmore Owings & Merrill LLP
Local Architect: Chang-Jo Architects

Liansheng Financial Center
Taiyuan, China
Project Team: John L. Wong, Alfred DeWitt, Bryon Hawley, Yoonju Kametani, Sergio Lima, Chih-Wei Lin, Nabyl Machas, Anna Park, Elizabeth Shreeve, Zhadjie Wu, Chuhan Zheng, Yang Zhang
Client & Architect: Skidmore Owings & Merrill LLP

Lite-On Technology Headquarters
Neihu Science Park
Project Team: John L. Wong, Roy Imamura, Hui-Li Lee
Client: Lite-On Technology
Architect: Kris Yao I Artech

Los Angeles Air & Space Museum
Los Angeles, California
Project Team: John L. Wong, Tom Adams, Michael Sardina
Client: California Science Exposition Center
Architect: Frank O Gehry

Marinaside Crescent
Vancouver, British Columbia, Canada
Project Team: John L. Wong, Sean O'Malley, Cinda Gilliland, Claudia Kath, Maureen Simmons
Client: Concord Pacific Development Corp.
Architect: James K.M. Cheng Architects

Mashreq Bank Headquarters
Dubai, United Arab Emirates
Project Team: John L. Wong, Minyoung Choi, Alfred DeWitt, Mandana Parvinian, Cendra Ramirez, Eric Story, Don Xu, Chuhan Zheng
Client: Mashreq Bank
Architect: Skidmore Owings & Merrill LLP

Minsheng Center
Shanghai, China
Project Team: John L. Wong, Zhao Jie Wu, Mandana Parvinian, Yang Zhang, Ming Yao Wang
Client: China Minsheng Jaiye Investment Co., Ltd
Architect: Kohn Pedersen Fox

Nanchang Greenland Central Plaza – Parcel A,B,C
Nanchang, Jiangxi, China
Project Team: John L. Wong, Alfred DeWitt, Christiane Dreisbusch, Pei-Ching Kao, Chih-Wei Lin, Bokyung Rhee, Kathy Sun, Travis Theobald, Amity Winters, Zhaojie Wu
Client: Nanchang Greenland Group
Architect: Skidmore Owings & Merrill LLP

Nanchang Greenland Gaoxin
Nanchang, China
Project Team: John L. Wong, Nicole Horn, Pei-Ching Kao, Huiqing Khang, Joseph Newton, Yuka Suganuma, Travis Theobald,
Client: Nanchang Greenland Group
Architect: Skidmore Owings & Merrill LLP

Nanjing Greenland Pukou Super Tall
Nanjing, China
Project Team: John L. Wong, Minyoung Choi, Ayaka Matthews, Yi Qu, Zishen Wen, Ao Zhang, Xiaowen Zhang, Yang Zhang
Client: Greenland Group
Architect: Skidmore Owings & Merrill LLP

Nanjing Hexi Yuzui Tower (Runmao Tower)
Nanjing, China
Project Team: John L. Wong, Junpei Asai, Minyoung Choi, Vincent Hsu, Ronald Lim, Ayaka Matthews, Yi Qu, Zishen Wen, Ao Zhang, Xiaowen Zhang, Yang Zhang
Client: Nanjing Jinmao
Architect: Adrian Smith + Gordon Gill Architecture

NeXT Seaport Center
Redwood City, California
Project Team: John L. Wong, John Loomis, Maureen Simmons
Client: NeXT

North Bund White Magnolia Plaza
Shanghai, China
Project Team: John L. Wong, Vincent Hsu, Alfred DeWitt, Yang Zhang, Yun Won Yunwo Choi, Wai Yan Choi, Erica Huang, Wei Chung Joong, Caroline Kim, Michael Odum, Zeinab Rabiee, Scott Slaney, Xiwei Zhang
Client & Architect: Skidmore Owings & Merrill LLP

Opera Plaza District, Downtown Dubai
Dubai, United Arab Emirates
Project Team: John L. Wong, Branden Capellari, Anya Domlesky, Arnizza Fernando, Jacob Glazer, Siyu Hou, Yuting Jiang, Shigeo Kawasaki, Mya Katalac, Abdallah Labib, Yikuan Li, Ronald Lim, Sergio Lima, Shaun Loomis, Ayaka Matthews, Eva Phe, Grace Prem, Yuzhou Zhao, Karl Sorensen, Chella Strong, Jie Xu, Jie Zhao, Tongtong Zhou, Mandana Parvinian
Client: Emaar Properties PJSC
Architects: CannonDesign, CRTKL, Kohn Pederson Fox

Pearl River Tower (Zero Energy Tower)
Guangzhou, China
Project Team: John L. Wong, Peichin Kao, Chih-Wei Lin, Zhoajie Wu
Client & Architect: Skidmore Owings & Merrill LLP

Pershing Square
Los Angeles, California
Project Team: John L. Wong, Kalvin Platt
Client: Pershing Square Management Association
Architect: Robert A.M. Stern

Project C
Bangkok, Thailand
Project Team: John L. Wong, Pawida Bualert, Minyoung Choi, Alison Ecker, Joe Runco, Vaan Surajuras,
Client: Central Pattana Plc.
Architect: Kohn Pedersen Fox

Robson Residence
Monte Sereno, California
Project Team: John L. Wong
Client: Name Withheld
Architect: Caroden Group, Terry Martin Associates

Ronald Reagan Presidential Library
Simi Valley, California
Project Team: John L. Wong, Maureen Simmons, Kalvin Platt, John Loomis
Client: Ronald Reagan Presidential Foundation
Architect: Kling Stubbins (now part of Jacobs)

Roppongi 6-6 Urban Redevelopment
Tokyo, Japan
Project Team: John L. Wong, Cinda Gilliland, Roy Imamura, Akiko Ishii, Jill Kuper, James Lee, Joseph Nootbaaar, Kalvin Platt, Maureen Simmons, Allison Towne, Corazon Unana
Client: Mori Building Company
Architect: Kohn Pederson Fox

Shanghai International Dance Center
Shanghai, China
Project Team: John L. Wong, Alfred DeWitt, Vincent Hsu, Caroline Kim, Jin Wook Lee, Sergio Lima, Mandana Parvinian, Xiayao Shi
Client: Shanghai International Dance Center
Architect: STUDIOS Architecture

Shanghai Tower
Shanghai, China
Project Team: John L. Wong, Chih-Wei Chang, Shih-Ying Chuang, Christiane Dreisbusch, Yoonju Kametani, Pei-Ching Kao, Huiqing Kuang, Huei-Lyn Liu, Joseph Newton, Sarah Peck, Bokyung Rhee, Travis Theobald, Amity Winters, Zhaojie Wu, Ying Zeng
Client: Shanghai Center Tower Construction & Development Limited Company
Architect: Gensler; Tongji Architectural Design

Shimao Shenzhen International Center
Shenzhen, China
Project Team: John L. Wong, Chen Hu, Steven Lee, Jing Li, Ao Zhang, Xiaowen Zhang, Yang Zhang
Client: Shenzhen Shimao Group
Architect: Adrian Smith + Gordon Gill Architecture

Shijiazhuang CBD Park and Office
Shijiazhuang, China
Project Team: John L. Wong, Abdallah Labib, Phoebe Cheng, Yuanyuan Guo, Chen Hu, Yuting Jiang, Xiaoyin Kuang, Ki Yau Lo, Mandana Parvinian, Yi Qu, Xiuxain Zhan, Ao Zhang, Chuhan Zhang
Client: Sunac Shiiazhuang
Architect: MAD Architects

Shimao Sheshan Garden
Shanghai, China
Project Team: John L. Wong, Gerdo Aquino, Juli Chiu, Shih-Ying Chuang, Thomas Fein, Nancy Flemming, Mary Gourlay, Roy Imamura, Akiko Ishii, Sehgyung Kang, Pei-Ching Kao, Conard Lindgren, John Loomis, Kui-Chi Ma, Bokyung, Rhee, Bonita Wahl
Client: Shanghai Shimao Manor Real Estate Co., Ltd.
Architects: Michael C.F. Chan Associates, Inc. ;Topo Design - Shanghai

SIP Administrative Center
Suzhou, China
Project Team: John L. Wong, Juli Chiu, Hye Choi, Shih-Ying Chuang, Thomas Fein Nancy Flemming, Ying Hu, Yoonju Kametani, Pei-Ching Kao, Han-Song Lee, Hui-Li Lee, Conard Lindgren, John Loomis, Chih-Wei Lin
Client: SIP Administrative Committee
Architects: Goettsch Partners Architects; Kling Architects; East China Architectural Design Institute

Skyview 4 5 6
Dubai, United Arab Emirates
Project Team: John L. Wong, Minyoung Choi, Taizo Horikawa, Jia Li, Sergio Lima, Adam Novack, Anna Park, Mandana Parvinian, Yi Qu, Darren Sears, Eric Story, Yang Zhang
Client: EMAAR PSJC
Architect: Skidmore Owings & Merrill, LLP

Sonoma Residence
Sonoma, California
Project Team: John L. Wong, William Hynes, Shaun Loomis, Travis Theobald
Client: Owners' names withheld
Architect: Walker & Moody Architects

Stanford University
Stanford, California
Alumni Center, Aquatics, Aquatics & Athletics Plaza, Arguello Mall Master Plan, Arrillaga Plaza, Arrillaga Recreation Center, Barnum Family Center, Branner Hall, Campus Center, Cantor Center for the Visual Arts Expansion, DAPER Master Plan, Excondido Village Master Plan, Ford Plaza, Graduate School of Business, Green Library, Hoover Inst. David & Joan Traitel Building, Lagunita Court, Lasuen Mall, Lathrop Library, Law School Courtyard, Liliore Green Rains Graduate Student Housing, Meyer-Buck Estate, Munger Graduate Residence, Panama mall, Ralph Landau Center for Economics & Policy Research, School of Education, SEQ Fountains, Stanford Inst for Economic Policy Research, Terman Park, Toyon Hall, West Gate, Stanford West Apartments, Sandhill Road
Project Team: John L. Wong, Sara Anning, Suvarna Apte, Gerdo Aquino, Jungyoan Bae, Simone Battersby, Rene Bihan, Herman Chein, Shih-Ying Chuang, Nancy Conger, Brennan Cox, Laura Curtis, John Dennis, Alfred DeWitt, Susan Durett, Alison Ecker, Thomas Fein, Cinda Gilliland, Mary Gourlay, Michael Grefe, Jill Ann Gropp, Natalie Harper, Ive Haugeland, Michael Herrin, Ying-Yu Hung, William Hynes, Roy Imamura, Akiko Ishii, Yuting Jiang, Yoonju Kametani, Andrzej Karwacki, Claudia Kath, Stacy Krajeweski, Xiaoyin Kuang, Jill Kuper, Nancy Larsen, Han-Song Lee, I-Hsien Lee, Hui-Li Lee, James Lee, Jessica Leets, Junyi Li, Bernard Lighter, Ronald Lim, Carson Lindley, John Loomis, Shaun Loomis, Kui-Chi Ma, Valerie Maillet, Carla Manzo, Kelly Mathiesen, David Mendelson, Joseph Newton, Nancy Noble, Adam Novack, Michael Odum, Sean O'Malley, Akiko Ono, Katherine Orff, Anna Park, Mandana Parvinian, Sarah Peck, Carolyn Perna, Eva Phe, Jamie Phillips, Michael Pon, Cendra Ramirez, Annabelle Reber, Larry Reed, William Reed, Juan Rivera, Elizabeth Shreeve, Maureen Simmons, Vaan Surajuras, Paul Stevenson, Eric Story, Katherine Strom, Ying Tan, Kathy Sun, Karen Tautenhalm, Caroline Templeton, Travis Theobald, Steven Tycz, Chryssa Udvaroy, Corazon Unana, Clotilde Viellard, Meredith White, Zhaojie Wu, Xiuxian Zhan, Hanqing Zhao
Client: The Board of Trustees of the Leland Stanford Jr University
Architects: Bar Architects; Brayton Hughes Design Studios; Cody Anderson Wasney Architects; Daniel Solomon Design Partners; ELS Architecture and Urban Design; Hoover Architects; Ike Kligerman Barkley Architects; James Polshek Architects now Ennead Architects; Kornberg Associates, Architects; Skidmore, Owings & Merrill, LLP; Perkins & Will; William Rawn Associates, Architects, Inc.

Suzhou Center
Suzhou, China
Project Team: John L. Wong, Conway Chang, Po-Shan Chang, Chenlu Fang, Vincent Hsu, Erica Huang, Fei-Ching Kao, Hui-Li Lee, Jinwook Lee, Chih-Wei Lin, Catherine McDonald, Mandana Parvinian, Yi Qu, Xiayao Shi, Travis Theobald, Zhaojie Wu, Don Xu
Client: SIP Jinji Lake Urban Development Co., Ltd., SIP Planning and Construction Bureau
Architect: Nikken Sekkei Ltd., Benoy Architects

Suzhou Convention and Exhibition Center
Suzhou, China
Project Team: John L. Wong, Po-Shan Chang, Minyoung Choi, Vincent Hsu, Ying Hu, Erica Huang, Josselyn Ivanov, Han Song Lee, Jin Wook Lee, Hui-Li Lee, Chih-Wei Lin, John Loomis, Yi Qu, Xiayao Shi, Travis Theobald, Chung-Hsun Wu, Zhaojie Wu, Don Xu
Client & Architect: Skidmore Owings & Merrill, LLP

Suzhou Greenland Center, Wujiang Lakefront District
Suzhou, China
Project Team: John L. Wong, Minyoung Choi, Christiane Dreisbusch, Byron Hawley, Yoonju Kametani, Pei-Ching Kao, Travis Theobald, Amity Winters, Zhaojie Wu, Don Xu, Yang Zhang
Client: Greenland Group Suzhou Office
Architect: Skidmore, Owings & Merrill, LLP

Tarrant County College
Fort Worth, Texas
Project Team: John L. Wong, Shih-Ying Chuang, Yoonju Kametani, Pei-Ching Kao, Hui-Li Lee, John Loomis, Travis Theobald
Client: Tarrant County College District (TCCD)
Architect: Bing Thom Architects
Local Landscape Architect: Studio Outside

Todos Santos Plaza Competition
Concord, California
Project Team: John L. Wong, John Loomis, Robert Behren
Client: Concord Redevelopment, NEA

Tokyo University of Foreign Studies Campus
Tokyo, Fuchu, Japan
Project Team: John L. Wong, Gerdo Aquino, Rene Bihan, Herman Chein, Roy Imamura, Akiko Ishii, Kalvin Platt,
Client: Landscape International, Ltd.
Architect: Kume Sekkei Co., Ltd., NBBJ

Tower Palace I, II, III
Seoul, Korea
Project Team: John L. Wong, Suvarna Apte, Gerdo Aquino, Roy Imamura, Clara Jimenez-Xiberta, Chen Chuang, Greg Matto
Client: Samsung Corporation
Architects: Skidmore Owings & Merrill, LLP; Kohn Pedersen Fox

The Ranch
Northern California
Project Team: John L. Wong, William Hynes, Carson Lindley, Shaun Loomis, Bokyung Rhee, Darren Sears, Caroline Templeton
Client: Name withheld
Architect: Walker Warner Architects

UC Davis West Village
Davis, California
Project Team: John L. Wong, Shih-Ying Chuang, Alfred DeWitt, Cinda Gilliland, Mary Gourlay, Yoonju Kametani, Pei-Ching Kao, Jessica Lee, Mandana Parvinian, Larry Reed, Carrie Rybczynski, Elizabeth Shreeve, Kathy Sun, Rick Story, Caroline Templeton, Travis Theobald
Client: West Village Community Partnership LLC
Architects: MVE Institutional, Student Housing Architects; Lim Chang Rohling & Associates, Residential Architects; Studio E Architects – Village Center

University of Chicago Booth School of Business, UCCHK, University of Chicago Francis and Rose Yuen Campus In Hong Kong, China
Hong Kong, China
Project Team: John L. Wong, Jungyoon Bae, Minyoung Choi, Christine Dreisbusch, Patrick Haesloop, Taizo Horikawa, Nicole Horn, Vincent Hsu, William Hynes, Ronald Lim, Adam Novack, Mandana Parvinian, Yi Qu, Cendra Ramirez, Rick Story, Travis Theobald, Xi Wei Zhang
Client: The University of Chicago
Architect: Revery Architects (formerly Bing Thom Architects)
Local Landscape Architect: Urbis Limited

Vi Living
Palo Alto, California
Project Team: John L. Wong, Suvarna Apte, Brennan Cox, Zachary Davis, Thomas Fein, Mary Gourlay, Susan Heiken, Hui-Li Lee, Sergio Lima, John Loomis, Caramanzo, Rick Story,
Client: Stanford Land, Buildings and Real Estate
Architect: Steinberg Architects

Victoria Ward Waiea Tower
Honolulu, Hawaii
Project Team: John L. Wong, Christine Dreisbusch, Patrick Haesloop, Nicole Horn, William Hynes, Jinwook Lee, Junyi Li, Anna Park, Michael Pon, Darren Sears
Client: Howard Hughes Corporation
Architect: James KM Cheng Architects

Wuhan Greenland Center
Wuhan, China
Project Team: John L. Wong, Chih-Wei Chang, Po-Shan Chang, Alfred DeWitt, Sergio Lima, Joseph Newton, Anna Park, Yi Qu, Travis Theobald
Client: Wuhan Greenland Bin Jiang Property Co. Ltd.
Architect: Adrian Smith + Gordon Gill Architecture, JERDE Partnership

XIQU Center
Hong Kong, China
Project Team: John L. Wong, Minyoung Choi, Byron Hawley, Vincent Hsu, Caroline Kim, Chih-Wei Lin John Loomis, Ayaka Matthews, Adam Novack, Anna Park, Mandana Parvinian, Yi Qu
Client: West Kowloon Cultural District Authority of the Hong Kong, China Special Administrative Region
Architect: Revery Architects (Formerly Bing Thom Architects), Ronald Lu and Partners

Zakin Residence
St. Helena, California
Project Team: John L. Wong, Sara Anning, Suvarna Apte, Gerdo Aquino, Carla Ernst, Haven Kiers, Conard Lindgren, Akiko Ono
Client: Zakin Family
Architect: Stanley Saitowitz, Architect

Zhangjiang Science City Parcelo 56, 57, & 58
Shanghai, China
Project Team: John L. Wong, Ayami Akagawa, Junpei Asai, Jungyoon Bae, Yuanyuan Guo, Pei-Ching Kao, Vincent Hsu, Xing Yue Huang, Jing Li, Shuyu Li, Xiu Zheng Li, Weixi Liu, Yani Liu, Yuzhe Ma, Hushou Shao, Yu Shi, Vaan Suraguras, Bosheng Wang, Don Yang Wu, Zhaojie Wu, Yijia Xu, Yuxin Yang, Shiya Zeng, Hangqing, Xijia Zhang, Yang Zhang, Zo Zhang, Chu Han Zhang
Client: Lujiazhui Group and Zhangjiang Group
Architect: Gensler, NBBJ, CRTKL

Zhongshan Int'l Exhibition Center
Zhongshan City, Quangdong Province, China
Project Team: John L. Wong, Emily Ang, Pei-Ching Kao, Hui-Li Lee, Chih-Wei Lin, Kui-Chi Ma, Zhaojie Wu
Client: Zhongshan City Construction Investment Company Ltd.
Architect: Skidmore Owings & Merrill, LLP

Zifeng Tower – Nanjing Greenland Int'l Commercial Center
Nanjing, China
Project Team: John L. Wong, Yunju Kametani, Han Song Lee, Hui-Li Lee, Chih-Wei Lin, Conard Lindgren, Huei-Lyn Liu, John Loomis
Client: Greenland Holding Corp
Architect: Skidmore Owings & Merrill, LLP

JOHN L. WONG
PLA, FASLA, FAAR

Education

Master of Landscape Architecture in Urban Design, 1978, Harvard University Graduate School of Design
Bachelor of Arts in Landscape Architecture with Honors, 1974, University of California at Berkeley
Associate in Arts with Honors, 1972, City College of San Francisco
Distinguished Alumnus Award, 2012, University of California, Berkeley, College of Environmental Design's CED/CEDA
Rome Prize in Landscape Architecture, 1981, American Academy in Rome, Rome, Italy
Fred B. Barlow Jr. Memorial Award for Excellence in Design, University of California, Berkeley, Department of Landscape Architecture, 1974
SWA Summer Program, 1972

Registrations

Registered Landscape Architect #1766, California
Registered Landscape Architect #595, Oregon
Registered Landscape Architect #964. Nevada
Registered Landscape Architect #002556-1, New York
CLARB Council of Landscape Architectural Registration Boards, #1650

Professional Affiliations and Recognition

CED/CEDA Distinguished Alumnus Award, University of California, Berkeley, College of Environmental Design, 2012
Fellow, American Academy in Rome
Fellow, American Society of Landscape Architects
Fellow, Institute of Urban Design
Member, Urban Land Institute
Member, Council on Tall Buildings and Urban Habitat (CTBUH)

Professional Experience

SWA Group, Sausalito, California; Managing Principal: 1987–Present; Board of Directors: 1999 – 2012; Chairman of the Board: 2012–2022
SWA Group, Sausalito, California; Principal: 1984–1987
SWA Group, Boston, Massachusetts; Principal: 1980–1984
SWA Group East, Boston, Massachusetts; Project Director, Office Manager: 1976–1980
POD, Inc., Orange, California; Project Landscape Architect: 1974–1976
Sasaki, Walker Associates, Inc., Sausalito, California; Project Designer: 1973–1974
Leo Tscharner, Landscape Architect, Pleasant Hill, California; Designer: 1972–1973

PROFESSIONAL ACTIVITIES:
UC Davis, Architecture Speaker Series – 'Green Building, Design and Materials: UC Davis West Village', 2022
ASLA Conference, Speaker/Presenter – 'Resiliency and Innovation; Evolution of Stanford's Olmsted Plan and Contemporary Design', 2022
Global Habitat Design Awards: Design Media Matrix and World Habitation Association, Shanghai, China, 2021
Thad International Academic Exchange Presentation – Speaker Beijing, China, 'Resilient Landscape', 2021
Stanford University Cantor Arts Center – 2019, Art Focus Lecture – 'The Spaces Between Buildings at Stanford University'. 2019
TCLF, Speaker/Tour – Stanford University Campus Landscape, 2019
Zhonghai Development Group, Shenzhen, China, Speaker, 'Humanity Entering the Clouds – Designing for the 22nd Century City Center', 2019
UC Berkeley College of Environmental Design Dean Search – Selection Committee, 2018–2019
Stanford University Women Alumni Council Group, Stanford University Speaker – 'The Spaces Between Buildings', 2018
UC Berkeley College of Environmental Design Annual Circus Soiree, Distinguished Alumnus Member, 2016, 2017, 2018, 2019, 2020
Sausalito Beautiful, Advisory Board 2016–Present
University of California, Berkeley, CED Dean Advisory Council 2013-present
Council for Tall Buildings and Urban Habitat (CTBUH): World Conference in Seoul, Presenter, "Humanity: Entering the Clouds" – 2011
The University of Hong Kong, China Advisory Council for the Division of Landscape Architecture in the Faculty of Architecture, 2010–Present
Stanford University, Guest Speaker, Landscape Architecture Practice, 2005–2012
Stanford University – Campus Lecture Series, Landscape Architecture Current Work, 2008
University of California, Berkeley, DRC – Design Review Committee: 2004–Present
University of California, Berkeley, College of Environmental Design Distinguishing Alumnus Award Committee: 2004–2009
University of California, Berkeley College of Environmental Design, Department of Landscape Architectural Annual Lecture Series, Guest Speaker, 'Landscape Design Works', 2004
University of California, Berkeley, Department of Landscape Architecture, Guest Panelist, Site & Insight Exploring Notable Bay Area Landscape Architecture, April 2002
University of California, Berkeley; College of Environmental Design Alumni Association (CEDAA), Board of Directors: 2000–2003
American Academy in Rome, Juror, Rome Prize Competition, School of Fine Arts, New York: 1994
Il Giardino Italiano: An Exhibition of Italian Gardens and Urban Plazas, Memphis Tennessee, 1992
City College of San Francisco, Guest Speaker, Department of Architecture 1990
Harvard University, Graduate School of Design, Guest Speaker, Department of Landscape Architecture 1989
Society of Fellows, Regional Representative, American Academy in Rome: 1988–1996
University of California, Davis, Jury Panelist, Arboretum National Design Competition, Davis, California, 1988
The Artists Foundation, Inc., Jury Panelist, Design and the Built Environment, Massachusetts Artist Fellowship, 1986
Harvard University Graduate School of Design Alumni Council, Council Member: 1985–1987
California Council of Landscape Architects, Guest Speaker, Annual Meeting, San Diego, California 1987; Annual Meeting, Monterey, California 1985
National Endowment for the Arts, Jury Panelist, Design Arts Program, Design Arts Demonstration, 1985
American Academy in Rome, Annual Exhibition, Rome, Italy 1981

Academic

Distinguished Visiting Farrand Professor, University of California, Berkeley, College of Environmental Design, Department of Landscape Architecture, Second Year Design Studio, spring 2005
Harvard University, Graduate School of Design, Department of Landscape Architecture; Visiting Critic, Second Year Option Design Studio, Fall 1989; Visiting Critic First Year MLA and Second Year MLA Core Design Studio, Advanced and Intermediate Graphic Communication: 1978–1982; Instructor, Graphic Communication, Spring 1977, Teaching Assistant – Design Studios In Site Planning and Design, Design Studio in Urban Open Space 1977, 1978
University of California, Berkeley, College of Environmental Design, Department of Landscape Architecture, Visiting Lecturer, Graduate Design Studio, 1986, 1987, 1988, 1992, 1993, 1994, 2005

Awards

Architecture MasterPrize (AMP), Recreational Architecture, Expo 2020 Al Wasl Plaza, Dubai, United Arab Emirates, 2022
ASLA Northern California Chapter, Merit Award, Shanghai International Dance Center, Shanghai, China, 2022
Re-Thinking the Future Awards, First Award, Cultural Built, Expo 2020 Al Wasl Plaza, Dubai, United Arab Emirates, 2022
The Chicago Athenaeum International Architecture Award - Exposition, Expo 2020 Al Wasl Plaza, Dubai, United Arab Emirates, 2021
The Chicago Athenaeum Green Good Design Award - Green Architecture, Expo 2020 Al Wasl Plaza, Dubai, United Arab Emirates, 2021
Canadian Architect Magazine, 2021 Award of Excellence, The Butterfly & First Baptist Church Development
ULI Americas Award for Excellence, Grosvenor Ambleside, Canada, 2021
Social, Cultural and Heritage Project of the Year MEED Awards 2019, Ministry of Education Headquarters, Kuwait
HKIA Medal of the Year of Hong Kong, China 2019 UCCHK University of Chicago Francis and Rose Yuen Campus, Hong Kong, China
Special Architectural Award - Heritage & Adaptive Re-use, HKIA Annual Awards 2018-2019 UCCHK, University of Chicago Francis and Rose Yuen Campus, Hong Kong, China

SCUP, Merit Award, 2019 UCCHK University of Chicago Francis and Rose Yuen Campus, Hong Kong, China

ASLA Northern California Chapter, Merit Award, 2019 UCCHK University of Chicago Francis and Rose Yuen Campus, Hong Kong, China

Prix Versailles – Campus Interior Award, 2019 UCCHK University of Chicago Francis and Rose Yuen Campus, Hong Kong, China

Future Arc Green Leadership Award, Merit Award, 2019 UCCHK University of Chicago Francis and Rose Yuen Campus, Hong Kong, China

CADSA Education & Religious Project, Gold Award, 2019 UCCHK University of Chicago Francis and Rose Yuen Campus, Hong Kong, China

International Architecture Awards, Restoration/Renovation Award, 2019 UCCHK University of Chicago Francis and Rose Yuen Campus, Hong Kong, China

Chicago Athenaeum Award, Merit Award, 2019 UCCHK University of Chicago Francis and Rose Yuen Campus, Hong Kong, China 2019

Architectural Design Awards (ASC), Architectural Design Award, Jiangxi Nanchang Greenland Zifeng Tower, Nanchang, China, 2018

Chicago Athenaeum, Green Good Design Award, Green Architecture, Wuhan Greenland Center, 2017

Real Estate Design China Award, Merit Award, Shanghai International Dance Center, 2017

The American Architecture Prize, Architectural Design/Tall Buildings, FKI Tower, 2017

Council on Tall Buildings and Urban Habitat (CTBUH) – Best Tall Building, Asia & Australia & Worldwide Awards, Shanghai Tower, 2016

Council on Tall Buildings and Urban Habitat (CTBUH) – Best Tall Building Award Asia, Australasia, Jiangxi Nanchang Greenland, Central Plaza, Nanchang, China, 2016

China International Exchange Committee for Tall Buildings (CITAB), Council on Tall Buildings and Urban Habitats – China Innovation Award – Honorable Distinction Jiangxi Nanchang Greenland, Central Plaza, Parcel A, Nanchang, China, 2016

Council on Tall Buildings and Urban Habitat (CTBUH) – Best Tall Building Award Asia & Australasia Beijing Greenland, Dawangjing Tower, Beijing, China, 2016

MIPM, People's Choice Award, Shanghai Tower, 2016

AIA Chicago Design Excellence Award, Federation of Korean Industries (FKI) Head Office, 2016

Center for Active Design Excellence Awards, Guthrie Green, 2015

Civic Trust Awards, Federation of Korean Industries (FKI) Head Office, 2015

SCUP Excellence in Landscape Architecture-Open Space Planning and Design, Honor Award, UC Davis West Village, 2015

MIPM Asia Gold Award, Best Chinese Futura, Mega Project, Suzhou Center, Suzhou China, 2015

SCUP Excellence in Landscape Architecture-Open Space Planning Design, Honor Award, UC Davis West Village, 2015

China International Exchange Committee for Tall Buildings (CITAB), Council on Tall Buildings and Urban Habitat (CTBUH), Best Tall Building China – Honorable Distinction, Zhengzhou Greenland Plaza, 2014

AIA Indiana Design Award, Columbus City Hall, 2014

Meddle East AIA, Non-built Category, Merit Award, Jeddah Tower, 2014

Institute of Classical Architecture & Art (ICAA), The Inaugural Julia Morgan Award, New Construction, Renovations & Additions – Stanford University John A. & Cynthia Fry Gunn Building (SIEPR), 2014

ASLA Northern California Chapter Merit Award, UC Davis West Village, 2014

Korean Architecture Award, Excellence Award, FKI Tower, 2014

Council on Tall Buildings and Urban Habitat (CTBUH) – Best Tall Building Asia & Australasia, FKI Tower, Seoul, Korea, 2014

Council on Tall Buildings and Urban Habitat (CTBUH) – Best Tall Building Middle East & Africa, Cayan Tower, 2014

Green Good Design Award, Pearl River Tower, 2014

Pacific Coast Builders Conference Gold Nugget Grand Award, Best Custom Home over 8,000 sq. ft., ARA Residence, 2014

Brownfield Renewal Awards, Guthrie Green, 2013

Architectural Engineering Institute Award of Excellence, Best Overall Project, Burj Khalifa, Dubai UAE, 2013

Architizer A+ Award, Cayan Tower, Dubai, UAE, 2013

ASLA Texas Chapter Honor Award, Tarrant County College, 2013

ASLA Northern California Chapter Honor Award, Guthrie Green, 2013

ULI Global Award for Excellence, UC Davis West Village, 2013

MIPIM Asia, Best Innovative Green Building, Silver Award, Pearl River Tower, 2013

Henry Bellmon Sustainability Award, Guthrie Green, 2013

Council on Tall Buildings and Urban Habitat (CTBUH) – Best Tall Building Finalist, Asia & Australasia, Pearl River Tower, Guangzhou, China, 2013

The Chicago Athenaeum International Architecture Award, Suzhou Greenland Center, 2013

WAN Awards: Urban Design, Guthrie Green, 2013

ABC (Associated Builders and Contractors) Oklahoma Chapter, Excellence in Construction Award, Guthrie Green, 2012

World Architecture News, WAN, Urban Regeneration Awards, Guthrie Green, 2012

Forbes Four-Star Award, Rosewood Sand Hill Hotel, 2011

Pacific Coast Builders Conference Gold Nugget Merit Award, Infill, Redevelopment or Rehabilitation Site Plan, Hummingbird Place, 2011

Pacific Coast Builders Conference Gold Nugget Merit Award, Infill, Redevelopment or Rehabilitation Site Plan, Mission Estates, 2011

The California Preservation Foundation (CPF) Preservation Design Award, Rehabilitation, Stanford Peterson Building, 2011

MUDA Co-Award, Urban Architecture (Mayor's Urban Design Awards, City of Calgary), SAIT Polytechnic Parkade, 2011

Times Properties Journal KinPan Award, Best Office Building of the Year, Nanjing Greenland International Commercial Center, 2011

Arab Investment Summit, Arab Achievement Award – Best Architectural Project, Burj Khalifa, 2010

California Landscaping Magazine, Herb Frank Memorial Trophy Award, Rosewood Sand Hill Hotel, 2010

Chicago Athenaeum, International Architectural Award, Burj Khalifa, 2010

Cityscape Awards for Real Estate in the Middle East and North Africa, Burj Khalifa, 2010

Council on Tall Buildings and Urban Habitat (CTBUH) Best Tall Building Asia & Australasia Nanjing Greenland Financial Center, Nanjing, China, 2010

Council on Tall Buildings and Urban Habitat (CTBUH) – Best Tall Building Middle East & Africa, Burj Khalifa, 2010

Council on Tall Buildings and Urban Habitat (CTBUH) – Global Icon Award, Burj Khalifa, 2010

Times Properties Journal Best Commercial Development, SIP Times Square, 2010

The Arnold Soforenko Award for Extraordinary Contributions to the Urban Forest, Vi Living, 2009

UN Habitat Scroll of Honour Awards Best Practice (in China), FuYang East Avenue, 2009

AIA Santa Clara Valley Award of Excellence, Historical Preservation Design, Stanford Branner Hall, 2008

Pacific Coast Builders Conference Gold Nugget Merit Award, Best Neighborhood Site Plan up to 20 Acres, Encanto, 2008

AIA San Francisco, Integrated Practice Honor Award, Camino Medical Group, 2007

ASLA Northern California Chapter Merit Award, Vi Living, 2007

ASLA Northern California Chapter Merit Award, Mayfield, 2007

Pacific Coast Builders Conference Gold Nugget Merit Award, Best Single Family Detached Home under 1,700 sf on a Compact Lot (under 3,200 sf), Encanto, 2007

ASLA National Honor Award, Lite-On Technology Headquarters, 2006

ASLA Northern California Chapter Merit Award, Stanford Alumni Center, 2006

Pacific Coast Builders Conference Gold Nugget Merit Award, Attached Suburban Project of the Year, Mayfield, 2006

Pacific Coast Builders Conference Gold Nugget Merit Award, Best Community Site Plan – 15 to 99 Acres, Mayfield, 2006

Pacific Coast Builders Conference Gold Nugget Grand Award, Best Seniors Housing Project, Vi Living, 2006

AIA Santa Clara Chapter, Certificate of Commendation, Vi Living, 2006

ASLA Northern California Chapter Award of Excellence, Lite-On Technology Headquarters, 2005

ASLA Northern California Chapter Merit Award, Tokyo University Foreign Studies Campus, 2005

California Construction Magazine 'Best of California', Vi Living, 2005

The California Preservation Foundation (CPF) Preservation Design Award, Stanford Branner Hall, 2005

Pacific Coast Builders Conference Gold Nugget Merit Award, Best Adaptive Reuse Project, Canyon Heights, 2005

ASLA National Merit Award, Tokyo University Foreign Studies Campus, 2003

AIA San Francisco, Honor Award, Stanford Graduate School of Business, (Knight Building Addition) 2002

Pacific Coast Builders Conference Gold Nugget Merit Award, Stanford West Apartments, 2002

Pacific Coast Builders Conference Gold Nugget Merit Award, Best Office Professional Building - over 50,000 sq ft, San Rafael Corporate Center, 2002

AIA California Council, Merit Award – Historic Preservation, Stanford Toyon Hall, 2001

The California Preservation Foundation (CPF) Preservation Design Award, Stanford Toyon Hall, 2001

City of Claremont Architectural Commission Excellence in Design Award – New Construction, Scripps College Residence Hall, 2001
Pacific Coast Builders Conference Gold Nugget Award – NorCal, The Old School House, 2001
Pacific Coast Builders Conference Gold Nugget Merit Award, Scripps College Residence Hall, 2001
National Preservation Honor Award, Stanford University 10-Year Renovation Project, 2000
National Preservation Honor Award, Stanford Green Library, 2000
National Preservation Honor Award, Stanford Cantor Center for the Visual Arts, 2000
ASLA National Merit Award, Stanford DAPER Master Plan, 1999
The Governor's Historic Preservation Award – California, Stanford Encina Hall, 1999
The Governor's Historic Preservation Award – California, Stanford Green Library, 1999
The Governor's Historic Preservation Award – California, Stanford Cantor Center for the Visual Arts, 1999
Pacific Coast Builders Conference Gold Nugget Merit Award, Carlsbad by the Sea, 1999
AIA California East Bay, Honor Award, Bentley School, Lafayette, California, 1998
ASLA National Merit Award – 190 Marlborough Street Roof Garden, Boston, Massachusetts, in Collaboration with Peter Walker and Martha Schwartz, 1998
Nagano Master Plan Competition, First Prize, Wakasado Complex, 1994
NAHB Grand Award, Stanford Manzanita Park Undergraduate Housing, 1994
Okayama Redevelopment Competition, Second Prize, City of Okayama, Japan, 1994
Pacific Coast Builders Conference Gold Nugget Grand Award, Stanford Manzanita Park Undergraduate Housing, 1994
Shanghai Government Center Competition – First Prize, Shanghai Government Center, 1994
Association of University Architects, Stanford Liliore Green Rains Student Housing, 1993
Los Angeles Beautiful Design Award, The Wilshire, 1993
Pacific Coast Builders Conference Gold Nugget Award, Stanford Manzanita Commons, 1993
ASLA Northern California Chapter Honor Award, Metrotown Resources Library Civic Center, 1992
ASLA Northern California Chapter Merit Award, Ronald Reagan Presidential Library, 1992
California Landscape Contractors Association Sweepstakes Award, Ronald Reagan Presidential Library, 1992
California Landscape Contractors Association, San Fernando Chapter, Landscape Beautiful Award, Ronald Reagan Presidential Library, 1991
ASLA National Merit Award, Stanford Liliore Green Rains Student Housing, 1990
Concrete Industry Award of Excellence, Outstanding Paving Project, Ronald Reagan Presidential Library, 1990
Harbor Island Hotel Competition – First Prize, 1990
Napa County Museum Competition - Finalist, 1990
ASLA Northern California Chapter Merit Award, Citicorp Plaza and Seventh Street Marketplace, 1988
City of Phoenix Visual Improvement Award, Southbank, Phoenix, Arizona, 1988
Oranges and Lemons Award for Achievement in Excellence, Citicorp Plaza and Seventh Street Marketplace, 1988
ASLA New England Chapter (BSLA), Merit Award, Citicorp Plaza and Seventh Street Marketplace, 1987
ASLA New England Chapter Merit Award, Charles Square, 1987
ASLA Northern California Chapter Award of Excellence, Stanford University Centennial Grove, 1987
ASLA Southern California Chapter Grand Award, Plaza Alicante, 1987
Landscape Architecture Foundation Honor Award, Plaza Alicante, 1987
Landscape Architecture Magazine Photography Competition, Opening Celebration, Citicorp Plaza and Seventh Street Marketplace, 1987
Los Angeles Beautiful Design Award, 400 South Hope Street, 1987
Los Angeles Beautiful Design Award, Citicorp Plaza and Seventh Street Marketplace, 1987
NEA, Design Arts Program – Finalist, Todos Santos Plaza, Concord, California, 1987
Portland Cement Association Award of Engineering Excellence, Plaza Alicante, 1987
ASLA Florida Chapter Award of Excellence, Boca Beach Club, 1986
ASLA Southern California Chapter Honor Award, Citicorp Plaza and Seventh Street Marketplace, 1986
Association for Multi-Image, Northern California Chapter Mayfest, Southbank, Phoenix, Arizona, 1986
City of Los Angeles Rose Award, Citicorp Plaza and Seventh Street Marketplace, 1986
Concrete Industry Award of Excellence, Plaza Alicante, 1986
NEA, Design Arts Program – Finalist, Pershing Square National Design Competition, 1986
Pacific Coast Builders Conference Gold Nugget Merit Award, Plaza Alicante, 1986

AIA/International Marmie Machine Carrara Marble Architecture Award, 400 South Hope Street, 1985
ASLA National Merit Award, 400 South Hope Street, 1985
ASLA New England Chapter, Honor Award, Jefferson Park Housing, 1985
ASLA Southern California Chapter Honor Award, 400 South Hope Street, 1984
ASLA New England Chapter, Merit Award, 400 South Hope Street, 1984
Columbus Carscape Competition, Honorable Mention, 1984
NEA, Design Arts Program – Finalist, Copley Square National Design Competition, 1984
National Association of Home Builders Project of the Year, Fairway Bay, 1983
Federal Copley Square National Competition – Finalist, 1979
Home For Better Living, First Honor Award, Rancho San Joaquin Apartments, 1979
Pin Oak Competition – First Prize, 1979
California Landscape Contractors Association, Beautification Award- Fist Prize, Rancho San Joaquin Apartments, 1977
Pacific Coast Builders Conference, Go Nugget Award for Best Apartments, Rancho San Joaquin Apartments, 1977
ASLA National Merit Award, The Market Place, 1976

Publications
100 of the World's Tallest Buildings, CTBUH, Edited by Antony Wood, 2015
Alwasl Plaza Dubai Expo 2020, Adrian Smith + Gordon Gill, 2022
2A Architecture & Art, Summer 2010, Quarterly Issue No. 14, Landscape Urbanism in Practice: SWA Group, Pg. 106–111
2A Architecture & Art, Summer 2009, Quarterly Issue No. 11, Racing to the Skies: Down to Earth Strategies for Super High Rise Buildings, Pg. 102 – 107
Architectural Digest, August 1996, Borlasca Reborn, Pg. 86 – 93
Architectural Digest, October 1999, Iris Cantor in Bel-Air, Pg. 294 – 301
Architects Newspaper, This Land, Chris Bentley, Guthrie Green, October 23, 2012
Architecture & Art, Summer 2009, Quarterly Issue No. 11, Racing to the Skies: down to Earth Strategies for Super High Rise Buildings, Pg. 102 - 107
Architecture of Kris Yao/Artech, Lite-on Headquarters, 032-049
Architectural Record, August 2010, Burj Khalifa, Dubai, Pg. 78-92
ArtPower International Publishing Co. Ltd, Landscape Housing II, UC Davis West Village
Best Tall Buildings – A Global Overview of 2010, 2011, 2013, 2014, 2016 Skyscapers, CTBUH, 2010–2016
Bing Thom Works, Tarrant County College, Pgs. 152–163
Building On the Past, The Making of the Iris & B. Gerald Cantor Center for Visual Arts at Stanford University, Richard Joncas, 1999
Chinese and Overseas Landscape – COL, Residential Landscape Design, Robson Residence, Pg. 36–41
City Builder: The Architecture of James KM Cheng, 2016
City Secrets, Robert Kahn, Series Editor, The Little Bookroom, New York, 1999
Rome: Pg. 59, 63, 80, 82, 87, 91, 118, and 150, Revised Printing Pg. 146
Florence, Venice and the Towns of Italy: Pg. 32, 41, 42, 53, 55, 86, and 185
Compasses – architecture & design, July 2010, Landscape Urbanism in Practice: SWA Group
Compasses – architecture & design, 2010–009, Ideas – Landscape Architecture, Pg. 126–131
Cowboys and Indians Magazine – Untamed Beauty of the Western Landscape – C&L Magazine, Vineyard Estate, April 26 2017
CTBUH, International Award Winning Projects – Best Tall Buildings 2010, Pg.92–95 Nanjing Greenland Financial Center; Pg. 144–149 Burj Khalifa.
Design Wanted – Containing a City Vertically – Interview with John Wong, July 7, 2020
Designed Landscape Forum I, Spacemaker Press, 1998, Burnaby Metrotown Civic Center, Pg. 104, 188; Center for Contemporary Graphic Art, Pg. 106, 189; LG Beijing, Pg. 30
Designed Landscape Forum III, Land Forum 13, Spacemaker Press, 2002, Bentley School, Pg. 46–47
Designing Places for People and the Environment, Kalvin Platt, 2014
The Dirt, Burj Khalifa Park Gets Starring Role in New Mission Impossible, 12/15/12
Drawing the Landscape, Second and Third Editions, Chip Sullivan, 2004, Pg. 34, 211
Emirates Business, January 4, 2010, Burj Dubai, Icon Rising, an Iterative Pattern, Pg. 38-43
Environment and Landscape Architecture of Korea, 08/2003, #184
Creating Landscape Oasis in Densely Developed Asian Cities, John Wong, The SWA Group, Pgs. 96–105
Frameworks, Fall 2012 (Berkeley's College of Environmental Design publication)
Interview with John Wong-Making Cities Livable: Burj Khalifa, Shanghai Tower, Suzhou Center, Kingdom Tower, Guthrie Green, 2012.

Gardens Without Boundaries, Paul Cooper, 2003, Pg. 56–57, 59
Gardenscapes – Designs For Outdoor Living, Carol Soucek King, PBC International, Inc. 1997 Structured Simplicity, Pg. 128–131
Gentry Design, April/May 2010, Toujour Provence, Pg. 66–71
Green and Design, July/August 2009, Firmly Planted, Ensuring Human Scale to Super-Tall and High Impact Structures, Pg. 18–21
Harvard Magazine, May – June 1982
How John Wong Found A Room With A View, By George Howe Colt, Pg. 58–64
Hi-Design International Publishing Hong Kong, China – Urban Water Landscape Architecture Book, Marinaside Crescent Waterfront Landscape Book, Marinaside Crescent.
Imprint, Fall 1999, Reconstructing the Heart of the University, The Associates of the Stanford University Libraries, 12 October 1999
Ingenieros Y Arquitectos, Arquitectura Del Paisaje
Inland Architect Volume 116, Number 2, Making Waves with Water, Pg. 32–34, Ranch – Style Landscaping, Pg. 22–25
J. Michael Welton. Landscaping and the Burj Khalifa, Pgs. 1–5.
Land Forum 14, 2002, The SWA Group: Recent Projects, Stanford University, Tokyo University Foreign Studies Campus, Dreamworks SKG Animation Studio
Landscape Architect and Specifier News, March 2010, Tulsa's New Water Playground, Pg. 90–98
Landscape Architect and Specifier News, February 2010, Arabian Tower, Pg. 98
Landscape Architecture, September 2009, Fellowships, There's No Place Like Rome, Pg. 80–99
Landscape Architecture, Nov./Dec. 1982
Spaces, Images and Ideas: Sketches From A Rome Prize Fellow, By John L. Wong, Pg. 63–65
Landscape Architecture China, Feb. 2008, Lite-On Technology Headquarters, Pg. 68–69
Landscape at Berkeley – The First 100 Years; Learning From the Best and Returning to Teach the Next Generation – John L. Wong, FASLA, FAAR, BLA, 1974, pg 170–174; pg 247, 2013
Landscape Design, January 20, 2010, No.1, Provencal Romance – Los Gatos Villa Residence, Pg. 34–39
Landscape Infrastructure – Case Studies by SWA, 2010
Landscape Journal, Vol. 12, Number 2, Fall 1993
Most Influential Landscapes, Pg. 170 –171
Landscape M.E., May 2010, Issue 35, Who's Who John L. Wong, Pg. 4–5
Landscape M.E., June 2010, Issue 36, The Back Drop Splendor of Burj Khalifa, Pg. 22–29
Landscape Record – SWA@60, Vol.2/2017.04
Landscape World, Vol. 06, Lite-On Technology Headquarters, Pg. 18–27
Landscapes for People, SWA Works, Selected Works by SWA, 2013
Master Planned Communities, Lessons from the Development of Chuck Cobb by Kalvin Platt, Urban Land Institute, Pg. 38, 56, 66, 106, 154
Paradise Transformed – The Private Garden for The Twenty-First Century, Guy Cooper and Gordon Taylor, The Monacelli Press, 1996, Tradition – John Wong, Pg. 140–143
The Place Itself, Richard Beard, AIA, and Dan Gregory, Selected Work of BAR Architects, Rancho San Joaquin Apartments, Liliore Green Rains at Stanford, Borlasca, UC Santa Cruz-Porter, Stevenson and Cowell, Scripps College Jungels-Winkler Hall, Pg. 17, 25, 33–35, 58–61, 88-91
Princeton Architectural Press – 'Good Energy: Renewable Poser and the Design of Everyday Life', UC Davis, West Village, 2021
Process: Architecture, Landscape Design and Planning at The SWA Group, #103, 1992
Progressive Architectural Magazine
Project Russia / International Edition, 2004
Tokyo University of Foreign Studies, Fuchu, Japan
Residential Landscape Design, 029, Chinese and Overseas Landscape, Robson Residence, Pg. 36–41
San Francisco Chronicle, Sunday, January 10, 2010, Sausalito Group Creates Oasis at Burj Dubai, Pg. C-3
Selected Works – Adrian Smith + Gordon Gill Architecture, 2006-2021, 2022
Shanghai Tower, Gensler, 2015
SOM: Work by Skidmore, Owings & Merrill, 984–1994, 1995–2000, 1984–1996, 1997-2008, 2009 - 2019
Super Tall/Mega Tall: How High Can We Go? Adrian Smith + Gordon Gill Architecture, 2022
Tasarim 104, Landscape Architecture, Urban Design and Planning of The SWA Group, Longboat Key, Ronald Reagan Presidential Library, Stanford University, Village of Woodbridge
Tasarim 135, 10/2003, Landscape Architecture
Tokyo University of Foreign Studies, Fuchu, Japan
The Campus Guide, Stanford University, Richard Joncas, David J. Neuman, and Paul V. Turner, Princeton Architectural Press, 1999
The Coalescing of Different Forces and Ideas: A History of Landscape Architecture at Harvard, 1900–1999, Melanie L. Simo, The Harvard University Graduate School of Design, 2000, Pg. 58, 72, 91
The Master Architect Series V, Kris Yao / Artech, Selected and Current Works, Images Publishing 2001
Lite On Headquarters, Pg. 33–35, Compal Park / Compal Headquarters, Pg. 36–45, Lot A-1 Tower, Pg. 72–73
The New American Garden – Innovations in Residential Landscape Architecture, James Grayson Trulove, Whitney Library of Design, 1998, Nagelberg Residence, Pg. 214–219, Collector's Residence, Pg. 220–225
The New American Swimming Pool – Innovations in Design and Construction, James Grayson Trulove, Whitney Library of Design, 2001, Chan Pool, 1994, Pg. 84–89, View Pool, 1997, Pg. 122–127, Hillsborough Pool, 1996, Pg. 198–201
The Structure of Design – Leslie Earl Robertson, 2017
The World's 118 Tallest Buildings, Edited by Antony Wood, CTBUH – 1, 3, -14, 22, 24, 66, 78, 9, 2022
Time Properties Magazine. Nanjing Greenland Tower
Urban Design International Magazine
Urban Design International, Contemporary California Competitions, Vol. 10, 1989, Pershing Square, Todos Santos Plaza
Urban Land, Case Study: Shanghai Tower, May/June 2013, pg. 140
Urban Land – Middle East, Spring 2009, Burj Dubai, Pg. 54–55
Veranda, September 2007, Passion for Provence for a California Family, Pg. 132–147
The Wall Street Journal, The Home Front, "Luxury Real Estate: Choosing to Live on the Edge in San Francisco', Friday, July 29, 2011
World Architecture Review 98:01, Landscape Architecture, Urban Design and Planning at the SWA Group:
Beijing Wellbond International Golf Club, Village of Woodbridge, LG Beijing, Shanghai Government Center, Citicorp Plaza and Seventh Street Market Place, Ronald Reagan presidential Library, Boca Beach Club, Nasu Highland Golf Club, Regus Crest Grand Golf Club, Nasu Highland Fantasy Pointe Park
World Architecture, SWA Group, Where Creativity Becomes Value, Issue No. 82, 12/1999–1/2000, Pg. 104–127
World Landscape Architecture – SWA and Thomas Balsley – Formation of SWA/Balsley, November 17, 2016

Representative Projects
83 Dalvey Road, Singapore
201 Mission Street, San Francisco, California
330 North Wabash, Chicago, Illinois
400 South Hope Street, Los Angeles, California
720 Beatty Street, Vancouver, Canada
41st Street Plaza, Tulsa, Oklahoma
1445-1455 West Georgia/Pender Street, Vancouver, British Columbia, Canada
6060 Minaret Road, Mammoth, California
Abu Dhabi Massnoua Island
Aerospace Museum Air and Space Garden, Los Angeles, California
Amaala, Red Sea, Saudi Araboia
Amazing Brentwood Town Centre, Burnaby, British Columbia, Canada
Angel No Mori, Ueno City, Nara-ken, Japan
Apple Computer Telecommunications and Computing Center, Sacramento, California
Apple DeAnza Courtyard, Cupertino, California
ARA Residence, Atherton, California
Arkansas River Conceptual Development Plan, Tulsa, Oklahoma
Arts Commons, Calgary, Canada
Asan-Baebang Mixed-Use Complex (ABMC), Asan-Baebang, Korea
Atomic City, Isfahan, Iran
Babcock Residence, Kentfield, California
Bank of China FTZ, Shanghai, China
Bank of China Hainan, Hainan, China
Baywood Canyon, Fairfax, California
Beach Villas, Jeddah, Saudi Arabia
Beijing CBD Development, Beijing, China
Beijing Greenland Center Dawangjing, Beijing, China

Beijing Wellbond International Golf Club, Beijing, China
Bella Vista / Villa Felice, Los Gatos, California
Bentley School, Lafayette, California
Bionic Hill Innovation Techno-Park Master Plan, Kiev, Ukraine
Bird Avenue, San Jose, California
Blair-Crow Creek Competition, Tulsa, Oklahoma
Boca Raton Hotel and Club, Boca Beach Club, Boca Raton, Florida
Boca Raton Hotel and Club, Main Hotel Master Plan, Boca Raton, Florida
Boston North End Parks, Boston, Massachusetts
Botown, San Jose, California
Bristol, Durres, Albania
Bukit Indah Park City and Industrial Park, Cikampek, Indonesia
Bund Finance Center, Shanghai, China
Burj Al Oula, Al Khobar, Saudi Arabia
Burj 2020 District, Dubai, United Arab Emirates
Burj Khalifa Downtown, Dubai, Dubai, United Arab Emirates
Burj Khalifa Tower Park, Dubai, United Arab Emirates
Burnaby Civic Square and Library, Burnaby, British Columbia, Canada
The Butterfly, (First Baptist Church), Vancouver, British Columbia, Canada
'C' Project, Bangkok, Thailand
C230, Seoul, Korea
Caldwell, Los Gatos, California
Camino Medical Group, Mountain View, California
Cantor Residence: La Belle Vie, Bel Air, California
Canyon Heights, Fremont, California
Carlsbad by the Sea, Carlsbad, California
Castilleja, Fremont, California
Cayan Tower, Dubai, United Arab Emirates
Center for Contemporary Graphic Art at Uzumine, Sukagawa, Japan
Chelsea Roof Deck, New York, New York
Chengdu Dongcun Greenland Tower, Chengdu, China
Chengdu Medical Center Master Plan, Chengdu, China
Chengdu Tianfu New District High Rise, Chengdu, China
Chongqing A13 Jiangbeizui International Center, Chongqing, China
CHIC Corporation Headquarters, Shanghai, China
Chongming Island Design Competition, Shanghai, China
Chongwen Menway Dajie Streetscape, Chongwen District 2 Master Plan, Beijing, China
Citicorp Plaza and Seventh Street Marketplace, Los Angeles, California
Cobalt – 1179 Campbell Avenue, San Jose, California
Columbus City Hall, Columbus, Indiana
Compal Park, T, T
Congregation Beth El of La Jolla, La Jolla, California
Copley Square Competition, Boston, Massachusetts
Cornell University East Hill Village, Ithaca, New York
Covington, Aliso Viejo, California
Crescent, The, Sunnyvale, California
CSU Chico Student Services Center, Chico, California
Daewoo Songdo, Inchon, Korea
Dallas Museum of Arts, Dallas, Texas
Dashen Lin HQ, Guangzhou, Guangdong Province, China
Day Ranch, Reno, Nevada
De Anza Boulevard, Cupertino, California
Dermody Farms, Reno, Nevada
DIFC Phase 1, Dubai, United Arab Emirates
DreamWorks SKG Animation Studio, Glendale, California
DUR, Doosan Haeundae U-Dong Residential, Busan, Korea
Dubai Four Seasons Residence, Dubai, United Arab Emirates
Dubai Hills, Dubai, United Areab Emirates
Dubai Mall and Fashion Promenade, Dubai, United Arab Emirates
Durres Master Plan, Durres, Albania
Edmonds Town Centre – Southgate, Burnaby, British Columbia, Canada
Encanto Campbell Avenue, San Jose, California
EPPF Eun-Pyeong Mixed Use, Seoul, Korea
Evans Residence, Los Gatos, California
Evergrande Shenzhen Center, Shenzhen, China
EXPO 2020 - Al Wasl Plaza, Parcel H, C209, C208, C38 Parks, The Loop, Dubai, UAE
Fantasy Pointe at Nasu Highland Park, Nasu, Japan
Federation of Korean Industries Head Office, Seoul, Korea
Foshan Chancheng Greenland Center, Foshan, China

Foshan Greenland Master Plan, Foshan, China
Franklin-McKinley Valley Health Center, San Jose, California
Fujita Landscape Training Program, Tokyo, Japan
FuYang East Avenue Phase I, FuYang, China
FuYang East Avenue, West Peninsula Planning and Design, FuYang, China
Golden Gate Center, Cairo, Egypt
Google Shorebird Campus, Mountain View, California
GS Kangnam Tower, Seoul, Korea
GTE Government Systems Master Plan, Mountain View, California
GTE Government Systems, Building #7, Mountain View, California
Guangzhou East Railway Station, Guangzhou, China
Guangzhou Greenland Luo Gang Central Plaza, Guangzhou, China
Guangzhou Jiangwan East Residential Tower, Guangzhou, China
Guthrie Green and Tulsa Arts District Streetscape, Tulsa, Oklahoma
Halla Bundang Head Office, Seoul, Korea
Halsey Lane Residence, Bridgehampton, Long Island, New York
Hangzhou Olympic Sports BinJiang International Business District, Hangzhou, China
Hangzhou Sunac West Station North Plaza, Hangzhou, China
Hato Montana Master Plan, Hato Montana, Panama
HDMC-1, Hwae Song Dongstan Mixed-Use Complex, Seoul, Korea
High Point Master Plan, Sandy City, Utah
Hone Shee, Hsinyi, Hsinyi, T, T
Hua Yang Industrial Area Development Project, Shanghai, China
Hummingbird Place, Fremont, California
Hyatt Regency Serenity Coast, Sanya, China
Irvine Spectrum, Irvine, California
Islamabad New City, Islamabad, Pakistan
Island Park, Dubai, United Arab Emirates
Island Outpost Resort, Park City, Utah
Iwaki City Cycle Park, Iwaki City, Fukushima Prefecture, Japan
Jinan Greenland CBD Super High-rise, Jinan, China
Jebel Ali Limitless Highrise, Jebel Ali, Dubai, United Arab Emirates
KA-CARE - King Abdullah City for Atomic and Renewal Energy, Al Riyadh, Saudi Arabia
Kezar Corner Master Plan, San Francisco, California
Jeddah Tower (Formerly Kingdom Tower), Jeddah, Kingdom of Saudi Arabia
Ko Olina Master Plan, Honolulu, Hawaii
Ko Olina, Four Seasons, Honolulu, Hawaii
Konjiam Resort, Gyeonggi-do, Seoul, Korea
Korea World Trade Center - COEX, Seoul, Korea
Koyang International Exhibition Center, Koyang, Korea
KUAF: Kuwait University Administrative Facilities, Shadadiyah University City, Kuwait
Kula Belgrade, Belgrade, Serbia
Grosvenor Ambleside, West Vancouver, British Columbia, Canada
Kuwait Ministry of Education Headquarters, South Surra, Kuwait
Laborers Trust Fund, San Ramon, California
Lafayette Town Center, Lafayette, California
Las Vegas Downtown Development Strategy, Las Vegas, Nevada
Lawrence Livermore Laboratory Business Center Conceptual Design, Livermore, California
Lawrence Livermore Laboratory Environmental Safety & Health Facility Concept Design, Livermore, California
Lawrence Livermore Laboratory Second Street Mall, Livermore, California
Lawrence Livermore National Lab NDERF and NTTC Buildings, Livermore, California
Lawrence Livermore National Laboratory DPRF/NTTC Buildings, Livermore, California
LG Beijing, Beijing, China
LG Twin Towers, Seoul, Korea
LG-GS Kangnam Ahjoo Site, Seoul, Korea
Liansheng Financial Center, Taiyuan, China
Lincoln Square, Bellevue, Washington
Lite-On Technology Headquarters, Neihu Science Park
Longmu Bay International Resort Beachfront and Town Center, Hainan, China
Longmu Bay International Resort City, Le Dong, Hainan, China
Longmu Bay International Resort Phase 1, Le Dong, Hainan, China
Los Coches, Milpitas, California
Lot A1 Tower, T, T
Lotte Mapo, Seoul, Korea
Lougheed Town Centre, Burnaby, British Columbia, Canada
Magnom Forbes Tower, Cairo, Egypt
Mahon Creek Restoration Plan, San Rafael, California
Malchicoff Residence, Thousand Oaks, California

Manor Spelling Residence, Holmby Hills, California
Marin County YMCA, San Rafael, California
Marina Lakes, Richmond, California
Marinaside Crescent, Vancouver, Canada
Mashreq Bank Headquarters, Dubai, United Arab Emirates
Mayfield Specific Plan, Fremont, California
Milpitas Public Park, Milpitas, California
Minsheng Center, Shanghai, China
Mission Estates, Fremont, California
MoD Headquarters Building, KSA-MOD, Riyadh, KSA
Moscow International Business Center, Plot 16, Moscow, Russia
Moscow Morgan Hotel, Moscow, Russia
Mountain Spa Resort, Las Vegas, Nevada
Muir Woods, Marin County, California
Nagelberg Residence – North Ranch, Thousand Oaks, California
Nanchang Greenland Central Plaza – Parcel A,B,C, Nanchang, China
Nanchang Greenland Jiangxi Gaoxin, Nanchang, China
Nanchang Greenland Melanwei, Nanchang, China
Nanchang Greenland Xiangshan Urban Infill, Nanchang, China
Nanjing Greenland Pukou, Nanjing, China
Nanjing Hexi Yuzui Tower, Runmao, Nanjing, China
Nanjing World Trade Center, Nanjing, China
Nasu Akebien Membership Hotel, Nasu, Tochigi-ken, Japan
Nasu Highland Fantasy Pointe, Woopy's World, Nasu, Japan
Nasu Highland Golf Club, Nasu, Japan
Nasu Highland Grand Hotel, Nasu, Japan
Nasu Highland Meeting/Sports Center, Nasu, Japan
Nasu Highland Vacation Homes, Nasu, Japan
Nature Group – Dianshan Lake, Dianshan City, Suzhou Province, China
NeXT Corporate Campus at Seaport Center, Redwood City, California
North Bund White Magnolia Plaza, North Bund, Shanghai, China
North Carolina State University School of Veterinary Medicine, Raleigh, North Carolina
North Natomas Community Plan, Sacramento, California
Nun's Island, Montreal, Canada
Ohlone College Campus Plan Update, Fremont, California
Okayama Competition, Okayama, Japan
Old School House, Fremont, California
Opera Plaza District, Downtown Dubai, UAE
Padmakara Garden, Berkeley California
Palamanui Master Plan, Kailua Kona, Hawaii
Palo Alto Medical Foundation, Fremont, California
Paradise Harbor, Shanghai, China
Paseo Padre: Mowry Mixed-Use Project, Fremont, California
Pearl River Tower (Zero Energy Tower), Guangzhou, China
Pebble Creek Resort Community, Goodyear, Arizona
Pershing Square, Los Angeles, California
PG&E Learning Center, Northern California
Plaza Rakyat, Kuala Lumpur, Malaysia
Point West Office Park, Framingham, Massachusetts
Point West Place, Framingham, Massachusetts
Popell Residence, Fairfax, California
Prime Computer, Framingham, Massachusetts
Project Duo, Red Sea, Kingdom of Saudi Arabia
Pusan Bumildong Residential, Pusan, Korea
Qingdao Fortune Center, Qingdao, China
Qingdao Golden Beach, Qingdao, China
Qingdao Ocean Science Park, Qingdao, China
Qingdao World Pole Project, Qingdao, China
Reagan Presidential Library, Simi Valley, Ventura County, California
Regus Crest Royal Golf Club, Hiroshima, Japan
Reno Golf and Country Club, Reno, Nevada
River Corridor Study for Tulsa, Tulsa, Oklahoma
Riverpoint Business Park, Phoenix, Arizona
Robert Young Winery, Geyserville, California
Robson Residence, Monte Sereno, California
Rockwell Urban Center, Manila, Philippines
Ronald McDonald House at Stanford, Palo Alto, California
Roppongi 6-6 Urban Redevelopment, Tokyo, Japan

Rosewood Sand Hill Hotel and Office Development, Menlo Park, California
Rule Lake, Nanchang, China
Sand Dune Residence, Bridgehampton, Long Island, New York
SAIT Polytechnic Parkade, Calgary, Canada
San Francisco War Memorial Veterans Building, San Francisco, California
San Joaquin Valley Agricultural Science Center (SJVASC), Parlier, California
San Rafael Corporate Center, San Rafael, California
San Rafael Corporate Center Phase 2, San Rafael, California
Santa Clara County Silver Creek Campus, Santa Clara, California
Sanya Serenity Bay Water Park, Sanya, China
Sapporo White Dome Competition, Sapporo, Japan
Sausalito Ice House Plaza, Sausalito, California
Scent of Orange: Integrated Rural Urbanization Project (IRUP), Chongqing, China
Scripps College Residence Hall, Claremont, California
Seoul Dome, Seoul, Korea
Sha Long Island Resort, Zhong Shan, China
Shanghai International Dance Center, Shanghai, China
Shanghai Government Center, Shanghai, China
Shanghai Grand Office Tower, Shanghai, China
Shanghai Jianqiao Pukai Zhangjabang, Shanghai, China
Shanghai Jianqiao Tod, Shanghai, China
Shanghai Riversong Community, Shanghai, China
Shanghai Tower, Shanghai, China
Shanghai Zhaofeng Mixed Use, Shanghai, China
Shanghai Zhoujiadu Project, Shanghai, China
Sheikh Mohammad Bin Rashid Boulevard, formerly Emaar Boulevard, Dubai, United Arab Emirates
Shenzen Evergrande Center, Shenzhen, China
Shimao Shenzhen International Center, Shenzhen, China
Shijiazhuang CBD Park and Office, Shijiazhuang, China
Shimao Shenzhen Tower, Shenzhen, China
Shimao Sheshan Garden E1 & E2, Shanghai, China
Shuangxin Hi-Tech District, Beijing, China
Silver Creek Master Plan, Santa Clara, California
Silverado Vineyards, Silverado Trail, Napa County, California
Sing Tran – Oriental Star Diamond Center, T, T
SIP Administrative Center, Suzhou, China
SIP Times Square, Suzhou, China
Sisters of The Holy Family Site, Fremont, California
Six Dynasties Museum/Grand Mansion Hotel, Nanjing, China
Skyview 4 5 6, Dubai, United Arab Emirates
Smart Dairy Property, Sandy City, Utah
Sonoma Academy, Santa Rosa, California
Sonoma Residence, Sonoma, California
Soul, North Coast, Egypt
South Bund Waterfront Open Space, Shanghai, China
South Street Seaport Center, New York, New York
Southbank, Phoenix, Arizona
St. Patrick's Seminary: Vintage Oaks, Menlo Park, California
Stanford Shopping Center Expansion, Palo Alto, California
Stanford Shopping Center, Bank of America, Stanford, California
Stanford Shopping Center, Saks Building Renovation, Stanford, California
Stanford University Albers Wall Relocation, Stanford, California
Stanford University Alumni Center, Stanford, California
Stanford University Aquatics and Athletics Plaza, Stanford, California
Stanford University Aquatics, Stanford, California
Stanford University Arguello Mall Master Plan, Stanford, California
Stanford University Arrillaga Plaza, Stanford, California
Stanford University Arrillaga Recreation Center, Stanford, California
Stanford University Bakewell Building, Stanford, California
Stanford University Barnum Family Center, Stanford, California
Stanford University Branner Hall, Stanford, California
Stanford University Buildings 160/320 Courtyards, Stanford, California
Stanford University Campus Center, Stanford, California
Stanford University Cantor Center for the Visual Arts Expansion, Stanford, California
Stanford University Center for Advanced Study in the Behavioral Sciences, Stanford, California
Stanford University CSLI/EPGY/MediaX Courtyards, Stanford, California
Stanford University DAPER Master Plan, Stanford, California

Stanford University Encina Hall East and Central, Stanford, California
Stanford University Escondido Village Central Spine / Maintenance Yard, Stanford, California
Stanford University Escondido Village Master Plan, Stanford, California
Stanford University Escondido Village, Wellesley Site, Studios 5 and 6 Stanford, California
Stanford University Faculty/Staff Housing Master Plan, Stanford, California
Stanford University Ford Plaza, Stanford, California
Stanford University Galvez House, Stanford, California
Stanford University Galvez Street Reconfiguration, Stanford, California
Stanford University Graduate School of Business (Knight Building Addition) Renovation, Stanford, California
Stanford University Green Library, Stanford, California
Stanford University Herbert Hoover Federal Memorial Building and Library, Stanford, California
Stanford University Hoover Institution, David and Joan Traitel Building, Stanford, California
Stanford University Hoover Institution, Schultz Building, Stanford, California
Stanford University Lagunita Court Infill Housing, Stanford, California
Stanford University Lagunita Court, Stanford, California
Stanford University Lasuen Mall, Stanford, California
Stanford University Lathrop Library, Stanford, California
Stanford University Law School Courtyard, Stanford, California
Stanford University Library Fountain, Stanford, California
Stanford University Liliore Green Rains Graduate Student Housing, Stanford, California
Stanford University Manzanita Housing, Stanford, California
Stanford University Manzanita Park Infill Housing, Stanford, California
Stanford University Maples Pavilion Renovation, Stanford, California
Stanford University Memorial Auditorium Parking Expansion, Stanford, California
Stanford University Meyer-Buck Estate, Stanford, California
Stanford University Munger Graduate Residence, Stanford, California
Stanford University Museum Way, Stanford, California
Stanford University North Stadium Area Study, Stanford, California
Stanford University Panama Mall, Stanford, California
Stanford University Peterson Labs Building, Stanford, California
Stanford University Ralph Landau Center for Economics and Policy Research, Stanford, California
Stanford University School of Education, Stanford, California
Stanford University SEQ Fountains - William R. Hewlett and David Packard, Stanford, California
Stanford University Serra Street Reconfiguration, Stanford, California
Stanford University SIEPR (Stanford Institute for Economic Policy Research), Stanford, California
Stanford University Soccer Field - DAPER, Stanford, California
Stanford University Stadium Elevator Tower, Stanford, California
Stanford University Stern Hall, Stanford, California
Stanford University Streetscapes - Bowdoin, Electioneer, Welch, Santa Teresa, and Searsville, Stanford, California
Stanford University Student Services Building, Stanford, California
Stanford University Terman Park, Stanford, California
Stanford University Toyon Hall, Stanford, California
Stanford University West Gate, Stanford, California
Stanford University Wilbur Hall, Stanford, California
Stanford University WindHover Center, Stanford, California
Stanford West Apartments, Palo Alto, California
Sun Cyber City Planning Workshop, Guangzhou, China
Sun Plaza, Las Vegas, Nevada
Suzhou Center Competition, Suzhou, China
Suzhou Center, Suzhou, China
Suzhou Convention and Exhibition Center, Suzhou, China
Suzhou Cultural Exhibition Center Plaza, Suzhou, China
Suzhou Golden Land, Suzhou, China
Suzhou Greenland Center, Wujiang Lakefront District, Suzhou, China
Taiwan Parliament Building Complex, T, T
Tarrant County College, Fort Worth, Texas
Tehran Center for the Performance of Music, Tehran, Iran
The Hollywood Palladium, Los Angeles, California
Tianshan Commercial Area, Shijiazhuang, China
Todos Santos Plaza, Concord, California

Tokyo University of Foreign Studies Campus, Fuchu, Japan
Tongxiang Retirement Community, Tongxiang, Zhejiang Province, China
Tongzhou Cultural District, Beijing, China
Tower Palace I, II, III, Seoul, Korea
Tribune East Parcel, Chicago, Illinois
Triple C Ranch, San Anselmo, California
Tulsa Arts District Streetscape and ONEOK Ballpark, Tulsa, Oklahoma
Tulsa River Parks Design Manual, Tulsa, Oklahoma
Tulsa River Projects, Tulsa, Oklahoma
Two Venture Plaza, Irvine, California
UC Berkeley Bowles Hall, Berkeley, California
UC Berkeley Computer Sciences Building, Soda Hall, Berkeley, California
UC Berkeley Stern Hall Feasibility Study, Berkeley, California
UC Davis Center for Comparative Medicine, Davis, California
UC Davis Central Plant Expansion, Davis, California
UC Davis Environmental Health and Safety Facility, Davis, California
UC Davis Medical Center Parking Garage II, Sacramento, California
UC Davis Medical Center, Research Building III, Sacramento, California
UC Davis West Village, Davis, California
UC Merced Student Housing, Merced, California
UC San Francisco Regional Medical Center, Fresno, California
UC Santa Cruz Academic Core Master Plan & Natural Sciences and Engineering Unit III, Santa Cruz, California
UC Santa Cruz Infill Housing - Stevenson, Cowell and Porter Colleges, Santa Cruz, California
Underhill, Kelowna, British Columbia, Canada
United Daily News Plaza, T, T
University of Chicago Booth School of Business, UCCHK, University of Chicago Francis and Rose Yuen Campus, Hong Kong, China
University of Incheon, Redevelopment & Replacement, Incheon & New Songdo City, Korea
University of Miami Master Plan, Coral Gables, Florida
University of Miami New Campus Master Plan, Coral Gables, Florida
Valley-Mercer Project, Seattle, Washington
Vanke Huang Pu East Road Project, Guangzhou, China
Vanke Zhongliang Golden Beach Blue Bay (Guangzhou Jin Sha Zhofu), Guangzhou, China
Vi Living, Palo Alto, California
Victoria Ward Master Plan - Ward Center, Honolulu, Hawaii
Victoria Ward Waiea Ward Village, Honolulu, Hawaii
Village of Woodbridge, Irvine Ranch, California
Wakasado Complex, Nagano, Japan
Walkerhill, Seoul, Korea
Waterfront Centre, Vancouver, Canada
Wenzhou Kean University Competition, Wenzhou, China
Wenzhou Lucheng Plaza, Wenzhou, China
Whole Foods, Fremont, Fremont, California
Wilshire, The, Los Angeles, California
Woodruff Arts Center, Atlanta, Georgia
Wuhan Greenland Center, Wuhan, China
Wuhan Hanzheng Street East, Wuhan, China
Wu Li Qiao Greenland Mixed Use, Shanghai, China
Xiongan SinoChem HQ, Beijing, China
XIQU Center, Hong Kong, China
Yangzhou Center, Yangzhou, China
Zakin Residence, Napa Valley, California
Zhangjiang R&D District Urban Design, Shanghai, China
Zhangjiang Science City parcel 56, 57 & 58, Shanghai, China
Zhengzhou Greenland Plaza, Zhengzhou, China
Zhongshan Administration Center, Zhongshan City, Quangdong Province, China
Zhongshan International Exhibition Center, Zhongshan City, Quangdong Province, China
Zhuhai Hong Kong, China - Macao China Bridge - Artificial Island Port Mixed use Master Plan, Zhuhai, Hong Kong, China
Zifeng Tower - Nanjing Greenland International Commercial Center, Nanjing, China

CONTRIBUTORS

Peter Walker has exerted a significant influence on the field of landscape architecture over a six-decade career. Educated at the University of California at Berkeley and at the Harvard University Graduate School of Design, Walker has taught, lectured, written, and served as an advisor to numerous public agencies while executing leadership of several firms including Sasaki Walker and Associates in 1957 (which became The SWA Group in 1979) and Peter Walker and Partners in 1983 (now known as PWP Landscape Architecture). The scope of his landscape inquiries is expansive as well as deep. Projects range from small gardens to new cities, from urban plazas to corporate headquarters and academic campuses. With a dedicated concern for urban and environmental issues, his designs shape the landscape in a variety of geographic and cultural contexts, from the United States to Asia, Australia, and Europe. Walker is a Fellow of the American Society of Landscape Architects and of the Institute for Urban Design and, in addition to numerous awards for specific projects, has been granted the Honor Award of the American Institute of Architects, Harvard's Centennial Medal, University of Virginia's Thomas Jefferson Medal, the ASLA Medal, and the IFLA Sir Geoffrey Jellicoe Gold Medal.

David J Neuman is the Founding Principal of Neu Campus Planning, a planning and programming consultancy, which utilizes a unique '360 degree' perspective and collaborative approach developed from experiences as both an internal administrator and an external consultant. His current clients range from research universities to leading preparatory schools to significant non-governmental organizations. The firm has a strategic alliance with the Architectural Resources Group (ARG), with offices in Los Angeles, San Francisco, and Portland. He brings more than 40 years of managerial and design experience in higher education/campus planning. Formerly, he served as the Chief Planning Official and Architect for the University of Virginia; Associate Vice Provost for Planning and University Architect at Stanford University; Associate Vice Chancellor for Planning and Campus Architect at the University of California, Irvine; and Consulting Campus Architect for the University of California, Santa Barbara, the University of Nebraska System and the University of Hawai'i, West O'ahu. He is a Fellow of the American Institute of Architects; is the recipient of the California Council AIA Corporate Architect Award; and has accepted major awards from the National Trust for Historic Preservation and the California Governor's Office. His publications include: *Critical Architecture and Contemporary Culture* (Oxford Press, 1994), *The Campus Guide: Stanford University* (Princeton Architectural Press, 1999 & 2006), *Building Type Basics for College and University Facilities* (Wiley and Sons, 2003 & 2013 English & 2005 Mandarin), and *The Campus Guide: University of Virginia* (Princeton Architectural Press, 2012).

Adrian Smith FAIA, is an architect of international renown, having designed many landmark buildings including the world's two tallest structures – Burj Khalifa completed in 2010 in Dubai (designed at SOM Chicago) and Jeddah Tower, now under construction in Jeddah, Saudi Arabia. His work has shown an evolving interest in the use of vernacular and indigenous forms and compositions together with state-of-the-art systems and technologies to integrate new buildings into the regional context. His designs are sensitive to each project's physical environment, taking into consideration conditions such as location, climate, geographical, geological, cultural, and social influences to achieve environmental sustainability. Over the last several years his work has embraced the principle of "on site" power generation using the building's design to harvest power from the sun, wind, and geothermal conditions to reduce the buildings' reliance on the local infrastructure. In many instances, this has had a dramatic impact on the expression of the architecture and has added an important influence for his philosophy: Global Contextualism. In 2006, he founded Adrian Smith + Gordon Gill Architecture (AS+GG), a firm dedicated to the design of high-performance, energy-efficient, and sustainable architecture on an international scale. Prior to AS+GG, he was Design Partner in the Chicago office of Skidmore, Owings & Merrill (SOM) from 1980 to 2003 and Consulting Design Partner from 2003 to 2006.

Gordon Gill FAIA, is one of the world's foremost exponents of performance-based architecture. Ranging from the world's tallest buildings to sustainable communities, his work is driven by his philosophy that there is a purposeful relationship between formal design and performance; and that there is a Language of Performance, which is the basis of his practice: Form Follows Performance. A founding partner of award-winning Adrian Smith + Gordon Gill Architecture (AS+GG), Gordon's work includes the design of the world's first net zero-energy skyscraper, Pearl River Tower in Guangzhou, China (designed at SOM Chicago); the world's first large-scale positive energy building, Masdar Headquarters; the world's tallest tower, Jeddah Tower in Jeddah Saudi Arabia; and most recently Al Wasl Plaza, the open space for the centerpiece of Expo 2020 Dubai, featuring an intricate domed trellis that is the world's largest immersive projection experience. These landmark projects pursue energy independence by harnessing the power of natural forces on site and striking a balance with their environmental contexts. Prior to founding AS+GG in 2006, Gordon was an Associate Partner at Skidmore, Owings & Merrill and a Director of Design for VOA Associates.

James K. M. Cheng is a Canadian architect recognized for his pioneering contributions to west coast architecture and city building. Born in Hong Kong, China and educated in North America, Cheng's approach represents a sensitive marriage of generous open environments with vibrant high-density living. He was a lecturer at the University of British Columbia, and a visiting design critic at Harvard University. Cheng launched his architectural career working for Fred Bassetti and Mithun Partners while earning his Bachelor of Architecture degree from the University of Washington in Seattle. A condominium project he designed during this time captured the attention of Architectural Record Magazine ("Young Architects" 1972 and "Record House" 1974) and garnered awards from AIA Seattle as well as the national AIA "Homes for Better Living" program. Cheng went on to apprentice with Henrik Bull in San Francisco, and then for three years with Arthur Erickson in Vancouver, before studying at the Harvard Graduate School of Design under Richard Meier. Cheng established James K.M. Cheng Architects Inc. in 1978 after winning a collaborative entry with Romses Kwan & Associates to build the Chinese Cultural Centre in Vancouver. Cheng has received over fifty design awards, including the Order of Canada, which is the country's highest civilian honour for lifetime achievement and merit of a high degree from the Governor General office of Canada; and Canada's Governor General's Medal in Architecture. His work has been published and exhibited all over the world.

James Moore McCown is a Boston-based architectural journalist who writes for numerous design publications including *Metropolis*, *Architect's Newspaper* and *AD PRO Architectural Digest*. He has collaborated with Oscar Riera Ojeda on several books including the Architecture in Detail series that comprised four volumes: *Elements*, *Materials*, *Colors* and *Spaces*.

McCown studied journalism at Loyola University New Orleans and holds an ALM (Master's Degree) in the history of art and architecture from Harvard University, where his thesis on modern Brazilian architecture received an Honorable Mention, Dean's Award, Best ALM Thesis (2007). He lives in Newton, Massachusetts.

Tom Fox SWA's former lead photographer and Director of Imaging and Media for over 35 years, Tom documented the firm's built projects around the world, "representing the intent of the designer through the camera lens," he explains. Tom also managed the firm's digital artists and photographers; collectively, they supported the firm's landscape architects and marketing efforts. A life behind the lens has lent Tom a unique view on what makes a project successful: "I am drawn to projects that have simple, clear but strong design ideas and that are built and finished in a precise way down to the finest details. These projects often translate into great photographs." He holds a Bachelors Degree in Professional Photography from Brooks Institute, recognized as one of the top professional photography schools in the world at the time.

David Lloyd is a commercial and editorial location photographer specializing in landscape architecture & design, industrial, drone-aerial, and environmental portraits. David is currently Director of Photography and Creative Media at SWA. He has over 25 years of experience working in the creative media field with a broad range of expertise in photography, video production, marketing, and web design. David is an award-winning photographer with a passion for documenting the interaction between people and the environment. He has documented a number of John Wong's more recent iconic projects around the globe, from residential to the tallest buildings in the world. David commented: "John's work is impressive in scale and impact, and always refreshing to photograph; the range of project types, the activity, the geometry and detailed patterns, makes for a compelling photograph and story."

Bill Tatham has been a photographer with the SWA Group for 20 years, capturing landscape architecture and the people in it through still photography, drones, and video. He manages the public website and digital asset system for the firm. Bill has captured many of John's projects throughout the United States and South Korea. "You can always tell when you step onto a John Wong project, the confident sense of balance in form conveys his deliberate hand in crafting the design and an experience." He is a graduate of the Brooks Institute of Photography in Santa Barbara, earning a bachelor's degree in advertising photography.

Oscar Riera Ojeda is an editor and designer based in the US, China, and Argentina. Born in 1966, in Buenos Aires, he moved to the United States in 1990. Since then, he has published over three hundred books, assembling a remarkable body of work notable for its thoroughness of content, timeless character, and sophisticated and innovative craftsmanship. Oscar Riera Ojeda's books have been published by many prestigious publishing houses across the world, including Birkhäuser, Byggförlaget, The Monacelli Press, Gustavo Gili, Thames & Hudson, Rizzoli, Damiani, Page One, ORO editions, Whitney Library of Design, and Taschen. Oscar Riera Ojeda is also the creator of numerous architectural book series, including Ten Houses, Contemporary World Architects, The New American House and The New American Apartment, Architecture in Detail, and Single Building. His work has received many international awards, in-depth reviews, and citations. He is a regular contributor and consultant for several publications in the field. In 2001 Oscar Riera Ojeda founded ORO Editions, a company at which he was responsible for the completion of nearly one hundred titles. In 2008 he established his current publishing venture, Oscar Riera Ojeda Publishers, a firm with fifteen employees and locations across three continents.

BOOK CREDITS

Graphic Design
Juan Pablo Sarrabayrouse

Art Direction
Oscar Riera Ojeda

Photography
Front endpaper: SIP Administration Center by Tom Fox
002-003: Guthrie Green by Tom Fox
006-007: SIP Administration Center by Tom Fox
010-011: Burj Khalifa by David Lloyd
014-015: Lite-On Technology Headquarters by Tom Fox
564-565: Stanford West Apartments by Jonnu Singleton
568-569: Expo 2020 by Jason O'Rear
586-587: Burj Khalifa by Tom Fox
Back endpaper: Zakin Residence by Tom Fox

Copy Editing
Kit Maude

OSCAR RIERA OJEDA
PUBLISHERS

Copyright 2024 Oscar Riera Ojeda Publishers Limited
ISBN 978-1-946226-78-5
Published by Oscar Riera Ojeda Publishers Limited
Printed in China

Oscar Riera Ojeda Publishers Limited
Unit 1331, Beverley Commercial Centre,
87-105 Chatham Road South, Tsim Sha Tsui, Kowloon, Hong Kong

Production Offices
Suit 19, Shenyun Road,
Nanshan District, Shenzhen 518055, China

International Customer Service & Editorial Questions: +1-484-502-5400

www.oropublishers.com | www.oscarrieraojeda.com
oscar@oscarrieraojeda.com

All rights reserved. No part of this book may be reproduced, stored in a retrieval system, or transmitted in any form or by any means, including electronic, mechanical, photocopying of microfilming, recording, or otherwise (except that copying permitted by Sections 107 and 108 of the U.S. Copyright Law and except by reviewers for the public press) without written permission from the publisher.